LOSING THE RACE

Explorations in Psycho-Social Studies Series
Published and distributed by Karnac Books

Other titles in the Series

Object Relations and Social Relations: The Implications of the
Relational Turn in Psychoanalysis
  Edited by Simon Clarke, Herbert Hahn, and Paul Hoggett

Researching Beneath the Surface
  Edited by Simon Clarke and Paul Hoggett

Social Symptoms: The Role of Identity in Social Problems and
Their Solutions
  Mark Bracher

Orders

Tel: +44 (0)20 7431 1075; Fax: +44 (0)20 7435 9076

E-mail: shop@karnacbooks.com

www.karnac books.com

LOSING THE RACE

Thinking Psychosocially about Racially Motivated Crime

David Gadd and Bill Dixon

KARNAC

First published in 2011 by
Karnac Books Ltd
118 Finchley Road, London NW3 5HT

British Library Cataloguing in Publication Data

A C.I.P. for this book is available from the British Library

ISBN: 978 1 85575 793 6

Edited, designed and produced by The Studio Publishing Services Ltd
www.publishingservicesuk.co.uk
e-mail: studio@publishingservicesuk.co.uk

Printed in Great Britain

www.karnacbooks.com

CONTENTS

ACKNOWLEDGEMENTS AND PERMISSIONS

The research could not have been without the generous support of the ESRC, who provided the large research grant (RES-000-23-0171) needed to conduct the fieldwork and then an impact grant, which gave us the opportunity to reflect on the issues further with a group of South African activists in Johannesburg at a workshop held in April 2007. This gave us a fresh and unique perspective on our research and we are very grateful to all of the participants for making it such a rewarding experience and to Brian Molewa in particular for co-ordinating the event on behalf of the Centre for the Study of Violence and Reconciliation. Too many people helped to make the research described in this book possible for us to thank them all here. Nor would all of them thank us for doing so, at least by name. But when it came to getting us started with the fieldwork, Damian Doherty, Peter Fieldhouse, Angela Glendenning, Jude Hawes, Clare Moran, Vince Simpson, Angela Staplehurst, and John Wood all deserve a special mention, as indeed do the many others who helped to set up, and then hosted, our focus group discussions.

As far as the analysis of our data is concerned there is one person—Tony Jefferson—we could not have managed without and to whom we both owe debts that extend some way beyond this project. We have benefited enormously from his enthusiasm for the research and his unrelenting dedication to meeting the interpretative challenges presented by the mountains of raw data we produced. Apart from Tony, many other people have given us invaluable feedback on early versions of parts of this book. They include: Nicole Asquith, Les Back, Gavin Bailey, Ben Bowling, Neil Chakraborti, Stephen Farrall, Stephen Frosh, Wendy Hollway, Mark Israel, Caroline Knowles, Ian Loader, Bethan Loftus, Eugene McLaughlin, Shadd Maruna, Matthew Millings, Barbara Perry, Scott Poynting, Graham Smith, Richard Sparks, Pnina Werbner, and Majid Yar. We are especially grateful to Simon Clarke and Paul Hoggett for helping to make this book a reality with Karnac. Particular thanks are also due to Diana Gadd, who faithfully transcribed all of the biographical interviews. It almost goes without saying that we both owe an enduring debt to our partners, Claire and Tania, who have lived with this project for too long and allowed it take precedence at more social engagements than we were entitled to expect, and to our sons, James, Thomas, and Alex, who have taught us much more about the complexities of identification and dealing with difference than can ever be captured on the pages of a book. It also almost goes without saying that the responsibility for what follows, including any omissions, errors, and shortcomings, is ours and ours alone.

Permissions

Parts of Chapter Four are reproduced (in revised form) by permission of SAGE Publications Ltd, London, Los Angeles, New Delhi, Singapore and Washington DC, from Dixon, B., & Gadd, D. "Getting the message: 'New' Labour and the criminalisation of 'hate'", published in *Criminology and Criminal Justice*, 6(2): 309–328, 2006.

We thank *Searchlight* for permission to reproduce the "Shutdown the Pedlars of Hate" image in Chapter Five, and *Unite Against Fascism* for permission to use their "Don't swallow their poison" bottle image.

The Joseph Rowntree Charitable Trust have given permission for us to use Table 13 from their publication, *539 Voters' Views*, in Chapter Five, although our version is slightly re-edited.

ABOUT THE AUTHORS

David Gadd has been conducting research on violent perpetrators since 1997. He is Professor of Criminology and Director of the Centre for Criminology and Criminal Justice at Manchester University Law School. **Bill Dixon** worked in local government and the third sector before moving into higher education in the early 1990s. He is Senior Lecturer in Criminology and Head of the School of Sociology and Criminology at Keele University. Between 2003 and 2005, they led a major research project on the perpetrators of racially motivated violence and harassment, funded by the Economic and Social Research Council (ESRC). In 2006, Bill and David received an ESRC Impact Grant to disseminate the findings from their research, and the methodology they had used in the course of their study, to a group of researchers and activists working on similar issues in South Africa's North West Province. This book arises out of these two research awards.

Introduction: Race, racism, and racially motivated offenders

> "The contrast between the vicious racism that drives predominantly young men to terrorize and kill and the supposedly unconscious variant that allows prejudice, ignorance and subtle bigotry to undermine democratic procedures is certainly not a new distinction. While the latter does not inevitably lead to or promote the former, it is a fundamental error to imagine, first that these are the only two options and, second, that they are not connected in significant ways"
>
> (Ware & Back, 2002, p. 5)

Racially motivated crime is a particularly, perhaps uniquely, difficult phenomenon to come to terms with. Its significance and immediacy cannot be ignored; the urge to do something, anything, is almost too hard to resist. Yet, the problem also remains strangely elusive; the complex, overlapping, often mutually contradictory set of conceptual, legal, cultural, and personal meaning frames with which we use to define it seem to keep the problem tantalizingly beyond our analytic reach. What do we mean by "racially motivated crime"? Are all those "racist incidents" recorded by the police motivated by hatred? How does racially motivated offending relate to "ordinary" prejudice and bigotry, to ignorance and fear of the unknown or unknowable? What do those who "terrorize and kill" have in common with those of us who do not? Do "we" share nothing but a common "whiteness"? Or are "we", at least potentially, liable to become just as prejudiced, bigoted, and ignorant as "them"? Do "we", at least to some extent, have similar unconscious thoughts and fantasies to "them"? If so, why do "we" behave differently? Under what circumstances would "we" behave as "they" do? When we fail to do something about racially motivated crime, as individuals and as a society, are "we" in some way complicit in "their" crimes?

As the sociologist Les Back (2004, p. 209) astutely observes, when our starting point is the kind of social science that merely points out "why racism is bad or wrong", we come little closer to answering any of these questions. Instead, we need analytic approaches which not only attend to what all of us feel as human beings, but also help us to deepen our understanding of the many ways in which notions of "race" slip through our minds, words, and deeds unnoticed, at least until they crystallize as indicators of difference, of what distinguishes "us" from "them". The problem for "us" as students of racially motivated crime has been that criminology, the sociological sub-discipline that has come to monopolize the study of unlawful behaviour, has largely abandoned its aetiological project (Young, 1994). As a consequence it has remarkably little to say about how certain attitudes, feelings, and ideas relate to particular kinds of behaviour. Despite a recent resurgence of interest in biographical and ethnographic methods (Ferrell, Hayward, & Young, 2008; Gadd & Jefferson, 2007; Maruna & Matravers, 2007), the perspectives of the marginalized, the excluded, and the criminalized, so central to the sociology of deviance, have largely disappeared from view in the face of criminology's growing commitment to the governmental project of controlling crime (Garland, 2002).

Moreover, and with a few honourable exceptions, criminology's engagements with the issue of racism have tended to be both casual and state-centred. The increasing attention being paid to the logics of social control in recent work on warfare, migration, the criminalization of foreign nationals, and the cross-border trafficking of people and goods is beginning to shake criminology out of its complacency (Bhui, 2008a; Bosworth & Guild, 2008; Hudson, 2006; Weber & Bowling, 2008; Whyte, 2007). But once it is accepted that racism is institutionalized within the state and its agencies (especially the police), it becomes all too easy to dismiss the relationship between the prejudices of "ordinary" individuals and their participation in racially motivated offending as irrelevant, since both appear to be determined by more macro-level processes. As one of the best sociological analyses of violent racism has demonstrated (Bowling, 1998), one of the ways in which the connections between racism and racially motivated offending is obscured is through the artificial separation of debates about prejudice and violence from those concerned with immigration, nationality, and citizenship. It is often forgotten that, while the first Thatcher administration was busy "getting tough" on immigration, the Home Office was also commissioning its first research on racial harassment. As Paul Gordon (1983, p. 22) remarked at the time, this was symptomatic of "a basic contradiction in state policy": "[Y]ou cannot consistently and openly discriminate in immigration control, and at the same time argue that discrimination is wrong". The paradoxical attitude towards racially motivated crime evident in these moves to tackle the problem of racist violence head on while simultaneously feeding popular fears of being "swamped" (in Margaret Thatcher's infamous phrase) by mass immigration, persists to this day and reflects a wider disjuncture not just in British political culture, but in public attitudes towards "race" more generally.

This curious mixture of xenophobic and authoritarian, anti-racist and liberal-reformist impulses is one of the things which cements the subtle but anti-democratic bigotry, referred to by Ware and Back (2002, p. 5) in our epigraph, to the more obviously racist attitudes of the "young men who terrorize and kill". It has also proved a significant obstacle to legislative reform and changes in institutional attitudes and behaviour in the area of racially motivated offending, fears about the links between crime and uncontrolled immigration often trumping proposals to take racism more seriously. So, in 1987, the Commission for Racial Equality's (CRE) report, *Racial Attacks*, repeated many of the recommendations made in the Home Office (1981) document of the same name six years earlier. Thereafter, in the late 1980s and early 1990s, a number of local initiatives took root in places such as North Plaistow, the site of

Bowling's (1998) influential study of the policing of racist victimization in east London. It was not until the late 1990s, however, that
most of the recommendations made in the 1981 Home Office report,
Racist Attacks, were implemented, following a change of government in 1997, the introduction of legislation on racially aggravated
offending in the *Crime and Disorder Act 1998*, and finally, and most
importantly, the publication of the report of the Macpherson
Inquiry into the failed investigation of the murder of the black
teenager Stephen Lawrence on the streets of South London in 1993.
Thus, it is only in the past decade or so that "hate crime" has risen
close to the top of the political agenda and the importance of tackling it become so widely acknowledged by the public sector bodies
required by the *Race Relations Amendment Act 2000* to monitor racial
discrimination and harassment both within their own organizations
and among the populations they serve.

As anyone who has studied hate crime in Britain since the implementation of the 1998 *Crime and Disorder Act* will know, however,
racially motivated crime is not caused by failures to legislate.
Despite some relatively radical reforms to the agencies of the criminal justice system, the problem of racially motivated crime has not
gone away. This much is evident from data published by the
Ministry of Justice under section 95 of the *Criminal Justice Act 1991*
(Ministry of Justice, 2009). The best estimates of the current extent of
racially motivated crime are obtained from the British Crime Survey
(BCS), which indicates that there were around 207,000 racially motivated incidents in 2007–2008, up from 184,000 the previous year
(*ibid.*, p. xi). Most of these incidents—in common with other forms of
victimization—were not reported to the police, who recorded only
57,055 racist incidents in 2007–2008, 7% fewer than in 2006–2007
(*ibid.*). The process of attrition does not stop there either, for, as
Ministry of Justice figures show, the police went on to record only
38,327 racially or religiously aggravated crimes in 2007–2008, a fall
of 10% on the previous year (*ibid.*, p. 13). Meanwhile, a total of 11,465
persons were cautioned or prosecuted for these offences in 2007, of
whom 5,403 (47%) were convicted in the magistrates' courts and 546
(5%) before the Crown Court (*ibid.*, p. 33, Table 3.3). A further 2,499
(21%) were cautioned. On this basis, it seems likely that the ratio of
racist incidents to *individual offenders either cautioned by the police or
convicted of racially aggravated charges by the courts* is around 18:1.

Of course, there are many reasons for this attrition. Many victims do not want to report being abused, attacked, harassed, or having their property damaged. Some see their victimization as too trivial to bring to the attention of the police, or believe that their complaint will not be taken seriously. Others may be too afraid to come forward, or see racist victimization as too commonplace for the police or anyone else to do much about. Sometimes, it is impossible to prove who the perpetrator was. But none of the difficulties associated with measuring the true extent of racially motivated criminal victimization or the pitfalls encountered in processing those responsible for it through the criminal justice system makes it any less important that we attempt to understand why offenders do what they do. On the contrary, that offenders so rarely provide full and verifiable accounts of what they think of their victims and the courts so rarely ask defendants to explain what motivated their behaviour make it all the more important that we attempt to explore perpetrators' motivations by other means.

The Home Office researchers who worked on the first official study of racial attacks in Britain, published in 1981, were well aware of the limited understanding of motive to be gleaned from what investigators and the courts were able to establish:

> Clearly a racial incident is one that is in some sense motivated by racial hatred or antipathy. Motives, however, are not open to direct inspection but have to be inferred from the circumstances of the incident or offence. Inferences of this kind may call for difficult and highly subjective judgments ... Ideally, the only reliable source of information on racial motivation would be from the offender ... [Home Office, 1981, p. 7]

Over the years since this report was published, neither policy-makers nor researchers have invested enough time and effort in tapping this "reliable source", that is, what offenders say about what they have done. Of course, there are a few studies that do attend to offenders' motives, but because most criminological research lacks an adequately theorized account of the relationship between the outward hostility articulated in racist attacks and the inner world insecurity, powerlessness, and disregard many perpetrators feel, most criminologists struggle to provide an analysis of motivation that is anything other than typological or "middle range". The failure either to talk to offenders or to attempt to make sense of the subjective judgements made about them on the basis of more circumstantial evidence has made it possible for politicians, criminal justice agencies, and anti-racist groups alike to advocate, and in some cases to deliver, uncompromising responses to "hate crime perpetrators", "racially motivated offenders", "extremists", and the "bias motivated" without giving much thought to the counterproductive consequences which their demonization may have. The consequences of this lack of attention to the motives of offenders is clear from a government sponsored study of the operation of the new laws on racially aggravated offending introduced under the *Crime and Disorder Act 1998*. This suggested that the courts in England and Wales have had to process a large number of cases brought "where the racist element is ancillary to the substantive offence, rather than the cause" (Burney & Rose, 2002, p. x). The researchers found that this has led to widespread disagreement among legal practitioners as to what constitutes the "hostility" needed to prove "racial aggravation" under the terms of section 28 of the 1998 Act. One view, "most often expressed by stipendiary magistrates [now district judges] and defence solicitors" was that "the law came down rather hard on people who, in the course of 'normal working class mayhem' as one person put it, uttered words which were part of their natural vocabulary" (*ibid.*, p. 20).

Other sentencers, however, took a rather different view: "Almost any reference to the victim's ethnicity in connection with an offence is seen as supplying the necessary element of racial aggravation, and it is believed that anything less condones racism" (*ibid.*, p. 114).

Burney and Rose (2002, p. 89) found that this second approach was often strongly opposed by defence lawyers, who were anxious to ensure that charges of racially aggravated offending against their clients were dropped. Indeed, "everyone involved in the process mentioned the vehemence with which racial aggravation is denied". Thus, and in spite of the attendant risk of eventually receiving a more severe sentence, not guilty pleas were entered for 87% of racially aggravated offences tried in the Crown Court in 1999, compared with no more than 47% for the basic (not racially aggravated) offences. While many defendants were prepared to admit to the basic offences, few were willing to plead guilty to their racially aggravated equivalents. Based on these findings, the researchers became convinced that defendants took the risk of pleading not guilty because they were

> genuinely upset and indignant at the prospect of a "racist" tag. Whatever anyone's overt or subconscious feelings on the subject, it is clearly socially unacceptable (except in a few circles) to be branded as a racist. A racially aggravated conviction is seen as a shaming event in a different class to a conviction for a basic offence ... [Burney & Rose, 2002, p. 91]

As a consequence, defendants were prepared to go to considerable lengths to resist allegations of racism:

> Friends and relatives of different ethnicities are often brought to court as character witnesses for somebody denying racism. Solicitors routinely seek demonstrations of this kind, or produce photographs of the defendant with a black girlfriend or similar alibi— this was a tactic that was met in every court. [ibid., p. 91]

Here, then, is another reason why so few racist incidents culminate in the conviction of a racially aggravated offender: what victims of crime may experience as racism may be perceived very differently by perpetrators, few of whom may be as unambiguously and incontrovertibly hostile to those from different ethnic groups as their behaviour might suggest, and many of whom may feel more ashamed of being seen as racists than of being known as offenders. For us, this tension between the way in which the perpetrators of what the law defines as racially aggravated offences see themselves, and how those on the receiving end of abuse, violence, and harassment experience their behaviour, is exactly why academic research needs to be directed at understanding perpetrators' motivations, and informed by approaches which help us to grapple with the complexity of their individual subjectivities. As researchers investigating racism, we must, as Les Back (2004, p. 209) has argued,

> allow the people we write about to be complex, frail, ethically ambiguous, contradictory and damaged. The tendency to write society as if it were populated by Manichean camps of people who are good or bad, angels or devils, is a strong temptation. When one is writing about stigmatised and excluded groups, this temptation

is particularly keen ... The danger here in creating heroic portrayals is that we make the very people whose humanity one may want to defend less than human. We don't allow them to be as complicated as we are, i.e. compounds of pride and shame, weakness and strength. Equally, when we make white racists into monsters there is a danger of organising racism into some—often very predictable white bodies—and away from others.

When we turn racists into monsters we allow ourselves to be deceived into believing that the problem of violent racism has nothing to do with us. We also allow those conveniently labelled as racists to conceal their prejudices and make it harder to challenge them. In the criminal justice system, the result of this is that everyday racism is routinely overlooked as not "real", as accidental or "unwitting", while a small minority of offenders are identified as forming an untreatable hardcore, beyond the pale of redemption, their bigotry too all-consuming to challenge (Ray, Smith, & Wastell, 2003a). In academic criminology, this seems to cause little concern, with some commentators too easily satisfied that punishing hate crime offenders more harshly is a step in the right direction: "an important symbolic cue against transgression by potential offenders"; and evidence of "the provision of equal concern and respect for all people ... a central plank of political liberalism" (Iganski, 2008, p. 86). As we argue throughout this book, it is only possible to make such assertions by oversimplifying both the ways in which the symbolism of race accumulates meaning in people's lives and the complex processes of identification that determine whether and how those invested in racism and violence can ever become receptive to the message that their values are at odds with well-established notions of "equality" and other core liberal democratic values.

Which way now?

What if legislating against "hate" has served, rather, to convince the law-abiding majority that they have nothing in common with the perpetrators of racist attacks, that they can be distinguished from a suitably criminalized minority solely by virtue of their superior values? If institutional racism really is endemic, how can we—to borrow from our epigraph from Ware and Back (2002, p. 5)—help people make the connection between the actions of violent racists and the "prejudice, ignorance and subtle bigotry" that undermines "democratic procedures"? It is our contention that it is the job of academic social scientists to rehumanize the demonized, even if in doing so we cast doubt on our own virtuousness. Les Back's (2004) call to transcend the kind of "moral absolutism" that denies racists their humanity provides some important clues about the kind of approach that is needed if we are to break down the barriers between a demonized, criminalized "them" and an ordinarily racist "us". As Back (*ibid.*, pp. 209–210), reflecting on the ambivalence of his own feelings, writes, we need to recognize racists for the "complex, frail, ethically ambiguous, contradictory and damaged" people they usually are:

> Perhaps, I am mindful of this precisely because people I have loved have also given popular racism a voice, including my own father . . . One of the paradoxes of this—and I am always compelled by the paradoxical effects of racism on our culture—is that towards the end of his life the only person who could reach through the cancer and morphine-haze was a black nurse. It was she who held his hand as he passed the brink of life. I want to believe that this was some kind of atonement or coming to terms.

In this book, we hope to be able to rise to the challenge of finding a way to capture both the paradoxical effects of racism and the biographical complexities that give rise to them. One of our central goals is, thus, to find a discourse that allows us to engage with the ways in which racism is connected to feelings of loss; how the loss of loved ones, of social status, and of physical and mental well-being may determine whether we feel seduced or repulsed by racism. Although much of this book attends to the question of why many people find it so difficult to identify with others with whom they have much in common, we recognize that racist attitudes are never absolute, and that there are many ways in which, despite their prejudices, people are able to identify with those who do not share their demographic characteristics or social status. Finally, we also hope to be able at least to begin to address the question of what atonement, forgiveness, and reconciliation might look like in the aftermath of racist aggression and violence.

In seeking to accomplish all of this, we draw upon a psychoanalytically-informed psychosocial approach to the problem of racially motivated offending. We do this not in the belief that it makes more straightforwardly sociological work unnecessary, but because we think that it complements and enriches our understanding of this kind of behaviour as a social phenomenon. Adopting a psychosocial approach means working with a model of subjectivity that takes seriously both the contradictory nature of individual social attitudes and the emotional conflicts that may underlie them. It also means avoiding the cultural determinism implicit in much criminological and legal thinking about hate crime in order to make sense of racialized fears and stereotypes without implying that they are the inevitable by-products of difficult social circumstances and/or class inequalities. For us, the key advantages of a psychosocial approach are: first, its *openness* to the possibility that, under certain conditions, all of us—righteous anti-racist and shameless hate-monger alike—are susceptible to change, either for better or for worse; second, its *conceptual specificity* in helping us to understand why some people are better placed than others to cope with uncertainty and confrontation without resorting to overt displays of hostility and aggression.

Based on a two-year research project, *Context and Motive in the Perpetration of Racially Motivated Violence and Harassment,* funded by the Economic and Social Research Council (ESRC), this book explores why many of those involved in racially motivated crime seem to be struggling to cope with economic, cultural, and emotional losses in their own lives. In doing so, we make use of conceptual insights from several recent revisionist engagements with the work of Melanie Klein. These include: Rustin's (2000) conception of racism as a container for unthinkable thoughts; Clarke's (2003) exploration of the momentum given to racism by shifts between depressive and paranoid–schizoid thought processes; and the relational thinking about identification and recognition explored in the work of Benjamin (1998). Drawing on these psychoanalytic ideas, we explore a second, more obvious sense in which "race" and "loss" are connected: the near impossibility of losing "race" from everyday conversations about community, difference, and inequality. Notwithstanding the development of new policy discourses about immigration, multi-culturalism, ethnicity, and the post-colonial, even those most committed to challenging racism still struggle to free themselves from what Gilroy (2004) calls "race-thinking". Using original life story and focus group data from our own research, we set out to expose the workings of "race-thinking" without compounding the demonization of the "race-thinker" as "racist". We also argue that, while it is difficult, if not impossible, to draw hard and fast distinctions between "ordinary people" and "real racists", a psychosocial approach enables us to detect and conceptualize important differences and significant similarities between the "merely prejudiced" and the perpetrators of hate crime.

Using our datasets to illustrate these arguments, the wider aim of the book is to provide the reader with a critical perspective on a series of debates in the academic and policy literature about the problem of racially motivated crime, which we suggest have not yet received the attention they deserve from criminologists. Among the issues we touch on here are the usefulness of typological, shame-based and structured action approaches in explaining racially motivated crime, the origins and impact of the creation of racially aggravated offences in England and Wales under the *Crime and Disorder Act 1998*, the promotion of "community cohesion" as a response to racism, religious extremism, and the threat of public disorder following disturbances in three towns in the north of England during 2001, the plausibility of the "protest vote" thesis as an explanation for the re-emergence of the far right in British politics and the electoral success of the British National Party (BNP), Paul Gilroy's account of the connections between loss, post-colonial melancholia, anti-immigrant xenophobia, and racial hatred, and, finally, the relationship between, on the one hand, racism, racial hatred, and racially motivated offending and, on the other, notions of respect and recognition current in government responses to "anti-social behaviour" and recent work by the sociologist Richard Sennett and the psychoanalyst Jessica Benjamin. In engaging with these debates, the book also attends to issues of wider criminological concern, including the role of group dynamics in offending behaviour, the nature of desistance from crime, the complicity of the state in some forms of victimization, and the difficulty of breaking cycles of hostility and vengeance in both liberal democratic nations and post-conflict transitional societies.

The structure of the book

Following on from this introduction, Chapter One describes the interview-based life history and focus group research we conducted in and around the city of Stoke-on-Trent in the English North Midlands. It provides an overview of our findings about those implicated in perpetrating racially motivated violence and harassment, and about the attitudes and experiences of other "ordinary" white people living and working in the same city. The chapter makes the case for endeavouring to humanize racist offenders and explores the connections between the response of the mother of the murdered Liverpool teenager Anthony Walker to her son's death and the emotional dynamics that developed between the victims and perpetrators of human rights violations during hearings before South Africa's Truth and Reconciliation Commission after the country's transition to democracy in 1994. This can be done, it is argued, by grappling simultaneously with the troubled emotional worlds of those who commit racist crimes and the defensive cultural functions served by racism in those communities that are overtly hostile to recent immigrants as well as to certain settled minority ethnic groups. The chapter goes on to highlight the fantastical, sadistic, and envious tendencies evident in the confrontational situations in which perpetrators become involved, often in interaction with like-minded others. The importance of recognizing the differences between perpetrators whose identities are inextricably bound up in the projective dynamics of racialized thought and those whose thoughts and words only become racialized under particular sets of conditions is signalled in the chapter's conclusion.

Chapter Two begins with the story of a teenage asylum seeker who was forced to return to her home country, much to the dismay of her classmates, many of whom came from families outwardly hostile to asylum seekers and open in their support for the BNP. This story is used to illustrate the need to move beyond the limitations of the critical criminological and sociological literature on the state and authoritarianism, and to resuscitate a model of the contradictorily racist subject that was the mainstay of classic works on authoritarianism, prejudice, and racism by Fromm (1942/2001), Adorno, Frenkel-Brunswik, Levinson, and Sanford (1950), and Allport (1954). We suggest that what needs to be overcome in this earlier work is a tendency to assume a singularly prejudiced personality too linear in its development from class-based or childhood experiences and too fixed and immutable once an authoritarian outlook has been adopted. It then goes on to explore the radical break made by psychoanalytically informed psychosocial approaches in understanding the contingencies that determine how and when race comes to matter so much to some individuals but not (at least in some key respects) to similarly placed others. These approaches are then used to re-read the multitude of psychosocial relations evident in the story of the schoolchildren distressed by their classmate's deportation with which the chapter opens.

The next chapter begins with a critique of the one-dimensional assumptions that have come to characterize criminal justice thinking about racially motivated offenders since Sir William Macpherson's (1999) report into the investigation of the murder of Stephen Lawrence. Applying insights derived from the revisionist psychoanalytic work discussed in Chapter Two, we analyse one of our own case studies of a young offender with a similar demographic profile and reputation to some of the men suspected of killing Stephen Lawrence. This analysis reveals the often-elusive ways in which anti-immigrant sentiments and notions of ethnic difference resonate in the lives of some troubled and troubling young white men. The chapter concludes by drawing attention to some of the parallels between our own case study and what is known about the young men widely assumed to have been involved in Stephen Lawrence's murder. We ask some critical questions about why all of these young men became so invested in hateful attitudes towards those they regarded as "immigrants", and consider what might have been done to help them to relinquish their investments in racial hatred.

Chapter Four sets out to interpret the "messages" about "hate crime" sent to perpetrators, and people from their local communities, by the creation of a new category of racially aggravated offences under the terms of the *Crime and Disorder Act 1998*. Two possible anti-hate crime messages and three potential audiences are identified and evaluated in the light of data generated from biographical interviews with perpetrators and a focus group discussion with young offenders from around the city of Stoke-on-Trent undergoing supervision in the community. Our conclusion is that the supposedly clear deterrent and denunciatory messages contained in the 1998 Act are either drowned out or distorted by other signals coming from successive "New" Labour governments about crime, immigration, nationality, and "community cohesion", and by the highly idiosyncratic and unpredictable ways in which they are mediated, and interpreted by their intended recipients.

In Chapter Five, we try to account for the rise, and continuing popularity, of the British National Party (BNP); a party which, until the early 2000s, was generally regarded as an extremist group on the margins of mainstream politics. Other social and political commentators have tended to explain the BNP's unexpected and still limited electoral successes as a result of the party's successful rebranding under the leadership of Nick Griffin, the failure of New Labour to live up to the expectations of white working-class voters, and the sustained scaremongering over immigration in which the established parties and the media have either colluded or indulged. Drawing on survey data, focus group material, and the biography of one local BNP activist in Stoke-on-Trent, this chapter reappraises these explanations and shows that, while they are not without merit, they tend to oversimplify the relationship between anti-immigrant attitudes and class, underplay the role of unconscious fantasies in sustaining support for the BNP, and overlook the hidden psychological injuries—sustained in the course of individual and collective experiences—that lure some individuals into adopting embattled, authoritarian-sounding, but, none the less, complex and contradictorily racist mentalities. Our exploration of how white working-class voters and sympathizers thought and felt about the BNP in the early 2000s leads us to the conclusion that the party's appeal has to be understood in terms of the unconscious emotional needs of individuals inflected by the development of a new politics of "race" and class, but not wholly reducible to it.

Chapter Six begins by re-examining the debate about community cohesion and the reasons why promoting cohesive communities came to be seen as a policy solution to urban disorder. In the course of this discussion, it considers what was overlooked in the evidence presented to government about the nature of the unrest in Burnley, Oldham, and Bradford in 2001. The chapter goes on to present data from focus group discussions with Asian young men, elderly white people, and public sector professionals living in

Stoke-on-Trent. Stoke makes an interesting case study for various reasons. In common with other northern towns and cities, it experienced escalating tension between young Asians and the police during the summer of 2001 before being awarded Community Cohesion "Pathfinder" status in 2003 (Home Office, 2003). Since mayoral elections in the city (also in 2001), Stoke-on-Trent has seen a steady growth in support for the BNP, with between a fifth and two-fifths of voters supporting the party in wards where it puts up candidates. Building on Sherwood's (1980) theory of racist spiralling, the chapter explores how anxiety and racialized hostility are connected by group dynamics. The chapter concludes by arguing that the rhetoric of "New" Labour's "third way" politics evident in the discourse of community cohesion means that the government has failed to capitalize on the genuinely containing—and cohesion-building—qualities of those most able to check the processes of demonization characteristic of public reactions to immigration, ethnic difference, and religious fundamentalism. We end by suggesting how these shortcomings might be overcome through a politics that prioritizes the creation of opportunities for identification over efforts to manufacture any artificial social consensus.

Some of the material presented to the Inquiry into the Murder of Zahid Mubarek in Feltham Young Offender Institute in 2000 is revisited in Chapter Seven. We ask why Mr Justice Keith's report began with "institutional racism" at its heart, but ended with a "focus" on "violence in prisons, specifically attacks by prisoners in their cells" (Keith, 2006a, p. 32, 2006b, p. 552). The answer, the chapter suggests, has to do with the nature of racism, especially when—as it seems to have been in the case of Robert Stewart, Zahid Mubarek's killer—compounded with mental ill-health. During the course of the chapter, we attempt to answer two questions posed by Dias (2006, p. 7), the Mubarek family's barrister: first, why "this country keeps producing men like Robert Stewart"; second, what it would take to "recognise" these men properly, to "see their hate and deal with it differently". By examining Robert Stewart's voluminous correspondence, and the records and reports about him placed in the public domain during the course of the Keith Inquiry, the chapter explores the acute loneliness, lack of self worth, and desire to be wanted betrayed by Stewart's peculiarly sexualized expressions of racism. We use the psychoanalytic concept of melancholia deployed by both

Gilroy and relational psychoanalysts to suggest that Stewart's racism was fuelled by powerful defences against loss. These defences were built up in childhood and reinforced during an adolescence and early adult life spent largely in custody and marked by estrangement from his parents, the break-up of the few friendships he had managed to establish, and anxiety about the stability of his relationship with the woman he considered to be his "girlfriend". Our view is that Robert Stewart, a disturbed and paranoid young man intimidated by his emotional dependency on others, came to feel persecuted by Zahid Mubarek precisely because his Asian cellmate was one of so few people in whom he could confide.

Chapter Eight begins by tackling the "Respect Agenda" that was at the forefront of the third Blair government's response to antisocial behaviour. Taking Richard Sennett's (2003) discussion of respect as its starting point, the chapter goes on to argue that rectifying the disrespect felt by the economically marginalized is only one part of the complex process needed to change racist mindsets. While not denying that feelings of disrespect are unevenly distributed along class lines (Sayer, 2005), we argue that whether the hidden injuries of class and criminalization are projected outwards on to racialized groups depends on the extent to which people feel sufficiently emotionally nourished in their own interpersonal relationships to withstand criticism directed at them, either by others or themselves. The chapter illustrates this point by exploring the intersubjective dynamics that fostered a disengagement from racist hatred in the life of a former far right activist we interviewed. Drawing on Benjamin's (1998, 2006) ideas about "identification" and "recognition", we show how it is necessary for those invested in racist hatred to reclaim the psychic parts of themselves that are projected on to victims through the kinds of symbolic "othering" that hate crimes entail. What we suggest is that, when those "others" are able to withstand and survive hostile projections, the possibility of psychic change—of losing the individual's dependence on race as a marker of difference—is significantly enhanced.

Finally, we conclude the book by analysing the different kinds of loss to be found in the lives of those involved in racist crime: loss of respect, jobs, and economic security; of a sense of shared identity, community and nation; of childhood, loved ones, health, and feelings of emotional well-being. We also attend to the question of how to respond culturally and politically to the contradictory nature of racism and the many losses that enliven it. Rather than anticipate these conclusions here, however, we end this introduction by reflecting briefly, and, we hope, given the biographical nature of much of the data on which we rely, appropriately on how we became involved in researching racially motivated offending in Stoke-on-Trent, and by acknowledging the help and support of those who contributed to that project and to this book.

About us

Identifying precisely where an intellectual idea began is something of an arbitrary task, but in relation to this research there was certainly an important moment in the summer of 2002, when the parameters of this project began to crystallize. I (Dave) had been attempting to mentor a young man who was becoming increasingly caught up in the criminal justice system, in part because of his addiction to heroin. "Liam" had spent much of his life moving between institutional care and his parents, something he blamed himself for, even if many of those working with him could not conceal their anger about the neglect he had suffered throughout his childhood. Liam was involved in robbing local shops and people on the streets. He often seemed ashamed of his crimes, and constantly promised to come off "the gear". However, he was unapologetic in his racism and "hated Pakis" with a vengeance.

Having spent most of my adult life in university settings, the harshness of Liam's racism shocked me. While I was not unaccustomed to hearing members of my extended family complain about minority groups having "taken over" parts of London and other cities with which they were familiar, I had not witnessed racism like this since leaving school. I began to consider connections between the deprivation that can be found in cities like Stoke-on-Trent, the rising profile of the BNP, and the complex and, at that time, underresearched problems the local populace faced as a consequence of the area's deindustrialization. While my academic interests shifted towards more locally based research projects on crime, ethnicity, and marginalization, I also began to reflect upon the extent to which racism had come and gone in my own life, the extent to which I was insulated from its pernicious effects and willing to suffer a level of quiet discomfort in the company of family and friends who expressed its milder, anti-immigrant variants. Perhaps this was why I decided to try to work on Liam's racism, asking him why he hated Asian people so much. He replied in a way that only served to underline the very real differences in life experiences between us. "They", he said, "were all born with silver spoons in their mouths." Asked to justify this, his only explanation was that "The Pakis get all the best rooms in the YMCA."

The research project described here was inspired by the discomfort I felt then, and still feel now, at my own incapacity to respond productively to attitudes like these, especially, but not only, when they are both energized by hardship and legitimized by the forms of xenophobia that have gained social acceptability during my own lifetime. I approached Bill about a research project on racial harassment, knowing that the issues I wanted to raise would be taken seriously by him, but also that he would feel able to tell me if he thought I had got it all wrong.

When Dave first approached me (Bill) about researching racially motivated offending in Stoke-on-Trent, I was still relatively new to an area more like the rural north Northumberland of my childhood in the 1960s than the cities—first London, then Cape Town— in which I had spent most of my working life. How better to get acquainted with this new city where words—"Paki" and "coloured"—were still used in much the same way as they had been in the 1970s? Growing up in a world where my first contact with anyone who neither looked white nor sounded northern came at the age of ten, when a Chinese restaurant finally opened in the small market town near my home, I was intrigued by the prospect of finding out more about this mysterious place where so many people still spoke the language of thirty years ago, even though chicken tikka masala had long replaced fish and chips as the signature dish of the British high street. After living for the best part of a decade in some of London's most ethnically diverse neighbourhoods, including a street in Southall where I was a member of one of only four even partially white households and could get everything from a new set of brake pads to a haircut on Christmas Day, Dave presented me with an opportunity to see the open, cosmopolitan Britain I had grown to love—maybe to idealize—through the eyes of people with very different experiences of whiteness, Englishness, and cultural change in the early twenty-first century. It never occurred to me when I duly decided to get involved in the research quite how unsettling, but also how strangely reassuring, an experience it would be. What I utterly failed to anticipate was just how sustained the assault would be on the sensibilities I had acquired over several years campaigning against racism in West London, or how easy it would be to put those bruised sensibilities to one side and feel the warmth of the welcome we received as researchers from their assailants. If I thought I knew what I was letting myself in for when I accepted Dave's invitation to join the research team, I was sadly mistaken. But I am very glad that I did accept, and have grown to appreciate Stoke-on-Trent and the rest of North Staffordshire for what it is, even if it is not always what I might like it to be.

CHAPTER ONE

Posing the "why?" question

"My heart is broken"

"The devastated mother of racist murder victim Anthony Walker said she would forgive his killers—but only when they showed genuine remorse. Special needs teacher Gee Walker, 49 . . . described Anthony as 'the man of the house' . . . who could defuse a family row by pointing out the humour in most situations. . . . [S]he wept as she explained the void his death created . . . Despite her obvious pain, Mrs Walker's strong Christian faith means she cannot hate [her son's murderers] Barton and Taylor . . . 'Hatred is a life sentence. . . . It eats you up inside like a cancer.' . . .

The fact that Anthony's killers grew up in the same area—Taylor attended the same junior school—is particularly hard for Mrs Walker to accept. . . . 'They played together, they stood in the same dinner queue. I believe that all kids are innocent and something went wrong along the way. Someone planted a seed of hate in their minds. Kids don't decide, "I'm going to hate." It's got to come from somewhere and it's down to all of us to find out where and why.' . . . And Mrs Walker was keen to stress the comfort she had

> taken from the huge outpouring of public sympathy . . . 'We
> wouldn't have survived without that'."
>
> (*The Sun*, 2005)

T he mushrooming literature on hate crime powerfully testifies to the harms caused by racially motivated forms of violence and harassment. Ehrlich, Larcom, and Purvis (2003, p. 158) observe that victims of "ethno-violence" are more likely to suffer a range of psychosomatic symptoms than victims of other crimes, including "nervousness, trouble concentrating or working, anger and a desire to retaliate . . . fear . . . and feeling exhausted or weak for no reason". Bowling and Phillips (2002, p. 114) describe how "serious and mundane incidents are interwoven to create a threatening environment which undermines" the "personal safety and freedom of movement" of people from black and minority ethnic communities. Racially motivated murders may be relatively rare in relation to other forms of homicide, but the horror these evoke is associated in the minds of many people from black and minority ethnic groups with the more commonplace phenomena of racially motivated assaults, racial harassment, racist graffiti, racist joking, and discrimination on the bases of skin colour, religion, and nationality. As we shall see in Chapter Four, the harsher sentences handed down to those convicted of racially aggravated offences under anti-hate crime laws in both Britain and the United States are open to criticism, but they have been widely welcomed by practitioners and academics on the grounds that "hate crimes hurt more", "are more likely to involve excessive violence", and "send out a terroristic message to members of the victim's group" (Iganski, 2003, p. 135).

Yet, as the story reproduced above suggests, better and harsher justice is not the only thing those who suffer the hurts caused by racially motivated crime want and need. Gee Walker, the mother of a black schoolboy killed when two white men wearing ski masks bludgeoned him to death with an ice axe, has talked repeatedly to the media about her desire to understand and forgive her son's killers. Knowing what to make of such news coverage, particularly the claim that the nation's sympathy enabled the grieving family to "survive" is not easy. Such sentiments mitigate the public's sense of culpability and obscure from view the many racist attacks, including some racist murders, which pass without media comment (Institute of Race Relations, 2008). However, Gee Walker's oft-repeated expressions of bewilderment at the killers' actions merit further consideration. In asking what had planted "the seed of hate" in their minds, the parameters of Gee Walker's own experience as both a single mother of six and a special needs teacher who successfully raised a young man emotionally adept enough to "defuse" many a family conflict come into play. Given that her son's killers were brought up in the same neighbourhood, played with Anthony, and that one of them went to his school, Gee Walker is understandably perplexed as to how they turned out so differently from her own son. From this perspective, her conclusion that something must have "gone wrong" for Barton and Taylor seems plausible, and her insistence that we all have a duty to "find out where and why" they became so hateful entirely justified.

Walker is not alone in taking this stand. As Pumla Gobodo-Madikizela's (2003) moving account of her interviews with Eugene de Kock, the South African police colonel who oversaw the murder and torture of many of apartheid's opponents demonstrates, coming to terms with the humanity of perpetrators can be part of the process of overcoming the dehumanizing impact of racism and the atrocities it facilitates. In South Africa, the desire to come to terms with loss, trauma, and brutalization was so great that, during the Truth and Reconciliation Commission's hearings, some victims offered to forgive perpetrators before they apologized for their crimes (*ibid.*, p. 98). Gobodo-Madikizela witnessed the wife of a man murdered in a bombing orchestrated by the security forces shed tears of forgiveness for Eugene de Kock (*ibid.*, p. 94). She further notes that, while many people find it hard to contemplate having anything to do with perpetrators, some victims need to be given the opportunity to engage with them, despite the emotionally disturbing consequences of doing so (*ibid.*, pp. 128–129). For these victims, identifying with the perpetrators' pain is one way of ridding themselves of the poisonous self-loathing instilled in them by victimization and oppression. Consequently, to

> ... dismiss perpetrators simply as evildoers and monsters shuts the door to the kind of dialogue that leads to an enduring peace. Daring, on the other hand, to look the enemy in the eye and allow

oneself to read signs of pain and cues to contrition or regret where one might almost have preferred to continue seeing only hatred is the one possibility we have for steering individuals and societies towards replacing longstanding stalemates out of a nation's past with genuine engagement. [*ibid.*, p. 126]

Of course, it is not necessarily the task of academics to facilitate dialogues between perpetrators and victims. But if criminologists are to make a contribution to alleviating the problem of racially motivated violence and harassment, and/or to helping people overcome the many hurts it causes, then we cannot afford to shy away from the challenge of rendering perpetrators' motives comprehensible, of searching for signs of pain and cues of contrition beneath the hatred, of teasing explanations out of excuses, and of finding the human within the dehumanizing. In sum, it is the job of academics to find a language capable of helping victims, perpetrators, and their wider communities to make sense of the phenomenon of racially motivated forms of crime and harassment, their most serious and apparently mundane manifestations included. In the rest of this chapter, we begin by looking at how criminologists writing from a range of different perspectives have tried to answer the "why" question. From there, we go on to summarize the findings of our research in North Staffordshire, parts of which form the empirical basis for our own attempts to answer this critical question later in this book.

Criminological perspectives

Criminological writing about perpetrators has largely shied away from attempting to answer the "why" question. The most cited works tend to be typological, or otherwise largely descriptive, profiles derived from secondary analyses of police incident data. These have enabled distinctions to be drawn between "thrill", "defensive", "retaliatory", and "mission" motivated offenders (McDevitt, Levin, & Bennett, 2003); "expressive and instrumental motives" (Berk, Boyd, & Hamner, 2003); "premeditated and unpremeditated attacks" (*ibid.*); and "versatile", generalist offenders tinged with "bias", and "specialist" hate crime offenders (Messner, McHugh, &

Felson, 2004). These typologies show that not all racially motivated offenders are the same, that motives and rationales vary, and that offences aggravated by the use of racist terms are not always initiated because of hateful feelings. But, in failing to grapple with how offenders' motives resonate with the contradictory mixture of popular prejudices, historically ingrained ideas about race and belonging, and contemporary concerns about nationality, entitlement and migration, typological approaches tend to oversimplify the distinctions between perpetrators and non-perpetrators.

From this base, Barbara Perry's (2001) attempt to apply structured action theory to the perpetration of hate crime was a radical move forward. Within western culture, Perry argues, difference is often constructed in negative relational terms as "deficiency", so that those who deviate from the hegemonic position in social relations—currently occupied by white, economically successful, heterosexual men—are constructed as inadequate, inferior, bad, or evil (*ibid.*, p. 48). From Perry's perspective,

> Hate crime . . . connects the structural meanings and organization of race with the cultural construction of racialized identity. On the one hand, it allows perpetrators to reenact their whiteness, thereby establishing their dominance. On the other hand, it coconstructs the nonwhiteness of the victims, who are perceived to be worthy of violent repression either because they correspond to a demonized identity, or, paradoxically, because they threaten the racialized boundaries that are meant to separate "us" from "them". [*ibid.*, p. 58]

Perry claims that the perpetration of hate crime serves multiple objectives. It reinforces the normality of white sexuality while punishing those who transgress, or who are imagined to have transgressed, the norm. Victims are often harassed for *transcending* normative conceptions of difference, for doing things white men think black and ethnic minority men are not entitled to do, but they may also be punished for *conforming* to relevant categories of difference, for behaving in ways whites consider to be stereotypical of non-whites. Although the process of victimizing others instils a positive sense of identity in those perpetrators who fear emasculation, and/or feel marginalized by their class position, knowledge of this victimization among the victim's community reinstates the

6   LOSING THE RACE

racialized injustices of the wider society. Grounding her work in the histories of slavery, segregation, and exploitation that initially defined white Americans' relationships with African and Native American people, Perry's thesis avoids the profilers' tendency to pathologize while also attending to the way in which so many racist attacks appear to be as much about gender, age, and sexuality as they are about "race". But in accounting for "hate" in terms of class and gender-related marginalization, Perry's analysis, like much of the structured action theory on which she draws, has a rather "deterministic feel", which makes it harder rather than easier to get to grips in any meaningful way with the inner worlds of the offenders in question (Gadd & Jefferson, 2007, p. 111).

In exposing the feelings of inadequacy contemporary racism so often conceals, some UK based researchers have offered a more humanizing perspective on the aetiology of hate crime. Rae Sibbitt attempted as much in her Home Office-funded study of racist victimization cases when she argued,

> For perpetrators, potential perpetrators and other individuals within the perpetrator community, expressions of racism often serve the function of distracting their own—and others'—attention away from real, underlying, concerns which they feel impotent to deal with. [Sibbitt, 1997, p. viii]

Likewise, Ray, Smith, and Wastell's (2004) study of those convicted of racially aggravated offences in Greater Manchester has drawn attention to the prevalence of racist crime in areas where white residents perceive themselves to be under threat from an expanding South Asian population, even though this population is no less affected by the decline of Britain's manufacturing industries. Ray and colleagues' interviews with those on probation for racially aggravated offences suggested that most (white) racially motivated offenders tend to share the values and prejudices of the communities from which they come. Deploying a framework developed by Scheff (1994), Ray, Smith, and Wastell detected unacknowledged shame in the verbal disclosures and body language of around two thirds of their thirty-six respondents. These racist offenders

> ... saw themselves as weak, disregarded, overlooked, unfairly treated, victimized without being recognised as victims, made to

feel small; meanwhile, the other—their Asian victims . . .—was experienced as powerful, in control, laughing, successful, "arrogant". (Ray, Smith, & Wastell, 2004, pp. 355–356]

But, while Ray and colleagues published many accounts of what offenders think about ethnic minorities, they provided few of their interviewees' explanations of their offending behaviour (see also Ray, Smith & Wastell [2003a,b] for further examples). This makes it hard to gauge whether "shame" was always the "master emotion" behind racist crime, whether loss of face or unacknowledged shame was more acute for those who committed acts of racist violence than for those who simply held racist views, and what caused the more acute shame supposedly felt by hate crime perpetrators.

Our research

Our own research, conducted in and around the city of Stoke-on-Trent in North Staffordshire in the English Midlands, set out to address these shortcomings. (For census and other official purposes, North Staffordshire is generally taken to mean the local authority areas of Stoke-on-Trent [of which more below], Newcastle-under-Lyme, and Staffordshire Moorlands.) The overall aim of our project was to tease out the connections and tensions between pervasive forms of racism and xenophobia, the expression of anti-racist sentiments, and the motivations of the minority of the population who perpetrate a range of racially motivated offences (Gadd, Dixon, & Jefferson, 2005). Focus group discussions were conducted with thirteen naturally occurring groups of local people. These included people from a residents' association, a neighbourhood watch, a working men's club, a day centre, and two anti-racist groups. We also talked to groups consisting of young offenders, asylum seekers, and white and minority ethnic users of two local authority run youth clubs. In addition to this, Free Association Narrative Interviews were conducted with fifteen people implicated in acts of racial harassment or violence (Hollway & Jefferson, 2000). Twelve of the fifteen were accessed via probation services and youth offending teams, although only five of them had ever been charged with racially aggravated crimes. Three participants, all of whom were politically involved in racist political groups, were recruited through more direct approaches. One activist was recruited from a focus group and put us in contact with another interviewee active in a local campaign against the dispersal of asylum seekers to North Staffordshire. The third was recruited by writing to him directly. Recordings of the focus groups and in-depth interviews were fully transcribed, with particular analytic attention being given to fragments of words, overlapping speech, changes of tone, and other non-verbal cues, as well as to emerging themes and intersubjective dynamics.

Racist crime in North Staffordshire

In 2005, one in every three minority ethnic residents of Stoke-on-Trent had experienced some form of racial harassment in the previous three years: one in four had been verbally abused; one in twenty had suffered a violent racist attack. These rates of victimization were higher than those found by the British Crime Survey for England and Wales as a whole (Salisbury & Upson, 2004). Local racist incident data for Stoke-on-Trent suggested that, by 2003, refugees and asylum seekers from Afghanistan, Iraq, and Iraqi Kurdistan were experiencing even higher rates of victimization than the (themselves heavily victimized) Pakistani and Bangladeshi populations. These high rates persisted, despite a more pro-prosecution approach than evident elsewhere. Perpetrators of racially aggravated offences in Staffordshire were less likely to be cautioned and more likely to be referred for prosecution than in most other counties in England and Wales. However, there was also evidence that most racist incidents never came to the attention of the police, let alone the courts. The police in Stoke-on-Trent recorded only 468 such incidents in 2002–2003 while, in November 2003, only one person in North Staffordshire was in custody for a racially aggravated offence, and only thirteen racially motivated offenders were listed in probation caseloads.

Deindustrialization and the rise of the British National Party

By the time we came to do our fieldwork in 2003–2004, Stoke-on-Trent had endured at least three decades of economic decline. By the end of the 1990s, the area's three major industries—ceramics, coal mining, and steel production—had almost disappeared. While other, similar cities had offset losses in manufacturing jobs by expanding service sector employment, Stoke-on-Trent had seen the workforce in financial services dwindle, forcing unemployment rates up and disposable incomes down far below the national average (Parkinson et al., 2006). With the area also experiencing greater out-migration than in-migration, these factors combined to erode the City Council's fiscal base and reduce its capacity to sustain adequate public services (Parker, 2000). This, in turn, enabled a succession of independent councillors to blame asylum seekers and travelling people for consuming scarce resources that "belonged" to local residents. As the electorate's long-standing support for the Labour Party ebbed away, the far right British National Party (BNP) began to benefit from the creeping racialization of social deprivation and persistent internecine rivalries between the historic "six towns" of Stoke-on-Trent and their near neighbour, the old market town of Newcastle-under-Lyme. (In strict alphabetical order, the "six towns" are Burslem, Fenton, Hanley, Longton, Tunstall, and Stoke. Although Burslem is, by tradition, the "mother town" of the area known as the Potteries in deference to the product for which it is still internationally famous, the main business district and shopping area is in Hanley. Stoke itself is only one of the "six towns", but we will risk irritating locals by occasionally using "Stoke" as a shorthand for "Stoke-on-Trent" here and throughout the rest of this book.) In the 2004 Stoke City Council elections, the BNP secured between a quarter and a third of the vote in the wards it contested, a level of support it maintains at the time of writing, notwithstanding subsequent declines in its fortunes elsewhere in the Midlands and the North of England.

The "white" community speaks

Perhaps predictably, given the city's increasingly straitened circumstances, white participants in our focus groups offered an overwhelmingly negative assessment of life in Stoke-on-Trent. Younger people dismissed it as a "shit-hole", a "dump", "crap". Their elders compared Stoke-on-Trent today unfavourably with the city they

had grown up in, though many paid tribute to the enduring friend-
liness of its people and could not contemplate living anywhere else.
Call centres, distribution hubs, and retail outlets had replaced major
industries. Skilled, relatively well-paid jobs had been lost, and
stable, self-sustaining communities broken up. Mining villages and
vibrant commercial centres full of hard-working, respectable people
had been reduced to wastelands. At the mercy of "absentee landlords" and uncaring housing providers, respectable neighbourhoods had become "dumping grounds" for "foreigners" and "riff-
raff". Older residents believed that parts of the city had come to
resemble a "war zone", "Beirut", "Africa", or "Bombay". They saw
evidence of a decline in social discipline everywhere. Children respected nobody. Parents and police alike seemed to lack the will to
do anything to control them. Drugs were ubiquitous, and binge
drinking and violence the apparently inevitable by-products of a
burgeoning night-time economy. By turns self-serving, uncaring,
and incapable of delivering adequate and affordable public services, national and local politicians were distrusted by people of all
ages, accused of favouritism, being out of touch, and allowing
Stoke-on-Trent to fall far behind nearby cities such as Birmingham
and Manchester.

Identity: "us" and "them"

Young and old alike associated industrial decline and social change
with the presence of people they saw as outsiders, sometimes from
elsewhere in the city or other parts of Britain, but most frequently
from southern and eastern Europe, the Middle East, south Asia, and
Africa. People described as "foreigners" or "immigrants" were
widely perceived as both symptom and cause of Stoke-on-Trent's
current malaise: evidence of the decline of "community" in previously homogenous working class neighbourhoods and responsible
for much of the crime, disorder, and drug abuse that affected the
quality of local people's lives. Although most participants made
exceptions for particular individuals or groups, discussions generally proceeded on the basis of a straightforward distinction between
"us"—people who belong in England, Stoke and/or "our" community—and "them"—people who do not. Who "they" were, and

what made "them" different, had little to do with participants' very imperfect knowledge of the law on immigration, asylum, and nationality. Birthplace, length of residence, and skin colour were much less significant in people's judgements than ethnicity, "attitude", and behaviour. Londoners, "gypsies", and "riff-raff" from other parts of Stoke could find themselves condemned along with "foreigners" and "immigrants", while "niggers", "half-castes", and "Chinks" (despite the offensive language used to describe them) were accepted as "safe" and "sound": hard-working, respectful, and appreciative. For many younger people, "they"—those who did not belong "here", who had a "bad attitude" and did not behave appropriately—were simply "Pakis". There was no necessary connection between "Pakis" and Pakistan: people of Indian, Iraqi, and Afghan origin could be "Pakis", too. Only "Kosovans" formed a distinct, but equally distrusted, alien group.

Immigration and asylum: who deserves what?

Asked for their views about the way in which immigration and asylum were being dealt with by the government, focus group participants rarely paused to distinguish between asylum seekers, refugees, and other newcomers to Britain. As we explore in more depth in Chapter Five, people in the younger groups often competed with each other to suggest the most lethal and fantastical responses to immigration. On reflection, many of them expressed similar views to their elders: the government should come clean about the scale of "the problem" (no one doubted that immigration *was* a problem); claims of persecution by those seeking asylum should be more thoroughly investigated; many more migrants should be "sent back" to where they came from; and access to benefits, housing, and healthcare should be restricted to dispel Britain's "soft touch" image. The crucial question for most participants was: who deserves what? "Genuine" asylum seekers fleeing persecution, well-qualified English-speaking professionals with valuable skills, and people prepared to live by "our" rules, speak "our" language, and work hard to make new lives for themselves all deserved to be allowed into Britain; illegal entrants, "scroungers", terrorists, disease carriers, people who refuse to "integrate", and "bogus" asylum seekers did not.

Victimization, entitlement, and disrespect

Participants' attitudes towards Stoke-on-Trent as a multi-ethnic "community" were often informed by quite limited personal experience of interacting with people from different backgrounds. Some participants gave first-hand accounts of adversarial and violent encounters with people from ethnic minority groups. The people who told such tales were inclined to see themselves as the innocent victims of abusive and aggressive "Pakis" and "Asians", although the details of their accounts often left scope for interpretations of events contrary to their own. Common to all of these stories was the feeling that the police and the criminal justice system were biased against white people, indifferent to "our" victimization, and obsessed with uncovering and punishing "our" racism. The health service, the benefits system, and local agencies responsible for providing social housing had also been coerced into favouring "them" as the only means of avoiding accusations of racism. While pensioners, ex-servicemen, and hard-working mothers providing for their children on meagre salaries struggled to survive, lazy, good-for-nothing "Asians" and "asylum seekers" were given new homes and money for cars, driving lessons, designer clothes, and mobile phones.

White people's feelings of relative disadvantage led us to conclude that part of the appeal of racism lay in its capacity to act as a receptacle for many unacknowledged emotions: shame about their inability to secure decent lives for themselves and their families; anxieties about ill-health and the risk of criminal victimization; and humiliation as their investments in the locality were exposed as unsophisticated or imprudent. It was as if the people we spoke to were aware that others perceived them as cultural and economic failures—as losers—and that, try as they might, there was little they could do counter this evaluation. In what were often quite paranoid-sounding polemics, migrants and ethnic minorities were accused of lacking respect for "us", "our" country, "our" rules, and "our" way of life. Britain and Stoke-on-Trent were being "swamped" as a result of mass immigration and unrestrained reproduction. Immigrants and their children were experienced as a constant, insubordinate, and intimidating presence on the streets, while a terrorist minority of "them" presented a profound threat to the nation's security. Instead of integrating and adapting to "our" way of life, "theirs" was being forced on "us": "our" children were "taught Muslim in school"; "they" thought they could treat women, including "white girls", as "second class citizens"; "they" chose not to adhere to "our" standards of public hygiene; "they" maintained "their" own impenetrable cultural traditions, and could speak in their own incomprehensible languages, while "our" culture and "our" language was there for everyone to understand but none to celebrate. Worse still, by working or being trained as doctors, some young people were afraid that immigrants could rapidly become better educated, wealthier, and more respected than they were— fears expressed even as they spoke highly of minority ethnic doctors who had treated them and their families in times of need. Rather than confront this uncomfortable contradiction, many participants fell back on the binary logic of racial politics. A vote for the BNP was equated with a vote for "us" whites against the intrusive presence, and potential one-upmanship, of a foreign "them".

Reading racist violence: "Brothers jailed for race attacks"

Nevertheless, when asked to review a local newspaper story about three white brothers who had been sent to prison for attacking a "black student" and a "fifty-year-old Turkish man" after a night out, nearly all participants condemned what were presented as unprovoked racially motivated attacks. In so far as the story could be taken at face value, the majority of participants thought that the three brothers—two of whom had been sentenced to four years, the other to eighteen months—had got no more than they deserved. Indeed, some older participants thought that the brothers had got off too lightly, and saw the sentences as further evidence of the malign influence of politically correct "do-gooders" on the criminal justice system. However, having condemned the attacks as reported, some participants went on to reinterpret them either as having been provoked in some way or as having little or nothing to do with "race". The most streetwise group of young people thought that the victims must have said or done something to provoke the violence—even a look from the Turkish man would have sufficed if, as they suspected, the brothers had been drinking. (This group's interpretation of the story is discussed in more detail in Chapter Four.)

They and others also wondered whether the brothers might have objected to the student having a white girlfriend. For many older people, the incidents were unexceptional evidence of the worrying effects of alcoholic excess and the impulsivity of youth, rather than any deep-seated racial antagonism. That the brothers had been convicted and punished at all, and the story reported so prominently in the local newspaper, was interpreted by some as yet another example of institutionalized bias against white people on the part of the criminal justice system and the media.

Perpetrators in perspective: multiple problems and mixed motivations

Of the fifteen people implicated in acts of racial harassment in Stoke-on-Trent who took part in our in-depth biographical interviews as "perpetrators", many of them would not have recognized themselves as such. Although at least seven of them had, at some point in their lives, been routinely involved in violent crime, none could justifiably be characterized as specialist racially motivated offenders. Drunkenness, using and/or dealing in illegal drugs, and the expression of territorial and institutional loyalties were more typical features of the violence in which members of this sample had been implicated. Five had been diagnosed with some kind of mental illness, including chronic or manic forms of depression. At least three had suffered paranoid delusions. Predictably, many of our respondents had experienced unhappy childhoods, been excluded from school, or were regular truants. Eight out of the fifteen disclosed childhood experiences of abuse, neglect, and/or domestic violence; nine came from homes "broken" by divorce, separation, and/or death.

Racist attitudes, hate, and denial

Our research found that criminal justice outcomes were often a poor indicator of racist attitudes. Some of the least racist interviewees we met had convictions for racially aggravated crimes; some of the more prejudiced had none. In fact, the stories most of our interviewees told suggested that racism was rarely, if ever, the sole factor motivating their offending behaviour and/or their political activism. This was not simply because our perpetrators were "in denial" about their racism. Only two of our interviewees, Marcus and Shahid (given pseudonyms here, like all our respondents), provided accounts that suggested that they were denying the racism evident at the time the incidents in question occurred. Another of our respondents, Alan, had been convicted in circumstances that suggested either that the evidence of racial aggravation had been fabricated by the victim, or that Alan had used racist language, to which he was self-consciously opposed, in the course of a psychotic bout (Gadd, 2009). Conversely, a number of the younger white males in our sample, such as Greg, Paul, Steve, and Stan, were relatively open about what they had done and unguarded in their often (but by no means universally) negative evaluations of different ethnic groups.

Stan was probably the only offender in our sample who could justifiably be accused of using race as a primary justification for violence, but even his behaviour could only be understood when contextualized in terms of his experiences of injustice and victimization. Stan was a nineteen-year-old prisoner who conceded that he was a "proper little racist back in school", "hate[d] Pakis", and wished that he was still involved with the far right National Front. Yet, when Stan recounted the brutal attack he had made on a worker in a Turkish takeaway, the breaching of standards of sexual and racial propriety were implicated. The story that unfolded was about Stan's desire to punish a "Paki bastard" who made suggestive remarks to a younger (white) woman with whom Stan had had a sexual relationship. Stan's story also revealed a life scarred by domestic violence, sexual abuse, drug-taking, and involvement in organized crime (Gadd, 2010).

Gender, heterosexism, and racial propriety

In Stan's case, as in several others, the meaning of what appeared to be racially motivated offending or racist political activism only made sense when placed in the context of the alleged perpetrator's wider experiences of social interaction. Issues of gender and sexuality featured in many of the stories we heard. Belinda, an eighteen-year-old probationer, complained about refugees "gawp-ing" at her, as well as black and Asian men who have "no respect for women". She also pointed to examples of friends of hers who had been sexually harassed or physically beaten by men from ethnic minority groups. Greg, meanwhile, complained about a Turkish man who had chased his younger sister because their brother had stolen from him (Gadd & Jefferson, 2007). When he saw a white woman at the Turkish man's window, Greg had thrown a glass bottle at her. Recalling his thoughts at the time of the incident, Greg had this to say:

> "The cheeky twat ... taking my white woman ... my race ... I don't mind about black men ... they can have as many white women as they want. It's just Asians, Turks, Albanians, whatever you want to call them ... I don't like seeing them with white women."

Emma, a twenty-eight-year-old street robber of mixed ethnicity, had frequently been called "a dirty lesbian" by black and Asian men in her neighbourhood. When she was younger, Emma had sent a letter purporting to be from the National Front to one of the black men who had harassed her, telling him that he was "going to get slaughtered". Ten years later, the racially aggravated assault for which Emma was currently on probation had taken place after an exchange of similar racial and sexual slurs between her and four Pakistani men, none of whom had been arrested or prosecuted.

Injustice, deprivation, and paranoia

The themes of less eligibility and unequal treatment also surfaced in many of our interviews. Paul, a fifteen-year-old aspiring member of the Young BNP, was particularly aggrieved by Asian youth ("dirty little things") who denied him access to play areas in a local park. However, Paul also got on well with the Asian shopkeepers, who gave him credit. He was most concerned with immigrants who were "claiming taxes" and "not working", unlike his parents, who had "worked all their lives". This discourse about the "burden" imposed by immigrants on public services was a frequent feature of interviewees' recycling of common myths about the benefits non-whites were assumed to be receiving. Darren, a disqualified driver and errant father, fantasized about putting a "bomb" to the "Pakis" he believed to be claiming "for everything" for their "90,000 children", and was outraged by rumours that asylum seekers were getting free driving lessons from which he, too, could have benefited. Others complained of unjust treatment at the hands of the police and other criminal justice practitioners. Marcus, a twenty-two-year-old prisoner, explained that he had been a victim of racial harassment by a group of immigrant men who had told him to stay away from the "half-Asian" woman his friend was dating. Marcus claimed that these men, with whom he and a friend had fought, had benefited from a system loaded in their favour: "If they say you are being racist, you can't get out of it." His experiences of a biased criminal justice system had destroyed his sympathy for the Asian people he had grown up alongside.

Both the Asian men in our sample of perpetrators had similar complaints. Kamron, a seventeen-year-old British Bangladeshi and erstwhile cocaine dealer, had been remanded in custody for eight months for a racially aggravated assault on a boy who had daubed racist graffiti on their school walls, even though the boy had conceded that Kamron had never said anything racist to him. Similarly, Shahid, a twenty-two-year-old man of Pakistani descent who had been disqualified for drink driving, complained that when the police approached the scene of an altercation in which he was not involved, they had singled him out for questioning because he was the "only Asian there". Shahid had been prosecuted for calling the arresting officers "white bastards" and for threatening to "kill their wives", but felt that these were "defensive" responses to the over-zealous and demeaning treatment to which the police had subjected him.

Two of our interviewees who had problems with alcohol indicated that paranoia sometimes fuelled their racism. Steve, a sixteen-year-old in trouble for a range of anti-social behaviours, had "filled in" three "Kosovans" who had looked at him while he was drunk. He also claimed that they had muttered incomprehensibly in their own language before he started behaving in a threatening way towards them. Likewise Carl, a recovering alcoholic at the age of twenty-five, complained about the asylum-seekers living in a nearby hostel who walked around in groups for their own protection, and whose presence made him feel nervous when he had not drunk enough to boost his confidence. Carl was on probation for calling the female police officer who had arrested him for drunk and disorderly behaviour a "black bitch". Having previously been arrested and imprisoned for crimes he claimed not to have committed, Carl felt aggrieved with the police, but insisted that he did not feel hostile towards established minority groups. Indeed, he expressed envious admiration for a group of Asian children who had thrown milk bottles at him because their mothers, unlike his own (a "dark-skinned" woman whom he had not seen since infancy), disciplined their children. Steve's views on other settled minorities were also broadly positive. He had "always" got on with "black" people, "black" being a term he used broadly to include Asians. His "best mate" was black, and he enjoyed going "rabbiting" with local gypsies. It was only "Kosovans" that Steve did not like, because they "come over here to get benefits". But even here Steve seemed prepared to make an exception: a Kosovan lad was the only person at work with whom Steve felt he could "have a laugh". We return to this case and the identity of the "Kosovan lad" in Chapter Three.

Safety, respect, and "blatant" racism

This kind of qualified racism ran through most of the accounts our interviewees provided, and was often contrasted with what one of the BNP candidates (Frank, aged forty-four) described as the "blatant racism" inherent in discriminating against all non-white people, including those born in Stoke. Frank himself had parted company with the BNP when he discovered that the party excluded "black and half-caste" people from membership. We have more to say about Frank in Chapter Eight. Similarly, Belinda, who complained about the threat posed to women by ethnic minority men, was just as critical of "wiggas", white boys "who talk as if they're black and wear all the big gold". Notwithstanding his qualms about "asylum-seekers" stealing "his white women" and his involvement in numerous fights with Asians laying claim to "his" school and "his" town, Greg also said that he was not racist because he had "sound Asian mates" to whom he sold skunk. Meanwhile, Kamron, despite his experiences of racism, felt sorry for those poor white people whose communities had been blighted by drugs. Kamron was also the most critical of "Kosovans", whom he branded, some-what contradictorily, as "tramps", affluent tax-evaders, "rapists", and "desperados". Kosovans had, in Kamron's view, given the local Asian community a bad name, something he felt justified his burg-lary of a Kosovan's flat.

It is these qualifiers that explain why themes such as "respect" and "safety" were as prominent as "hate" in many of the life stories we elicited. Among our sample of perpetrators, feelings of hatred were often inspired by what was perceived to be disrespectful or threatening behaviour on the part of others. From their perspective, the violence in which some of our perpetrators were implicated had been provoked by threats to their own safety or reputations. Most of those who were routinely violent tended to be young people who were generally not well respected by their teachers, parents, the police, or other adults in positions of responsibility or authority, and who could recall earlier periods in their lives when older people had compromised their safety only to find those in a posi-tion to protect them unable or unwilling to respond. For two of the older interviewees, Terry, an anti-asylum activist, and Nigel, an active campaigner for the BNP, the lack of respect shown by both the City Council and young Asian people for local war memorials and graveyards was a source of considerable anger and frustration. Nigel's life story and the background to his involvement in the BNP is considered at much greater length in Chapter Five.

Conclusion: why do they do it?

At a time when globalization processes routinely restructure ethno-nationalist sentiments so that they assume peculiarly localized forms, it is difficult to know whether the findings of a locally based study like ours can be used to shed any light on the phenomenon of racially motivated crime and harassment elsewhere in Britain, let alone in the rest of the world. Our view is that racist violence can rarely be fully understood without also understanding the histories of the places in which it takes place and the people implicated in perpetrating it. That said, and to the extent that working-class people in many regions of the global North have witnessed an upsurge of in-migration at a time when the security provided by traditional industries has waned, we believe our study of racism in Stoke-on-Trent has some wider purchase. Our research found racist attitudes to be widespread among the white working-class population of Stoke-on-Trent. Thinking and talking in terms of "us" and "them", of people who belong and people who do not, was something that perpetrators shared with people of all ages from across North Staffordshire. Older focus group participants felt an obvious sense of loss that merits much closer inspection. On the one hand, industries, jobs, communities, a whole way of life, had gone never to return. Though they had never known the good times (real or imagined), younger people living with the consequences of deindustrialization identified with their elders' sense of themselves as victims of discrimination imposed by a distant, "politically correct" elite that consistently expected the worst of people like them. On the other hand, this cultural narrative of economic decline and political marginalization could be invoked to mask, if not always successfully, some of the very painful personal losses individuals had endured: losses of "face", respect, and reputation, of course, but also, and more troublingly, of loved ones, relationships, faith, peace of mind, financial security, and physical and mental health. Darren, a dangerous driver, was a case in point. He had recently lost his job, his relationship was "going down the drain" because he was "continually losing [his] temper: screaming, shouting, not coping", and a brief period of economic security had gone when the (uninsured) house he had bought with some money from an inheritance had gone up in flames. Yet, these were not the losses that appeared to upset Darren most. Instead, he remembered how "gutted" he had been when he recently went to look at the boarding school for "unruly children" he had attended as a teenager, only to discover that it had been converted to a care home for the elderly. Visibly upset at what he saw as the loss of his past ("they've nicked me good years"), Darren was left wondering "how can they do this?"

Coupled with the extent to which anti-immigrant sentiment has gained global respectability, this kind of layering of meaning makes it all the more difficult to make out clear differences between perpetrators and non-perpetrators. Meanwhile, the abhorrence of racist violence expressed by most of the ordinary people we spoke to, like the public sympathy for Gee Walker, renders Sibbit's (1997) concept of the "perpetrator community" too simplistic, and the notion that hate crime reproduces pre-existing structures of domination (Perry, 2001) overly general. In Stoke-on-Trent, the vast majority of ordinary white people we interviewed associated immigration with everything that was wrong with their lives: crime, unemployment, inadequate health-care, substandard housing. Increasingly diverse migrant and minority ethnic populations were perceived by many members of the local white population as both a cause of the city's decline and as an indicator of their own inability to "have a nice home and a nice life", as one young mother expressed it; evidence, in other words, of the extent to which they, working-class whites, appeared to be "losers" or cultural and economic failures. For some, racism was a defence against the shame of redundancy, as Ray and colleagues (2004) argue. But it tended to be the exposure of other, more enduring losses that gave racism its more sadistic quality and most destructive features. Many of the ordinary white people we spoke to in focus groups took pleasure in imagining the suffering of ethnic others, particularly when encouraged to do so by fellow participants. This pleasure was often connected to their own feelings of powerlessness and/or persecution. Contemplating the humiliation of ethnic minority individuals who appeared to have achieved success in the face of adversity was one way in which some white people imagined they might win back their own sense of self-respect.

Among people who worked, relaxed, or studied together, shame, sadism, powerlessness, envy, and humiliation coalesced, turning minor and specific grievances into a generalized fear of a menacing ethnic other about to destroy everything good in the world. That many white working-class people feel themselves to be under attack by a political elite which blames the poor for their own poverty, and the many for the "anti-social" behaviour of a few, feeds into the feelings of persecution that render the politics of blame superficially soothing. However, as we will go on to argue in subsequent chapters in this book, it is also true that many of these same people can identify with the pain of bullying and physical victimization and freely acknowledge debts of gratitude to black and minority ethnic people who have befriended them and their families or helped them as professionals. For some, this ability to identify with the other may provide enough of a reality check on paranoid thinking to stop the spiralling of racial hatred. Such checks, however, are much less effective when the demonized other—whether in the form of the newly arrived "asylum seeker" or the densely mythologized "Paki"—is rendered so completely unknowable that no familiar individual or identifiable ethnic group can be related to it.

Paradoxically, the perpetrators we met and interviewed on a one-to-one basis tended to appear much less totalizing in their animosities than the non-perpetrators we interviewed in groups. While the former tended to locate their grievances in specific conflicts with identifiable individuals on particular occasions, the latter were more inclined to express themselves in terms of negative feelings towards all-embracing stereotypes. When it came to recalling disputes which had culminated in the perpetration of acts of racial harassment or violence, however, it usually became evident that similar spiralling dynamics had come into play, with specific grievances and insecurities rapidly giving way to more general racialized fears and hatreds, fuelled, on occasions, by like-minded accomplices, friends, and relatives. Seen in the context of their own biographies, we found that it was possible to identify with the anger and hurt associated with many perpetrators' feelings of aggression without in any way condoning their racist attitudes and behaviour. At least some measure of pain and contrition could be detected behind most perpetrators' expressions of hatred, if only we, as researchers, were prepared to be receptive to it.

The defensive processes that help some "ordinary" white people cope with unsettling and uncertain circumstances, their fears of loss, inferiority, and insignificance, are very similar to those employed by the perpetrators of racial harassment in coming to terms with their experiences. But the perpetrators we met often had particularly acute reasons for feeling ashamed, worthless, humiliated, and fearful, and for feeling very much alone in these sorrowful states. While a few of them had gained a modicum of respectability among similarly criminalized peers, they were, by and large, some of the least respected people in their communities: excluded from school; deserted by their parents; unjustly treated, neglected, or abused by those who owed them a duty of care. White and non-white perpetrators alike had upbringings that seemed brutal and devoid of the kind of containing care and affection young people generally need to help them cope with experiences of threat and anxiety in later life. Predictably, they suffered more than their fair share of the drink, drug, and mental health problems that feature so prominently in the lives of the poor and the criminalized. For all their tough talk, almost all of them had racially abused others when they had themselves been feeling vulnerable, lonely, and troubled.

Certainly, there are crimes of *hate*, in which perpetrators either satisfy some thrill-seeking, retaliatory, defensive, or missionary goals, as the profilers have documented, or physically project into their victims parts of themselves they wish to counter or disown, thus enabling them—as the "doing difference" approach predicts— to accomplish a form of racialized identity by attacking someone else. The investment of many of the perpetrators we interviewed— Greg, Stan, Darren—in the idea that migrants were guilty of things they themselves had done, such as committing petty crime, carrying concealed weapons, harassing women, driving dangerously, and hanging around in menacing groups, is testimony to the role played by these kinds of projective processes and the extent to which they remain outside the conscious awareness of those most caught up in them. But the many acts of racial harassment that occur when vulnerable people—like Shahid, Emma, and Carl— suddenly feel under attack and lash out, suggest a rather different aetiology. In these instances, racial harassment is not simply motivated by "hate" and racist epithets are used to defend against the humiliation of having lost control by those whose prejudices are not ordinarily strong. As we shall see in Chapter Four, such conceptual distinctions make little difference to the administration of justice. Nor do they generally count for much from the victim's perspective, since, in both cases, the offender compounds the hurt caused by disowning her or his feelings of worthlessness by projecting them into another. But to the extent that it is not possible to change either perpetrators or the communities from which they come without first recognizing the complex mix of hard-to-admit feelings upon which racism and violence feed, it is important to find ways of engaging with the specificities of particular offenders' motives. If there is to be any prospect of securing lasting change among those who cause pain by carrying out acts of racist violence and harassment, we must take care not to give the impression that we think that they, too, are "all the same".

CHAPTER TWO

Recovering the contradictory racist subject

"Protests against decision to deport schoolgirl"

"A headteacher is organising counselling for his pupils
because they are so distressed by the imminent deportation
of a Kurdish asylum seeker . . . Lorin Sulaiman, 15, who
joined the school a year ago unable to speak any English. She
has since been placed on the gifted and talented register, and
was chosen to represent her year on the school council. But
the Home Office has rejected appeals for Lorin, her mother,
Amina Ibrahim, 51, and Lorin's 16-year-old sister, Eva, to
remain in Britain, which means they could be ejected at any
time.

Although Portsmouth has gained a reputation as a hotbed
of hostility towards asylum seekers, a campaign is being
mounted on the family's behalf. Derek Trimmer, the headteacher of the 1,306-pupil school, said: '. . . There is a great
feeling of helplessness in the school community of having a
pupil plucked away from us like this.' Mr Trimmer said the
anti-asylum BNP had been active in Portsmouth. 'Some of
our older students whose views on race were a bit hostile
needed counselling because they had very strong feelings

25

about what was happening to Lorin, and had difficulty in bringing their two views together.' . . .

Lorin and a group of relatives arrived in Britain in 2002 after escaping Syria in the back of a lorry . . . Her parents were both active in Weketi, a Syrian political party which campaigns for Kurdish human rights and full citizenship. Her father was jailed for putting up posters in 1993. Nothing has been heard of him since, and he is thought to have been murdered. . . . Lorin's schoolmates say their fears have been heightened by a letter she sent while detained at Tinsley House, near Gatwick . . . [I]f they returned to Syria, she wrote: 'They will kill us straight away'"

(Taylor & Muir, 2005)

Class, racialization, and revelatory racism

W hat seems to make a story like the one above newsworthy, at least to readers of the *Guardian*, is the revelation that the children of white working-class BNP supporters could be troubled enough by the deportation of a foreign-born classmate to require "counselling". In this chapter, we want to argue that "discoveries" like this are only revelatory because, over the past thirty years, our understandings of racism have become decreasingly psychosocial and, hence, insufficiently attuned to the complex, contradictory, and often transient role racism plays in people's lives. This intellectual flaw is particularly evident in the case of criminology (the discipline in which both of the present authors are grounded), where the explanatory capacity of class has often been over-stated. For the past forty years or so, most critical scholarship on "race and crime" has taken the position that it is less important to understand the dynamics of racially motivated offending than it is to appreciate the macro-phenomena that make for a structurally racist class society. Unravelling the relationship between the authoritarian tendencies of the state, the discriminatory workings of the criminal justice system, and the demonizing rhetoric of the media have been part of the core business of critical criminology since the early 1970s. A great deal of effort has quite rightly been expended on deconstructing what Gilroy (1987) referred to as "the myth of black criminality" and attempting to explain why young black men have long tended to be stopped, searched, and arrested more frequently by the police, and then to be more harshly treated by the rest of the criminal justice system, than other social groups (Reiner, 1993). However, this emphasis on the political economy of race in a capitalist society and its impact on the treatment of black people—and, more recently, of other minority ethnic groups—by the apparatus of criminal justice has often been at the expense of studying racism itself: what it is, the forms that it takes, and the different ways in which it works for those drawn to it.

For many, criminologists Hall, Cricher, Jefferson, Clarke, and Roberts's (1978) analysis of the the phenomenon that came to be known as "mugging" remains a seminal "race and crime" text, anticipating, as it did, the rising tide of "authoritarian populism" (Hall, 1980) which brought Margaret Thatcher to power, and left the Labour Party in opposition for the best part of two decades. In *Policing the Crisis* (1978), Hall and his colleagues at the Centre for Contemporary Cultural Studies at the University of Birmingham used the notion of a "signification spiral" (p. 223) to analyse the way in which the identification of a specific issue of concern ("mugging") associated with a "subversive minority" (black youth) became linked through a process of "convergence" to a much wider range of problems flowing from the loss of Britain's empire, its declining political and military standing in the world, the impact of economic recession and widespread industrial unrest, and the long-term effects of the "cultural revolution" of the 1960s. They argued that the racialized figure of the "black mugger" created by the media, politicians, and the judiciary became a political and ideological scapegoat on to which the anxieties associated with the hegemonic crisis of contemporary capitalism could be displaced:

> [T]he nature of the reaction to "mugging" can only be understood in terms of the way society—more especially the ruling class alliances, the state apparatuses and the media—responded to a deepening economic, political and social crisis. [Hall, Critcher, Jefferson, Clarke, & Roberts, 1978, p. 306]

Though it deserved a more exhaustive analysis "in terms of the capitalist mode of production", they presented it "at the level, or in

the form of the slow construction of a soft 'law-and-order society'"
(*ibid.*).

Thus it was that a—sometimes willful, often inadvertant—mis-
reading of some controversial statistics was used to convince
people that "mugging", a supposedly new form of crime endemic
in the USA, had spread to Britain. As politicians moved sharply
to the right in an effort to be seen to be doing something about
a problem partly of their own making, the National Front (still
in those days the dominant force on the far right of British politics)
did its best to lure minority ethnic men into violent confrontations with white racists and the police, feeding ordinary white
people's fears about the civil unrest, crime, and violence that
uncontrolled migration might bring. In the discourse of politicians
and social commentators, and the minds of many others, migration
and the black presence in Britain became inextricably linked with
crime and disorder and a negation of everything for which the
country had once stood. Against this background, as Hall (1980,
p. 4) was to argue elsewhere, the "drift" towards a "law and order
society" secured "a degree of popular support and legitimacy"
from below.

It is a tribute to the prescience of Hall and his colleagues' analysis that, over the thirty years since it was delivered, many criminologists—in the USA and Australia as well as in Britain—have
concurred with their prognosis and detected signs that the "drift"
towards authoritarianism has not only continued, but gathered
momentum (Keith, 1993; Scraton, 1987; Weber & Bowling, 2002,
p. 130) as the state has become increasingly adept at modulating
public opinion (Poynting, Noble, Tabra, & Collins, 2004). In Britain,
the erosion of the rights to silence and trial by jury, the scrapping of
the rule against double jeopardy, the criminalization of "anti-social
behaviour", successive "clamp downs" on asylum seekers, and the
compromising of the presumption of innocence in suspected terrorism cases are ample evidence of this trend. Yet, at a time when
widespread public opposition has been expressed to the "war on
terror", a duty to root out institutional racism imposed on almost
all public institutions, and increasing (though still scandalously
small) numbers of black and Asian people elected to political office,
the argument that there is any obvious relationship between state
authoritarianism, public attitudes towards black and minority

ethnic people, and racist violence has begun to look a little less convincing than it might have done in the 1970s.

This is why, in the second edition of *There Ain't No Black in the Union Jack*, Gilroy (2003, p. xii) referred to the gradual, if still incomplete, awakening of "Britain's racial conscience". As popular culture has embraced black celebrities, music, and sport stars, the "unconvincing caricature" of racial purity espoused by the National Front has been exposed and its racist sloganeering has lost much of its popular appeal. Meanwhile, "the convivial metropolitan cultures of the country's young people" have become "a bulwark against the machinations of racial politics" (*ibid.*, p. xxix). Of course, Gilroy is well aware that "racism and nationalism" remain all too comfortable bedfellows (*ibid.*, p. xxiii), Islamophobia and hostility towards immigrants proliferate in an "insecure and perennially anxious nation", and the Left has moved rightwards, loosely decoupling the "language and symbols of British patriotism" from colour-based racism in order to prolong its political advantage (*ibid.*, p. xxxi). But, as our opening quotation suggests, British working-class culture is by no means uniformly and uncomplicatedly racist. Indeed, Hall and colleagues (1978) themselves cautioned against implying an overly tidy relationship between class and social values. Under capitalist relations of production, "race relations" are inseparable from "class relations": for "black labour", race is both "the modality in which class is lived" and "the medium in which class relations are experienced" (*ibid.*, p. 394). If racial divisions have been ". . . elaborated and transformed into practical ideologies, into the 'common sense' of the white working class, it is not because the latter are dupes of individual racists, or prey to racist organisations" (*ibid.*).

Organizations and individuals who "articulate working-class consciousness into the syntax of a racist ideology" are "key agents" in an ideological struggle,

> But they succeed to the measure that they do because they are practising on real relations, working with real effects of the structure, not because they are clever at conjuring demons. [. . .] Capital reproduces the [working] class as a whole, structured by race. [*ibid.*, pp. 394–395]

It is to the shame of criminology that neither the left realism that became the dominant critical current of the 1980s and early 1990s

(Lea & Young, 1984; Young, 1997) nor the cultural criminology that has recently supplanted it (Ferrell, Hayward, & Young, 2008) have ever grappled with the complexity of popular racism and its relationship to individual and collective loss, social inequality, and the institutional biases of the state (Sim, Scraton, & Gordon, 1987, p. 43).

Beyond the confines of criminology, there seems to be a consensus among many social commentators that there is something distinct about, in Engels's (1958) famous phrase, "the condition of the working class in England" and their relation to racism. Sivanandan (2002, p. 117), for example, argues that deprivation has given a new "face" to racism among the white "have nothings" living in the "pockets of poverty where mills and mines, docks and shipyards, steel and textiles" are no more. Seabrook (2004) also perceives a resurgence of support for the BNP in the places of "broken" working-class identity, where "disused railway lines, rusty metal and buddleia have been landscaped into retail gallerias and up-market housing". And, writing twenty years after *Policing the Crisis* was published, none other than Stuart Hall (1999, p. 193) has detected a "growing sense of defensive embattlement" among "a section of white working-class young men, living in some of Britain's most depressed and forgotten corners":

> They have few employment or educational prospects, feel a deep sense of national shame and dispossession, they are the small seedbed of that form of violent collective projection which follows the classic logic—"We are poor because the blacks are here".

There is, indeed, much empirical evidence to support the claim that white racism manifests itself most virulently not in those parts of the country where ethnic diversity is at its greatest, but where whites living on the fringes of ethnically homogenous enclaves see themselves as the last line of defence against "foreigners" liable to "invade" their communities: the East End of London housing estates where white residents can trace their ancestry back several generations (Hewitt, 1996, p. 29: Back & Keith, 1999), the deindustrializing towns and cities of the north of England to which asylum seekers are "dispersed" (Webster, 2003), and the costal and agricultural communities where the transient presence of (legal) migrant labour from Eastern European accession states and (often illegal) migrant labour from further afield satisfies the demand for ever cheaper food products in Britain's supermarkets (French & Möhrke, 2007; Garland & Chakraborti, 2004). Explaining why racism becomes virulent in these places without diminishing the difficulties faced by the people who live in them is a much more difficult task, however, and some commentators have accused sociologists of abandoning the white working class when the issue of racism became politically sensitive (Collins, 2004). Others, though committed to recognizing the humanity and autonomy of the socially excluded necessary for them to acquire self-respect, appear unwilling to extend the conditional recognition on which self-esteem depends to individuals or groups who "behave in ways that do not warrant recognition": "not all forms of life are worthy of esteem, for example, those of racists or paedophiles" (Sayer, 2005, p. 60).

The ascendancy of a victimological perspective within criminology, to which left realism contributed by undertaking detailed survey research in the inner city areas inhabited by both black and minority ethnic people and many of the most marginalized working-class whites, did little to resolve the issue (Crawford, Jones, Woodhouse, & Young, 1989; Jones, MacLean, & Young, 1986; Kinsey, 1984). Bowling's (1998, p. 18) term, "violent racism", is now widely used to connote the "dynamic and complex" processes through which "the experience of repeated and systematic victimization" is lived, and the "continuity between violence, threat and intimidation", endured by members of minority ethnic populations. But, as he and Phillips (2002, p. 114) have since observed, the major problem with the victimological perspective is its inability to tell us much about why people perpetrate racist crimes:

What is now required is a shift away from the victimological perspective to an analysis of the characteristics of offenders, the social milieu in which violence is fostered, and the process by which it becomes directed against people from ethnic minorities.

Authoritarianism and the conflicted psyche

Put crudely, then, much of the sociological and criminological work on racism—and especially that which is victimological in its emphasis—tends to predict too much racism among certain sections of the working class and too little in other, less deprived sections of society. Too often, such academic analyses fail to differentiate between those who are vocal in their racism from those who are not, while implicitly assuming that the perpetrators of hate crimes come predominantly from the former group. As a result, the tolerant resident of the sink estate is lost from view along with those who, but for their affluence and erudition, would be easy to dismiss as unashamedly racist. This causes two problems. First, it creates analyses that make stories like Lorin Sulaiman's seem more exceptional than they probably are. Second, it leads to the pessimistic conclusion that there is little prospect of making things better while class-based inequalities persist. In the next section of this chapter, we explain why the first of these problems was less of an issue for the psychoanalytic and psychological work that attended to authoritarianism just after the Second World War. We then go on, in the last section, to detail how the second problem (that of unduly pessimistic prognoses) has become the focus of much of the new relational work emerging within psychosocial studies. Hence, in what follows, we engage first with Fromm's (1942) *The Fear of Freedom* (now republished as a Routledge Classic (Fromm, 2001)), Adorno, Frenkel-Brunswik, Levinson, and Sanford's (1950) monumental thesis on *The Authoritarian Personality*, and Allport's (1954) landmark psychological text, *The Nature of Prejudice*, before turning to the advances made by recent psychosocial analyses of racism to be found in the work of Rustin (2000), Clarke (2003), and Benjamin (1998, 2006).

The Fear of Freedom

Fromm's primary concern was not with racism per se, but, rather, with the rise of European fascism and why, despite the bloodshed of the First World War, endured by their fathers in the name of freedom, it was so actively welcomed by large swathes of the population. For Fromm, fascism represented a state of "unfreedom", calling into question Marx's prediction that liberal capitalism was a necessary phase on the road to socialism, and posing some difficult questions about the relationship between culture and psyche inadequately answered by Freud. Fromm argued that psychic conflicts were culturally specific, not Oedipal pre-givens, and that the liberal freedoms ushered in by industrial capitalism, modern individualism, and democracy had placed a heavy psychological burden on the population of Western Europe. They, in turn, had begun to feel "more isolated, alone and afraid" (2001, p. 90). Fascism appealed to the "diabolical forces" (p. 5) aroused by the terrifying fears of loneliness and insignificance that accompanied the growth of freedom and the loss of traditional bonds of deference and authority under capitalism. Fromm detected three types of hostile reaction to the anxiety these new contingencies evoked in 1930s Germany.

1. *Authoritarianism.* This manifested itself in a desire to "give up the independence of one's own individual self and to fuse with somebody or something outside oneself in order to acquire the strength which the individual is lacking" (p. 122). This could involve a "striving for submission and domination" (*ibid.*) because, in submitting to the will of a higher power in order to overcome feelings of inferiority, the authoritarian also becomes aware (again) of his or her own longing for submission and, hence, dependency. Awareness of this dependency is, thus, kept at bay by adopting a kind of "blind admiration" (p. 142) for the authority figure and a bitter contempt for the powerless who are sadistically attacked, dominated, and humiliated for their weaknesses (p. 144). The authoritarian, Fromm observed, was liable to become unconsciously dependent on the objects of his contempt: he "needs the person over whom he rules, he needs him very badly, since his own feeling of strength is rooted in the fact that he is the master over someone" (p. 125)

2. *Destructiveness.* According to Fromm, those who perceived themselves to be "blocked in realizing" their "sensuous, emotional, and intellectual potentialities" (pp. 155–156) relative to others often seek to destroy what they believe to be good in the world. The destructive person exists in a state of "splendid isolation" in which he deludes himself that he cannot "be crushed" (p. 154). Sometimes, when an alternative object cannot be found, the destructive person turned his passion against himself causing "physical illness . . . even suicide" (p. 155).

3. *Automaton conformity.* This was the solution that Fromm thought
    "the majority of individuals"—and the working class masses in
    particular—were pursuing (p. 159). It entailed the adoption of
    "pseudo" personalities offered up by cultural patterns.

> The discrepancy between "I" and the world disappears and with it
> the conscious fear of aloneness and powerlessness ... The person
> who gives up his individual self and becomes an automaton, iden-
> tical with millions of other automatons around him, need not feel
> alone and anxious any more. But the price he pays is high; it is the
> loss of his self. [*ibid.*]

Constantly "obsessed by doubt", the automaton conformist feels
"compelled to conform, to seek his identity by *continuous approval
and recognition by others*" (pp. 175–176, our emphasis).

Applying this analysis to the rise of German Nazism, Fromm
pointed to the importance of differentiating between those (mostly
either "working class" or "bourgeois Catholic") individuals who
became resigned to Nazism more through fear of being seen as
unpatriotic than because of any particular affinity with its ideology,
and those (predominantly lower middle-class) individuals who
were gripped by it, and who actively embraced its hatred of minorities. While the former group, whom Fromm considered to be primarily automaton conformists, had retained reasons to be proud—
they had fought well during the war and had benefited from the
change of regime at home—the latter, more fanatical group tended
to be those most threatened by monopolistic capitalism, and the
most evidently authoritarian and destructive in "social character".
The fall of the monarchy jeopardized the authority the lower middle
class had traditionally gained through their identifications with the
aristocracy, while developments in the post-war period created a
generation of young people who were not willing to accept uncritically the precepts of middle-class morality laid down by their
fathers. In this context, Nazism appealed directly to the lower
middle classes, as it offered "a rationalization, projecting social inferiority to national inferiority" (p. 187). Thus, the ascendancy of
Nazism, Fromm concluded, had to do with Hitler's ability to satisfy
"the desires springing from the character structure" of the lower
middle class, while giving "direction and orientation" to those
working-class populations who, though not enjoying domination

and submission, were "resigned and had given up faith in their own decisions, in everything" (*ibid.*, p. 204).

The Authoritarian Personality

Written by a collective of European émigrés who had fled the terrors of Nazism only to discover troubling expressions of American "pseudopatriotism" among their Los Angeles contemporaries (Adorno, Frenkel-Brunswik, Levinson, & Sanford, 1950, pp. 147–148), *The Authoritarian Personality* tackled head-on the question of difference among those similarly located in the social structure. Why, at "this moment in history", asked Horkheimer and Flowerman in the volume's preface, is "anti-Semitism . . . not manifesting itself with the full and violent destructiveness of which we know it to be capable" (p. v). "What is there in the psychology of the individual that renders him 'prejudiced' or 'unprejudiced,' that makes him more or less likely to respond favourably to the agitation of a Goebbels or Gerald K Smith?" (p. vii). "Why does an individual behave in a 'tolerant' manner in one situation and in a 'bigoted' manner in another situation?" (p. viii). And; "To what extent may certain forms of intergroup conflict, which appear on the surface to be about ethnic difference, be based on other factors, using ethnic difference as content?" (p. viii). The "authoritarian type" which he and his colleagues sought to understand was, from the outset, considered to be a complex and conflicted character: "enlightened and superstitious, proud to be an individualist and in constant fear of not being like all others, jealous of his independence and inclined to submit blindly to the power of authority" (p. xii). In order to get at this complexity without compromising scientific validity, Adorno and his colleagues pooled together a range of studies and approaches from the fields of social theory and depth psychology, content analysis, clinical case analysis, political sociology, and projective testing. The outcome was an empirically rich, methodologically sophisticated 990-page volume.

What made Adorno and colleagues' work particularly prescient, though, was its commitment to discerning how the complex, often incommensurable, forms racist, anti-Semitic, and authoritarian thinking took related to individual "psychological wants and needs" (p. 609). Hence, Adorno's deconstruction of "Prejudice in the Interview Material" noted: the appeal of "stereotypy" to subjects whose "ignorance and confusion ... when it comes to social matters" makes them feel "uncomfortable" (p. 618); the relatively common tendency to overlook the victimization of minority ethnic groups by "reasoning" that victims must have brought their victimization upon themselves (p. 630); the prejudiced person's need for the objects of racist stereotyping to both "possess features" which "harmonize" with their own "destructive tendencies" (for example, to appear aggressive, weak, or clannish), and seem "tangible enough" to enable "destructive projections to be sustained by a wider social group" (p. 608); and the "legitimized psychotic distortions" that mark out committed anti-Semites from the tacitly prejudiced. Their

> ... more-or-less cryptic hints frequently reveal a kind of sinister pride; they speak as if they were in the know and had solved a riddle otherwise unsolved by mankind (no matter how often their solution has been already expressed) ... Probably it is this delusion-like security which casts its spell over those who feel insecure ... [p. 619]

The F-scale, for which Adorno and his colleagues became infamous, was an attempt to formulate a measure more capable than the ethnocentric and anti-Semitic scales they had also devised to discern the shape of the many different psychological dispositions associated with anti-democratic, authoritarian outlooks. Application of the scale to various populations in Los Angeles revealed greater authoritarian tendencies among prisoners than non-prisoners, and among the working classes compared to those with a university education. Importantly, however, Adorno and colleagues noted that there was no neat relationship between authoritarianism and class or gender; contact with "liberal organizations" and "liberal thought" seemed to be more influential than socio-demographic variables (p. 268). Using the F-scale, Adorno, Frenkel-Brunswik, Levinson, and Sanford (1950) identified six types of "high scorers" and five types of "low scorers". The high scorers were classified as follows:

1. *Surface resentment* is a common response to "justified or unjustified social anxieties". Through it, prejudices are accepted

from outside "as ready made formulae" without any "deep-lying, unconscious aspects", but used, none the less to, "over-come overt difficulties" (pp. 753–754).

2. The "conventional" syndrome entails the integration of "in-group" and "out-group" thinking within the personality. Prejudice is not "particularly outspoken, on account of a characteristic absence of violent impulses, due to wholesale acceptance of the values of civilization and 'decency'" (p. 756, original emphasis).

3. The "authoritarian" syndrome involved an addiction to the inter-play of obedience and subordination. Adorno and colleagues suggested it arose out of an

> "internalisation" of social control which never gives as much to the individual as it takes ... The subject achieves his own adjustment only by taking pleasure in obedience and subor-dination ... Stereotypy, in this syndrome, is not only a means of social identification, but has a truly "economic" function in the subject's own psychology: it helps to canalize his libidi-nous energy according to the demands of his overstrict super-ego. [p. 759]

4. The rebel and the psychopath have "an irrational and blind hatred of all authority, with strong destructive connotations, accom-panied by a secret readiness to 'capitulate' and to join hands with the 'hated' strong" (p. 762, original emphasis). This "syndrome is characterized, above all, by a penchant for 'toler-ated excesses' of all kinds, from heavy drinking and overt homosexuality under the cloak of enthusiasm for 'youth' to proneness to acts of violence ..." (p. 763, our emphasis).

5. The crank, "whose whole inner life is determined by denials imposed on them from outside", is "driven by isolation" and occupies a "spurious inner world, often approaching delusion ... They can only exist by self-aggrandizement ... an affinity to psychosis cannot be overlooked: they are 'paranoid'" (p. 765).

6. The "manipulative" type is "defined by stereotypy as an extreme", is potentially "schizophrenic" and preoccupied with sexual matters, and manifests a

> compulsive overrealism which treats everything and every-one as an object to be handled, manipulated, seized by the

subject's own theoretical and practical patterns ... [T]heir
sober intelligence, together with their almost complete
absence of any affections makes them perhaps the most merci-
less of all. [p. 767]

The low scorers consisted of:

1. *The "rigid" low scorer*, whose lack of prejudice arises not from
    "concrete experience", but from "some general, external, ideo-
    logical pattern" that disposes them "towards totalitarianism",
    that sees "*only* minority problems", or otherwise belittles
    "racial discrimination ... as a byproduct of the big issues of
    class struggle". Despite being "identified ideologically with
    the progressive movement", rigid low scorers tended to hold
    ideas that "contained features of compulsiveness, even para-
    noid obsession" and "rigidity" that "could hardly be distin-
    guished from the high extremes" (pp. 771–772, original
    emphasis).
2. *The "protesting" low scorer* who is "thoroughly guided by
    conscience". They protest "out of purely moral reasons against
    social repression", are "frequently guilt-ridden and regard the
    Jews *a priori* as 'victims'", and are often found "among people
    who underwent serious family troubles, such as divorce of
    their parents" (p. 774, original emphasis).
3. *The "impulsive" low scorer* is someone who sympathizes

    > with everything they feel to be repressed ... [T]hey are
    > attracted by everything that is "different" and promises some
    > new gratification ... They certainly do not think in stereo-
    > types, but it is doubtful to what extent they succeed in concep-
    > tualization at all. [p. 777]

4. *The "easy-going" low scorer*, who has a

    > marked tendency to "let things go", a profound unwillingness
    > to do violence to any object ... an extreme unwillingness to
    > make decisions ... [and] a sense of humor which often
    > assumes the form of self-irony ... They are rarely radical in
    > their political outlook, but rather behave as if they were
    > already living under nonrepressive conditions ... [pp.
    > 778–779]

5.   The genuine liberal, who is

> very outspoken in reaction and opinion ... [and] has a strong
> sense of personal autonomy and independence ... One of his
> conspicuous features is moral courage ... He cannot "keep
> silent" if something wrong is being done, even if he seriously
> endangers himself. [p. 781]

Using these typologies, *The Authoritarian Personality* offered a
more emotionally sophisticated conceptualization of the multitude
of investments people make in racisms and violence, tolerance and
pacifisms, than many contemporary criminological and sociological
analyses achieve. In so doing, it alerted the reader to the fact that not
all racists condone violence, not all violent people are particularly
ideological, and that many of those who oppose racism are no less
authoritarian in their outlook than some of those committed to it,
often for reasons to do with "troubles" in their own lives. That the
capacity to "identify with" another's "humanity" was demonstrated
to be more critical as a defence against authoritarianism than demographic characteristics is certainly worthy of further reflection. Yet,
in their typologies and explanations, Adorno and colleagues, like
Fromm, simply could not see beyond their enthusiasm for classical
Freudianism and almost all the types—from the "authoritarian"
through to the "manipulative type", the "protesting low scorer", and
the "genuine liberal"—were ultimately conceptualized in terms of
Oedipal dynamics: "hatred against the father ... transformed by
reaction-formation into love" (p. 759); "early and deep emotional
traumata, probably on a pregenital level" (p. 768); "a strong mother-
fixation" (p. 776); and "erotic character ... connected with a lack of
repression" (p. 783). As even the most sympathetic reappraisals of
Adorno and colleagues' evidence were to show, while parenting
styles and personality development are almost certainly connected,
such a broad brush psychological determinism is no more helpful
as a predictive instrument than the infinitely simpler model of the
subject assumed by social learning theory (Altemeyer, 1988).

The Nature of Prejudice

Despite these problems, *The Authoritarian Personality*, proved a
major—if now often overlooked—influence on the work of Gordon

Allport. Allport's view was that there are two natural capacities of
the human mind that help to explain why people slip so easily
into ethnic prejudice: "erroneous generalization" and "hostility".
Allport argued that erroneous categorical prejudgements are
formed because of our need to simplify and generalize. In order to
negotiate the millions of different events that they experience each
day, people have to use categories in order to make "rational"
judgements about what is likely to happen. Thus, according to
Allport (1954, p. 26), people have a "normal and natural tendency
to form generalizations, concepts and categories, whose content
represents an oversimplication of . . . [their] world of experience".
And categorization gives rise to prejudice because we "prize our
own mode of existence and correspondingly underprize (or actively
attack) what seems to threaten us" (p. 26).

This focus on the necessity of categorization and generalization
was to prove the starting point for several generations of psychological researchers interested in the "cognitive aspects of prejudice", as Tajfel (1969) was to restate them. It was also to give rise to
the "contact hypothesis". This is the notion embedded in much of
the community cohesion rhetoric of today, which holds that, far
from breeding contempt, familiarity can unravel prejudices and
allay hostility towards those formerly defined as members of an
out-group by enmeshing people in "larger circles of loyalty"
(Allport, 1954, p. 45; Crisp & Turner, 2007, pp. 15–17). As Allport
(1954, p. 267) argued,

> Prejudice (unless deeply rooted in the character structure of the
> individual) may be reduced by equal status contact between major-
> ity and minority groups in the pursuit of common goals. The effect
> is greatly enhanced if this contact is sanctioned by institutional
> supports (i.e. by law, custom, or local atmosphere), and if it is of a
> sort that leads to the perception of common interests between
> members of the two groups.

In other words, and as Fromm's and Adorno's analysis also anticipated, in favourable circumstances all but the most prejudiced
members of in-groups and out-groups can come to identify with
each other to some extent. People are rarely irredeemably prejudiced, because "prejudiced attitudes are almost certain to collide
with deep-seated values that are central to the personality" (Allport,

1954, p. 309). Anti-attitudes alternate with pro-attitudes. "Often the see-saw and zig-zag are almost painful to follow" (*ibid.*, p. 310).

Many individuals feel shame and guilt about their own prejudices, especially because these tend to conflict with other religious and political values. At the same time, the liberal democratic "habits and beliefs" Westerners learn "by subsidiation" tend to clash with their own "infantile egoism, needs for status and security, material and sexual advantage, and sheer conformity" (*ibid.*, p. 313). For Allport, whether prejudice became "lockstitched into the very fabric of [an individual's] personality" (*ibid.*, p. 383) was determined by a whole range of factors, including: the prevalence of anxiety and its enmeshment in issues of economy and sexuality; the weight of the burden of guilt felt by the individual; how successfully patterns of "identification" with parents were resolved; the extent to which aggression arising out of unresolved conflicts is displaced (*ibid.*, p. 339); ongoing experiences of "love" arising from "affiliative" relationships; and the extent to which the disruption of affiliative relationships gives rise to "hate" (*ibid.*, p. 342). Among the principal projective mechanisms through which the prejudiced person seeks to manage inner conflicts were: attributing to another person the "emotions, motives and behavior that actually belong to the person who projects them" ("direct projection"); exaggerating the qualities in other people "which both they and we possess, though we may not realize that we possess them" ("mote beam projection"); and "explaining and justifying our own state of mind by reference to the imagined intentions and behaviors of others" ("complementary projection") (*ibid.*, pp. 365–367).

The contradictory racist subject

Taken together, we think there are many lessons to be learnt from these three classics. The notion of the contradictory racist subject— sometimes bigoted, sometimes tolerant, vulnerable to change when crises occur, protected in part by strong relationships, occasionally able (if not always willing) to identify across social differences, zig-zagging between different positions—offers, as the empirical material presented later in this book testifies, a more convincing account of how and why prejudice tends to manifest itself than is generally

provided in sociological and criminological work. Fromm's observation that we are often submissive in the face of prejudice because
we are beholden to the continuous approval of others is one way to
make sense of bystanding. It may also help us to understand the
converse phenomenon, why many people moderate their racism
when they find themselves in the company of others who may not
share their views. This, of course, makes it all the more important
to understand how, when, and why prejudice is liable to become, as
Allport conceived it, "lockstitched" into certain personalities as
well as why some, no less authoritarian people identify so strongly
with "minority" or anti-fascist "positions", as documented by
Adorno and his colleagues.

The key question for us is whether it is possible to do this without falling foul of the determinism of both classical Freudian theory
and structural sociological analysis. What we want to do now is to
argue that the Kleinian refashioning of the notion of psychic
defence mechanisms provides one way of retaining a less deterministic model of the subject, as well as a means of recognizing the
ways in which the social and psychic, inner and outer worlds,
become intricately entwined. The relational revisionism that has
gained prominence within psychoanalysis and psychosocial studies
also offers up further ways of understanding how racism is negotiated *inter*subjectively between individuals, as well as *intra*subjectively within their own minds, and is especially important for
understanding why identification is crucial to both the "lockstitching" of prejudice into some "authoritarian-looking" personalities
and, just as importantly, to its unravelling, when people begin to
distance themselves from a racist past.

Race as the container of psychotic thought

It is intriguing to recall that, writing some time before the recent
relational turn in psychosocial studies, Sherwood (1980) attempted
to do just this in her weighty empirical examination of the psychodynamics of race in three families of different ethnic origins. We
will return to this unjustly neglected classic and its examination of
the intersubjective negotiation of racism, and the centrality of identification to both "lockstitching" and unravelling it, in more detail

in Chapter Six. In its stead, we begin this section with the more influential work of Mike Rustin, first published in 1991 in *The Good Society and the Inner World* (Rustin, 1991), and then reproduced as Rustin (2000) in du Gay, Evans, and Redman's *Identity* reader. In this piece, Rustin begins with the question of how the scientifically meaningless category of "race" has become such a powerful and destructive form of social categorization. His answer to this conundrum is that it is the very emptiness of race as a social category that enables its signifiers—colour, face shape, hair, and, increasingly, religion, language, nationality, and citizenship—to become invested with the kinds of feelings about which people feel most uncomfortable, including, among others: anxiety, inadequacy, envy, and guilt. At their most intense, these feelings are among those that fuel "the mechanisms of psychotic thought". As Rustin argues, these feelings

> . . . find in racial categorizations their ideal container. These mechanisms include the paranoid splitting of objects into the loved and hated, the suffusion of thinking processes with intense, unrecognized emotion, confusion between self and object due to the splitting of the self and massive projective identification, and hatred of truth and reality. [Rustin, 2000, p. 187]

The irrationality of investments in race, Rustin argues, can only be grasped if we are prepared to take irrational thoughts as a serious subject of study, as psychoanalysis does. One unconscious source of racialized projections is anxieties about bodily sensations from touch, smell, the feel of air, and the perception of family resemblance, which may get suffused with incomprehensible emotions when we are very young and unavoidably dependent on our primary carers. It is at this stage of development that the schizoid mechanisms of splitting, idealization, and denigration, which Klein (1935, 1940, 1946, 1955, 1957) observed in infants, begin to take shape, largely in response to the contingencies of separation and the ways in which they are negotiated by parents and their children. During this process, psychic defences are often mobilized against reflexive self-knowledge, enabling us to hide away from truths that are painful or to shut out experiences that are too confusing to fully comprehend, a process famously described by Bion (1984) as consisting of "attacks on linking".

Given experiences of good enough care, most of us develop less destructive ways of coping with things that make us anxious. But, from the Kleinian perspective, such defences never really leave us. They can be rapidly reawakened in subsequent adult relationships, especially when other life crises emerge. Racism can become socially "useful" to those who cannot manage crises of the self, because it legitimates the projective identification through which "hated self attributes of members of the group gripped by prejudice are phantasized to exist in members of the stigmatized race" (Rustin, 2000, p. 191). It also—as Fromm noted—has the potential to become addictive, the racist becoming dependent on racism in ways that are ultimately self-destructive.

> Sadistic attacks on absent or lost external objects . . . lead to a perverse idealization of the "bad self"—that is the self as the author of denigratory and sadistic attacks. Such destructive narcissism could extend to the self's own pathological and destructive ways of thinking. The lie in this system of personality organization becomes positively valued, as carrying for the self an important aspect of defences against weakness, loss, or negative judgment. [*ibid.*, p. 192]

Through a re-reading of the work of Klein, Bion, and those who followed in their wake, Rustin thus provides an answer to the question posed by Allport, Fromm, and Adorno and colleagues as to why racism can become, in Allport's phrase, lockstitched into some personalities and not others: "the lie in the system of personality organization becomes a defence against weakness, loss and negative judgment" (*ibid.*). And, because what counts as loss, weakness, and negative judgement are all mediated biographically, culturally, and interpersonally, the racist in Rustin's account is no longer determined by Oedipal pre-givens or a crisis in contemporary capitalism, but emerges as a psychically complex negotiator of a multitude of socially meaningfully contingencies.

Can the racist self ever recover once he or she has become dependent on these schizoid defence mechanisms? Rustin suggests that this is unlikely if the anti-racist challenge simply charges the prejudiced with being untruthful, or otherwise persecutes them for their ignorance. Rustin argues that, if we are to avoid intensifying the persecutory feelings on which racism thrives then we need first to help people access "an experience of thinking about states of mind and their origins and meanings in relatively free and non-accusatory settings" (ibid., p. 197), and second, to promote "the dissolution of the empty object of [the] signifier 'race' into more real and individuated kinds of difference". For Rustin, then, a "good society would be one which was not anti-racist but non-racial in its identities" (ibid., p. 198).

Reparation in the depressive position

So how do we lose the "race" from our everyday thought processes? And why has this proved so difficult to achieve? Interests, power, and historical legacies provide part of the answer to these questions. But, as Clarke (2003) has explained, the kind of knowing about feelings that the undoing of racism requires cannot be accomplished without a working through of feelings of guilt, shame, and loss. Building on Rustin's argument, Clarke explores what a move towards the depressive position would mean in terms of thinking about race. For Kleinians, the depressive position involves a move beyond the polarized splitting of the paranoid–schizoid position towards a more reconciliatory mode of thinking through which it becomes possible to perceive others as neither all bad nor all good. In the depressive position, conflicts are better managed, the individual is less dependent on projective defences, and a capacity to care develops (Hollway, 2006), often as the individual confronts their guilt at having attacked another whom they can now perceive as less demonic and more likeable or redeemable than they previously imagined. As Clarke explains, the individual in the depressive position "hates the hating self and tries to repair, to make reparation for the damage that has been done" (ibid., pp. 137–138). This necessitates a "mourning for the lost good object" imagined to have been destroyed by hate (ibid., p. 138). The anxieties that working through this mourning evokes in us may, however, be experienced as too persecutory to bear, and may encourage a return to the paranoid–schizoid position through the spiralling of hostile projective identification. Put more plainly, attempts to lose the race from our thinking can be painful, so painful, in fact, that we return once again to seeing those to whom we attributed our bad bits forcing their way back into our minds, bodies, and cultures, accusing us of doing them harm, and of being ungrateful for our attempts to "tolerate" them.

The challenge, then, is how to keep open the possibility of identifying with others which the depressive position opens up without feeling so threatened that a return to the paranoid–schizoid position becomes imminent. How, in the face of our guilt about our own complicity, can we remain emotionally connected to the fates of those we might otherwise find it psychologically more comforting to cast as outsiders? And what would it take for the once hateful individual to become the emotionally reflexive thinker about thinking whom Rustin suggests is best able to assume a non-racial identity; or, indeed, whether, under particularly favourable conditions, a more enduring reparativeness in relation to the hate previously caused by racism can be productively sustained? There is some evidence to suggest that this is indeed possible, in the literature on the process of truth and reconciliation in post-apartheid South Africa (Gobodo-Madikizela, 2003), in the case material documented in this book, and in the news story with which we began this chapter. In any event, we would argue that it is only in theoretical work which attends to the psychosocial challenges of recognition that the conditions and processes needed for this kind of transformative change to take place are adequately explained.

Losing race through recognition

Critical to relational work on recognition is the insight that the process of projective identification—often used to put hateful feelings into another, and/or to block out thinking—is also a means through which we learn to empathize with what others are feeling, to see parts of ourselves in them. But what exactly is it that transforms the demonized from being a repository for our unwanted projections into someone able to teach us something new about ourselves? Benjamin's (1998) view is that it is only when the demonized other is able to retain a sufficient sense of their own history and independent subjectivity that they become psychologically capable of withstanding the destructiveness of their attacker's projections. The demonized other's capacity to withstand these hostile projections is what makes it possible for the attacker to work through the psychic losses exposed in the depressive position, to come to terms with their hate for their hating self, and to begin to perceive the hitherto demonized as irreducible to the sum of the projective attacks mounted against them.

> Identification can serve as a means for bridging difference without denying or abrogating it, but the condition of this form of identification is precisely the other's externality. The other's difference must exist outside; not be felt as a coercive command to "become" the other, and therefore not be defended against by assimilating it to the self. It is here that the notion of recognition as mediated not only through identification, but through direct confrontation with the other's externality, makes a difference. [Benjamin, 1998, p. 96]

As Benjamin argues in relation to the end of apartheid in South Africa, the racist may need the victim of their aggression to identify with them, to extend a gesture of recognition towards them, if they are going to be able to contemplate relinquishing their dependence on racism, a point that is well illustrated in Coetzee's (1999) novel *Disgrace*, and in *Goodbye Bafana*, August's (2007) film about the prison officer who guarded Nelson Mandela. It is the other's capacity to extend a gesture of recognition which, according Benjamin, opens up an intersubjective space—"the third"—where "self and other recreate recognition after breakdown; a space in which historical responsibility for injury, failure, loss, and suffering can be acknowledged and the wounds and scars of destructiveness healed" (Benjamin, 2006, p. 121). To reach this position of "thirdness", both parties have to overcome the dissociative processes that make for the denial of responsibility and the nexus of denials that enable both parties to convince themselves that they are the "done to", not the "doers", the victims of the other's misdeeds and accusations, not the aggressor. In order to move forward, someone has to take ownership of some of the helplessness and destructiveness felt by both sides. One party, at least, must show that they can survive the other's negation, that they are unwilling to become what the other assumes they will be, that they are able to take an ethical responsibility for the consequences of trying to move things forward, and that they can recognize something of themselves, something of value, in the character of their hostile detractor. If the process is sustained, each party becomes a little more able to live in the mind of the other, a little more able to mourn the losses—both physical and developmental—that have contributed to the structure of their defensiveness, and a little more able to reclaim parts of the self hitherto disowned through projection so as to use these to recognize the autonomous existence of others. The challenge for those interested in tackling experiences of injustice and disrespect, including those that fuel violence, racism, and other extremist attitudes, is how best to achieve the level of identification needed to confer this recognition on disadvantaged *groups* more divided in their experiences, outlooks, and interests than they ever have been. How should we respond to what Honneth (2007) calls an "uncoordinated complex of reactive demands for justice" and a "highly sensitive sensorium for injuries" (p. 84), among a populace that is, if the notion of the unconscious is taken seriously, always liable to be "confronted by the unexpected possibilities of their own selves" (p. 191)?

Conclusion

In this chapter, we hope to have demonstrated that there is something complex and contradictory to be understood about the subjectivities of people who are, or appear to be, racist. Moving beyond some of the better known criminological and sociological commentaries, we tried to recover some of this complexity by exploring the models of the authoritarian and/or prejudiced subject to be found in the classic works of Fromm, Adorno and colleagues, and Allport. We also used the revisionist work of those who have borrowed from the Kleinian and relational schools of psychoanalysis to show how a less deterministic, more socially contingent, and, ultimately, less politically pessimistic model of the subject can be constructed. From this, it becomes possible to see how all of us are at risk of identifying with authoritarian characters, racist and anti-racist, of enviously seeking to destroy that which we perceive as admirable in others and deficient in ourselves, or otherwise unthinkingly going with the flow of believing what others think we should believe. The difference between Fromm's "automaton conformist" and Adorno and colleagues' "easy going liberal" might be slight, but those, including Adorno and colleagues' rebels, psychopaths, cranks, and manipulative types, who appear irredeemably racist and who seem to have prejudice "lockstitched" into their personalities, are, we hypothesize, likely to be among the more troubled sections of the population. They are people who not only have more hurt to project outwards, but are also haunted by the force of their own troubling projections, people with whom it is hard to identify, and for whom the challenge of recognition is most acute. When we witness change in these cases, we may learn most about the possibilities of changing those more "conventional" cases consisting of the majority of people who, even while they tend to think in terms of in-groups and out-groups, are not particularly outspoken in their prejudices or violent in their impulses.

The value of this theoretical detour can be assessed by looking again at the story of Lorin Sulaiman and her classmates with which we opened this chapter. On the surface, this is a story based on the revelation that the children of working-class BNP supporters may not be as racist as is often assumed. But it can also be read as a report on the state of the nation, a story about a majority identified (again) with the authoritarian anti-immigrant rhetoric of a government that has contributed to the construction of a problem it is not really able to address, a minority torn between the state's authoritarianism and the more explicitly racist rhetoric of a resurgent British National Party that claims to be standing up to the government on their behalf, and a more critical elite of teachers, counsellors, journalists, and *Guardian* readers, situated predominantly, but not exclusively, between the extremes of Adorno and colleagues' "conventional low scorer" and their "genuine liberal". As the crisis experienced by some of the more racist pupils would suggest, the identifications between these groups are shifting, or, at the very least, are open to being shifted. We would not expect it to be otherwise in the case of young people at an early stage in their social and psychological development who find themselves caught up in conflicts between groups with whom they are multiply identified: their classmates, parents, peers, and teachers.

Predictably, as their headteacher discovered, many of the students encountered a contradiction between their own views on race and their feelings about Lorin's imminent deportation. For some, no doubt, their "distress" stemmed from their identification both with the anti-immigrant views of their parents and the sense of injustice and helplessness they felt about their own inability to prevent Lorin's deportation. Some may have been able to identify with Lorin's personal experiences, her house raided by the police, her mother unwell, and her father missing, presumed murdered, others with her struggle in the face of adversity. She was also the daughter of parents who had campaigned on behalf of the disen-franchised—much like the BNP claims to do on behalf of white working-class voters disillusioned by the indifference of more mainstream political parties. For her classmates in Portsmouth, Lorin had become not just "any" refugee but an exceptionally talented and gifted young woman who represented their interests on the school's council. In some senses, she had become one of them. It is possible, then, that, long before Lorin was taken into custody, a process of mutual recognition may well have been unfolding in which some pupils had already confronted the substance of their hostile projections about immigrants. But it is also possible that the "distress" was more severe for those who did not consciously identify with Lorin, who saw her academic ability as a threat and her engagement with the school as kowtowing to adult authority, or who simply perceived her as another asylum seeker to be bullied, intimidated, and, as far as possible, excluded from the life of the school. What kind of counselling do such people need and what difference, if any, can it make? How can one make reparation for hostile projections to someone who fears she may be killed if she is forced to leave the country? If we are to have any hope of changing racist mindsets, we must be able to find a frame-work within which these questions can be addressed and this kind of psychosocial diversity recognized. The empirical analyses put forward in the next six chapters are offered in the hope that such a framework can be constructed.

CHAPTER THREE

Understanding the "racially motivated offender"

> "[T]here are many flaws in the [Macpherson] report which do need to be acknowledged ... There is ... a woefully inadequate understanding of the constitution of white ethnicities, violent masculinities and white territorialization. The five prime suspects have been transfixed into the racist 'other' where their *witting* racism is presented as a totalizing condition of their being. This one-dimensional conceptualization is one of the reasons why the inquiry, like the inquest before it, could make no headway during the cross examination of the five young men"
>
> (McLaughlin & Murji, 1999, 374–375, original emphasis)

As McLaughlin and Murji note, a preconception of the racist "other" as someone totally consumed by prejudice and hate effectively prevented both the Macpherson Inquiry and the inquest into the death of Stephen Lawrence which preceded it from developing all but the most rudimentary understanding of the five young white men widely suspected of the black teenager's brutal murder. The legacy of this one-dimensional way of thinking about "racial motivation" is now becoming apparent in the criminal justice system. When offenders demonstrate that they have black friends or partners, or insist that they do not hold racist views, those working with perpetrators feel torn between one of two conclusions: either the offender is not really racist or s/he is "in denial" (Dixon, 2002; Docking & Tuffin, 2005; McGhee, 2007; Ray, Smith, & Wastell, 2003a). This chapter sets out the conceptual moves needed to transcend this debilitatingly one-dimensional model. Drawing on Jackson and Pratt's (2001) analysis of the identities of the "prime suspects" in the Lawrence case, this chapter explores the relationship between psychic defences and racist fantasies as developed by those who have followed in the psychoanalytic footsteps of Klein. The chapter also uses the account provided to us by a perpetrator we have called "Steve" to help reveal how persecutory thoughts can become infused, through the process of projective identification, with *racialized* hostility. It concludes by signalling the importance of deconstructing the symbolic dimensions of hate crimes and responses to them, and urging scholars and policymakers to reappraise the disclosures of the men suspected of killing Stephen Lawrence in the light of what is known about the suspects' life histories.

Witting and unwitting racism in the Macpherson Report

The frustration caused by the failure of both the Macpherson Inquiry and the earlier inquest to persuade the five suspects, Neil and Jamie Acourt, David Norris, Gary Dobson, and Luke Knight to reveal anything of themselves under cross-examination is evident in the following passages from the report of the Stephen Lawrence Inquiry: "In 1997, the youths were summoned to appear at the full Inquest. . . . None of them gave any evidence. They all claimed 'privilege'" (Macpherson, 1999, par. 7.38).

> Their final appearance [before the Lawrence Inquiry] was on 29 and 30 June 1998. All five suspects came into the witness box, and answered questions under oath or affirmation. To say that they gave evidence would be to dignify their appearance. They all relied upon alleged lack of memory. They showed themselves to be arrogant and dismissive. (*ibid.*, par. 7.39]

Elsewhere in the same chapter in his report, Macpherson reviewed allegations that the five suspects and / or their associates in a "group of youths ... who always carry knives and threaten people" (*ibid.*, par. 7.11) had been involved in a series of apparently racially motivated attacks in and around Eltham, where Stephen Lawrence was murdered. Then, after referring to recordings made when four of the five "prime suspects" were subject to intrusive surveillance during the second police investigation into the killing in late 1994, Macpherson concluded that "[W]e have confirmation that the suspects were then and certainly before that date infected and invaded by gross and revolting racism" (*ibid.*, par. 7.31).

Though Jamie Acourt had not been subject to the surveillance because he was in custody at the time, Macpherson had "no reason to believe that he was any different from others so far as overt racism is concerned" (*ibid.*). The Inquiry report went on to reproduce extracts from the surveillance transcripts that "showed violent racism at its worst ... both in language and in the brandishing and pretended stabbing [of people described as 'niggers' and 'Pakis'] with knives" (*ibid.*, pars. 7.33–34).

> In themselves the recordings showed abundantly that the suspects were the type of people who could or would have committed a crime of this kind. There was never any doubt but that the killers were rabid racists". [*ibid.*, par. 7.36]

For McLaughlin and Murji (1999), the Inquiry's view of the suspects as "others" consumed by "witting" racism of the most blatant and vicious kind, and its inability to go beyond this and begin to understand how their identities as young white men routinely involved in territorial violence were constructed, left it unable to cope with their intransigence in the face of cross-examination. The following exchange between Acourt and counsel to the Lawrence Inquiry, Edmund Lawson QC, reported in the *Guardian* (1999a), illustrates just how quickly an impasse could be reached:

Lawson: What about the allegations of racism, are they wholly untrue?

Acourt: Yes.

Lawson: You attended a committal hearing when you were charged with Stephen Lawrence's murder. Did you see a surveillance video made by the police?

Acourt: Yes.

Lawson: That was peppered with references to racial comments?

Acourt: I can't remember.

Lawson: Did you remember all the references to niggers, Pakis?

Acourt: No.

Lawson: Have you ever come across racists?

Acourt: No.

Lawson: Is that the truth?

Acourt: Yep. Not what I know of.

Counsel's questions, and his slightly incredulous reaction to Acourt's denials, seem to have been premised on the assumption that "racists" are a distinct population that should have been clearly identifiable to Jamie Acourt because of the memorably offensive language such people use. Anyone would know a racist if they heard one speak. Hence, Acourt must have been lying when he claimed never to have "come across racists", since his brother Neil and their friend David Norris had both been so brazen in their use of racial epithets in the video he had been shown. It did not seem to have occurred to Lawson that it might not be possible to distinguish between "racists" and "non-racists" by the relative offensiveness of the language that they use. Nor did he appear to have considered the possibility that many people who hold racist views do not identify themselves as "racists". It was as if Lawson considered racists a breed apart, prejudiced through and through, in everything they think, say, and do. It was in this respect that the Inquiry operated, as MacLaughlin and Murji (1999) argue, with a set of one-dimensional assumptions about the "constitution of white ethnicities".

As we have seen, Macpherson had no difficulty in condemning the "overt" racism displayed by the five suspects, even going so far as to remark on how the "appalling words" they uttered "sully the paper upon which they have been recorded". Yet, when it came to the police, his criticisms of not dissimilar, if less extreme, language were more muted, and the conclusions drawn about the individuals using it more nuanced.

> In this Inquiry we have not heard evidence of overt racism or discrimination [on the part of the police], unless it can be said that the use of inappropriate expressions such as "coloured" or "negro" fall into that category. The use of such words, which are now well known to be offensive, displays at least insensitivity and lack of training. A number of officers used such terms, and some did not even during their evidence seem to understand that the terms were offensive and should not be used. [Macpherson, 1999, par. 6.3]

The critical distinction made by Macpherson was between the "overt" racism of the kind displayed by the five "prime suspects" and the "institutional racism" which, as the Inquiry report put it, "exists both in the Metropolitan Police Service (MPS) and in other Police Services and other institutions countrywide" (ibid., par. 6.39). Twelve years before Stephen Lawrence's murder, Lord Scarman (1981, par. 9.1) had found no evidence of institutional racism either in the police service or anywhere else in Britain, and Macpherson (1999, par. 6.13) went to some lengths to make it clear that the racism evident in the MPS's handling of the case was, in Scarman's words, "unwitting" or "unconscious", to which he added a third adjective, "unintentional". According to Macpherson's (1999, par. 6.34) now famous definition, institutional racism consisted of:

> The collective failure of an organisation to provide an appropriate and professional service to people because of their colour, culture, or ethnic origin. It can be seen or detected in processes, attitudes and behaviour which amount to discrimination through unwitting prejudice, ignorance, thoughtlessness and racist stereotyping which disadvantage minority ethnic people.

The finding that institutional racism existed in the MPS did not imply either that "the policies of the MPS are racist" or that "every police officer is guilty of racism" (ibid., par. 6.24). Unlike the five suspects who were seen as "overtly" and totally racist, Macpherson's view of the MPS and its officers was more complex: some individual officers were insensitive in their inappropriate use of offensive language, while the organization was guilty of institutional racism, of being "unwittingly" discriminatory in the implementation of policies which were not racist in themselves. Macpherson's account of police racism was as subtle and multifaceted as his analysis of the "prime suspects" was one-dimensional and simplistic.

Unfortunately for Macpherson, reactions to his analysis of police racism were distinctly mixed. One commentator, Brian Cathcart, came, perhaps rather prematurely, to the conclusion that Macpherson had "transformed" the "debate about race in Britain", claiming that "notions that were easier to live with, such as the bad apple theory" had "lost much of their authority" (Cathcart, 1999, p. 416). By contrast, the *Daily Mail*, having branded the five suspects in the Lawrence case "murderers" and challenged them to sue if the newspaper's claims proved unfounded, carried a column by Lynda Lee-Potter (1999) which tried to breathe new life into the one-dimensional "bad apple theory" as she railed against Macpherson's "politically correct McCarthyism":

> The botched investigation . . . was not only a damning indictment of the police, but a betrayal of every law-abiding citizen, irrespective of colour. But to conclude, as Sir William apparently has, that the Metropolitan Police is sunk in "pernicious and institutionalised racism" is a different matter. The words could hardly be more chilling. However he tries to define them, they must damn every member of the Force, irrespective of personal beliefs or behaviour. It is precisely the kind of prejudiced blanket condemnation in which genuine racists like to indulge.

In likening MacPherson to "genuine racists", not dissimilar to Stephen Lawrence's killers, Lee-Potter was being entirely consistent with her newspaper's long-standing view that there is no connection between the attitudes of the "law-abiding" majority and the motives of the rotten minority who perpetrate racist attacks. Within this framework, the notion that many people are unwittingly or unconsciously racist simply did not compute. Rightly or wrongly, a great many police officers did indeed feel that they had been unjustifiably "branded as racists" (Foster, Newburn, & Souhami, 2005, p. 33), a stigma that the finely calibrated distinctions in Macpherson's explanation of "institutional racism" did little to prevent from attaching not just to police organizations, but also to the individuals serving within them (Bowling & Philips, 2007; FitzGerald, 2001; Holdaway & O'Neil, 2004; McLaughlin & Murji, 1999, p. 374; Webster, 2007, p. 77).

The psychic defensiveness of the "prime suspects"

For a more sophisticated view of the *Daily Mail's* "murderers" than is offered in the report of the Macpherson Inquiry, we must turn to Jackson and Pratt (2001), whose analysis of the masculinities of the five suspects drew attention to the role of defensiveness in shoring up the subjectivities of racial harassment perpetrators. Extraordinarily envious of the "bigged up" masculinities of some black men (*ibid.*, p. 27), the five teenagers suspected of killing Stephen Lawrence were prone, according to Jackson and Pratt, to paranoid, largely unconscious, fears that the physically menacing figures of their imaginations were out to get them. Applying the psychoanalytic insights of Klein to some of the things the suspects said after the murder, Jackson and Pratt hypothesize that, when they stumbled across Stephen Lawrence, flustered and "less visibly armoured and perhaps more vulnerable than many other black men who were more streetwise", the murderers spotted an opportunity to fulfil a fantasy of themselves as "heroic white warriors", "no longer failures to themselves . . . because they had triumphed over their imagined persecutor" (*ibid.*, p. 28). In so doing, they were shielded from seeing both the real Stephen—an ambitious, studious, and unthreatening young man worried about being late home—and "the changing complexity of black men's lives—the real pain, the everyday heartache of white racism, the occasional power and contradictions . . . hidden under this carapace of seeming hardness" (*ibid.*, p. 27). Stephen Lawrence was attacked, Jackson and Pratt surmise, by five men who were deeply afraid of "being seen as white losers" and highly defensive about their own failings (*ibid.*, p. 25). Our view, however, is that, while Jackson and Pratt's analysis is penetrating, it underplays the complexity of Klein's insights and, in so doing, understates the benefits of adopting a Kleinian approach to understanding both the motives of those who perpetrate racially aggravated crimes generally, and the thinking of the suspects in the Lawrence case in particular.

What, then, was Klein's central hypothesis? Whereas Freud studied neurotic adults to discover their repressed inner childhood conflicts, Klein's (1946) view—controversial in the 1950s, but almost *passé* now—was that, by studying infants, we could make inferences about the inner psychic worlds of adults and older children

(Sayers, 2000). Whereas Freud conceptualized sexuality as a primary source of human anxiety, Klein argued that many childish anxieties arise from the infant's feelings of emotional ambivalence towards its parents (Minsky, 1998, p. 33). Klein observed that children often express very destructive feelings towards those upon whom they are dependent—babies sometimes quite literally attacking the nipple that feeds them, for example—alongside more loving and generous sentiments. Applying "play techniques" with her own children, as well as those of others, Klein (1955) came to the conclusion that infants struggle to come to terms with being both the centre of their parents' attention (and, hence, powerful and in control) and being dependent on their parents (and, hence, controlled and vulnerable). In this context, phantasies of omnipotence, together with projective attacks on their primary caregivers, are the child's defences against persecutory feelings of anxiety.

Klein's observations about this process led her to the conclusion that people fluctuate between different ways of thinking about their relationships with others, between the poles of what she was to refer to as the *paranoid–schizoid* and *depressive positions*. Klein explained that, in the paranoid–schizoid position, people tend to feel uncomfortably vulnerable and unfairly criticized, and are preoccupied with the idea that hostile others are out to get them. Consumed by their own inner turmoil, people in this position typically respond to persecutory anxieties very defensively. This defensiveness often takes the form of *splitting*, where the self is divided into good and bad parts, and *projection*, where disowned parts of the self that the individual perceives as threatening are attributed to significant others. Thus, people in the paranoid–schizoid position adopt a dichotomous all good/all bad view of the world, and feel envy towards those they assume possess things or qualities they crave, often unconsciously, for themselves. In the short term, projective mechanisms help the individual to fend off their anxieties. In the longer term, however, the processes of *projective identification* on which the paranoid–schizoid person becomes reliant can compound feelings of persecution causing them to act aggressively towards both the recipients of their original projective attacks and anyone imagined to be associated with them. This is because

> Projective identification [entails] . . . splitting off and projection of parts of the self and the forcing of them upon another person who

may then be attacked for seeming to be responsible for those parts
... Sometimes the recipient of the projective identification feels
taken possession of and may shout out phrases such as, "Stop it,
you'll drive me mad!" Such outbursts are not meaningless expressions of intolerance. Sometimes aggression is unconsciously
designed to put madness into somebody else, that is, to drive him
or her mad in the hope and expectation that the subject may remain
sane. [Hyatt Williams, 1998, p. 69]

In other words, as the attacked other starts to resemble the split-off
parts projected into them, the paranoid–schizoid person begins to
imagine the attacked other as someone who is irreconcilably fear-
some, menacing, dirty, corrupt, and/or incorrigible, a dim but
persistently nagging reminder of the very person the paranoid–
schizoid person is afraid they themselves have become.

"Race" as the ideal container of psychotic thought

Applied specifically to the question of how and why some people
become consumed by racial hatred, the Kleinian perspective can
help us transcend the limitations of one-dimensional assumptions
about offenders. First and foremost, the Kleinian perspective
enables us to offer a much more nuanced account of how, why, and
when people become susceptible to polarized forms of thinking. As
Mike Rustin (2000, p. 187) surmises:

[P]sychotic states of mind are universal, original and latent compo-
nents of human mentality; never wholly banished from the self;
liable to become more salient in conditions of fear and anxiety than
in more benign settings; and of course more central and pathogenic
in some individuals than in others, sometimes for explicable
reasons in an individual's psychic history.

Refashioned in this way, it is possible to see how almost anyone can
become susceptible to paranoid–schizoid thinking, but also why
certain individuals, because of the biographical and socially structured contingences of their own lives, are more prone to persecutory anxieties than others. The uncertainties of the world we live in
constantly evoke fears in all of us, perhaps explaining how it is that

we are sometimes shocked to find those whom we would not ordinarily consider prejudiced making hostile or stereotypical assumptions in times of crisis or stress. The pain of redundancy, estrangement, loss, and victimization may prove too much for some people to contain psychologically, increasing the allure of culturally sanctioned modes of disowning vulnerabilities. On the other hand, there are some individuals who, because of experiences of uncontained trauma, often in the earlier parts of their lives, become so dependent on paranoid–schizoid defences that dichotomized thinking becomes ingrained in their personality structures, giving the appearance, in certain contexts, of an unshakably authoritarian outlook.

Second, and as Rustin goes on to argue, a Kleinian perspective also helps to explain why these polarized, potentially authoritarian modes of thinking often manifest themselves in highly racialized, or racializable, forms. Because "race" "is both an empty category and one of the most destructive and powerful forms of social categorization", negative affect, including all that is loosely related to forms of intimacy and bodily function, can easily be loaded into it (Rustin, 2000, p. 183). In other words, as we saw in Chapter Two, it is precisely because differences in skin colour and facial features are relatively meaningless markers that "race" has become so frequently used as a repository for the divestment of negative sentiment: it readily lends itself to the "pseudo-thinking" in which the paranoid–schizoid indulges, offering up a convenient menu of stereotypes, prejudices, and generalizations that render it culturally permissible to attack the ethnic other with relative impunity. This, in turn, helps to explain why racism is so difficult to challenge, and confrontational interventions so frequently counterproductive (Bhavnani, Mirza, & Meetoo, 2005, p. 135). If accusations, especially accusations of prejudice, are liable to generate the persecutory feelings that mobilize the same kind of schizoid defence mechanisms— splitting, projection, denial—that inform expressions of racist hate, how, from a Kleinian perspective, can racist mindsets best be changed?

Having discovered that children could sometimes learn to cope with troubling anxieties if she, the analyst, was able to find a way of meaningfully symbolizing them back in a more bearable form, Klein's (1955) view was that the spiralling of projective hostility was not the inevitable fate of the person in the paranoid–schizoid position. Following the work of Bion (1984), this *detoxifying* mode of symbolization is sometimes referred to by Kleinians as *containment*, a process that can give rise to psychologically enriching forms of projective identification whereby the individual reintrojects—takes in—the good parts of the self attributed to the "containing" other. It is through this process of having one's anxieties contained that people learn how to manage their own worries and those of others, to occupy what Klein called the *depressive position*. Once in this mode of mentalization, people are better equipped to tolerate ambivalent feelings about themselves and others, to make psychic reparation for hostile projections, to feel gratitude for the emotional warmth they have received from others (as opposed to envy at the warm person's capacity to give), to manage guilt without being overcome by feelings of persecution, and to begin to imagine the world from the perspectives of others. For the cycle of hostile projective identification to be interrupted, guilt has to be confronted and the pain of making reparation tolerated and endured. As Clarke (2003, p. 142) explains,

> The depressive position can be viewed as recognition of the plurality of difference in which the individual hates the hating self and tries to repair, to make reparation for the damage that has been done. Care for others develops, as does guilt in realisation that the attacked "other" contains both good and bad. Thus, depressive anxiety fuels the need to make reparation. The depressive position involves fear, anxiety and despair about the ability to both make reparation for those destroyed in phantasy and to overcome one's own destructiveness.

The problem is that the "fear, anxiety, and despair" encountered in the depressive position can all too easily prove overwhelming, giving rise to the paranoid fear that the other is either aggrieved with us and set on taking revenge, or desperate to become one of us and liable to attempt to take us over. When such reactions become culturally commonplace, as they have periodically in Britain, expressions of outright hostility to those perceived as "foreigners" are able to co-exist quite comfortably with an ostensible abhorrence of bigotry, hatred, and violence.

Perpetrators' biographies and the psychodynamics
of racist motivation

We believe that attending to the mental shifts between depressive and paranoid–schizoid ways of thinking about "race", ethnicity, and difference provides a means of surmounting one-dimensional ways of conceptualizing racism and the illusory "now you see it, now you don't" quality these confer on offenders' "racial motives" (Ray, Smith, & Wastell , 2003a). But this is only possible if—and this is not always the case—sufficient space is made for the full contradictoriness of offenders' subjectivities to become apparent. Capturing both the hostility and the tolerance of which offenders are capable requires methods that allow them to "recreate" in the telling particular occasions on which they have felt threatened or aggrieved, while simultaneously providing them with opportunities to speak about their thoughts, feelings, and experiences with a level of detachment that is not threatened by accusatory questioning. It was for this reason that we deployed Hollway and Jefferson's (2000) Free Association Narrative Interview method in our research.

The Free Association Narrative Interview method is an approach which encourages research participants to "freely associate" in relation to an invitation to tell their own life stories, including stories relating to particularly critical incidents, whether racist, criminal, or otherwise. Hence, we often encouraged participants not only to tell stories of their own schooling, upbringing, work, and family lives, but to return more specifically to their recollections of adversarial situations, relationships with members of other ethnic groups, and encounters with criminal justice professionals. Through the use of active reflection, where participants' meaning frames are presented back to them, and follow-up interviews during the course of which participants' defences, avoidances, and rationalizations are carefully probed, the Free Association Narrative Interview method elicits rich life story accounts well suited to psychoanalytical interpretation. It was using this method that we interviewed all the perpetrators described in Chapter One, including Steve, to whose story we now return. We have chosen to focus on Steve because, in our initial readings of his interview transcripts, we were undecided about whether Steve was or was not a "racially motivated offender". Armed with a Kleinian approach, however, it became possible to see how ideas about race had informed Steve's violence while simultaneously resolving, albeit only temporarily, other psychic conflicts that were of much more immediate concern to him.

A pen portrait of Steve

When he was first invited to participate in an interview about his life, Steve, a sixteen-year-old young offender undergoing supervision in the community, adopted a cocky, if wilfully evasive, attitude. Asked if he was married or single, he mocked the interviewer, exclaiming, "I'm married. Sixteen. I'm married . . . six kids." Invited to tell the story of his life from as far back as he could remember, Steve retorted, "I can't remember last week." The disclaimers with which he commenced the second interview—"I can't remember nothing today. I got tonsillitis. Me head's mashed", and "I can't remember nothing, I can't. I swear on it"—seemed to serve a similar function to Jamie Acourt's rather convenient memory failures during cross-examination before the Macpherson Inquiry. Yet, once he had begun to relax a little, Steve was willing and able to provide an informative outline of his life as he remembered it. The first recollection Steve offered was of the time when, aged between three and five, his "mum and dad split up". Following the break-up, his mother had to find a new home on a neighbouring estate for Steve and herself. At first, his father maintained contact, taking Steve out on a motorbike at weekends, but this ceased abruptly when Steve was no more than six years old. Thereafter, Steve claimed to have "got on well with everyone" in his new neighbourhood, despite "a few ifs". This turned out to be something of an understatement of the problems he faced. Disliked as a newcomer to the area, Steve's first fight was at primary school when "a big fat guy" called him "a prick". Steve ended up "filling him in"—"punching" and "stamping on him"—and was promptly suspended. Picked on by one of the "fat guy's mates" on his return from suspension, Steve got into a second fight—"filled him in" too—and was suspended again.

Things settled down once his mum got to know the other children's mothers, and Steve claimed at one point that he "never got in any trouble". However, the story he told suggested that, once again, this was not strictly the case. His mum having got to know their mums, Steve and his new mates started to "terrorize the estate". As Steve recalled, with more than a hint of nostalgia, this entailed making too much noise, robbing and selling "anything we could get our hands on", chucking bricks at "anyone [who] used to give us trouble" or "filling them in": "We all used to be little bastards, man." Steve's nostalgia was soon tinged with regret, however, as he remembered how he, and he alone, became known to the adults in his neighbourhood as "the little bastard of Basford Green": even today, if "anything goes missing, they blame me . . . anyone gets hit . . . they blame me". Only in the second interview did Steve provide some clues as to why, when so many of his contemporaries were also involved in childish pranks and petty crime, he alone became so stigmatized. One particularly significant incident involved Steve posting matches through his primary school's mailbox, leading to an "accident" in which three of the school's offices were burnt out. As a result of this escapade, Steve's mother faced a £5,000 compensation order and, from then on, "loads of people's mums didn't like" him. Urged to recall his mother's reaction, Steve conceded that he had known that she was "cross", but also remembered that "she didn't say nothing to me, because I'd start going at her if she [said] anything to me".

At high school, Steve became part of an ethnically mixed gang of white and Asian "lads". He was routinely "chucked out" of class, only to roam the school and "chat the birds up". Aged fourteen, Steve was eventually excluded for hitting a teacher with a crutch, but claimed that he had done so only in retaliation for the teacher doing the same thing to a girl. Immediately after he had hit the teacher, and knowing that expulsion would follow, Steve had set off on a "wild one round school", swearing at everyone, setting off a fire extinguisher, and "causing loads of trouble". By his mid teens he was already consuming alcohol quite frequently, a habit that escalated when his dad re-entered his life and provided Steve with some short-lived employment as a painter and decorator, rounded off with a trip to the pub at the end of the week. Having discovered vodka, Steve was soon "on litres . . . near enough every night". Being "pissed" made him particularly touchy: "If anyone says anything to me when I'm pissed . . . I'll hit them . . . I lose me temper dead easy." And there were plenty of people saying "things" about him. In addition to being known as the "bastard of

Basford Green", "little kids" called Steve a "gyppo" because (or so he claimed) his clothes were often ripped and dirty from riding his motorcycle across local waste ground. Worse still, adults living locally—his peers' "aunts and uncles"—publicly attacked him for being a "bully" and a "thief", accusations that Steve found particularly upsetting: "I'm not a bully . . . get on with everyone as long as they get on with me."

The trouble was that Steve's reactions to things that bothered him—even when sober—often made him extremely difficult to get along with, even for those interested in trying. So, for example, Steve fell out with his father when he realized that the payments his dad received for painting and decorating jobs were not shared equally between the two of them. A confrontation about this led to Steve refusing to talk to his father, his father threatening to withhold Steve's wages, and Steve threatening to smash the windows of his father's van. When he eventually lost his job, Steve's contact with his father rapidly diminished again. Around the same time, Steve also started having "a few ifs" with his mum. This began with her "flipping" because Steve's father had not delivered the new bed he had promised him, and ended with her "putting her fist" in Steve's face when he refused to turn the volume down on his music. With no apologies exchanged, the conflict culminated in Steve's mother telling him to "get out" and consider himself "thrown out" of "her house". Steve responded to this confrontation by telling his mum to "Get out me face before I hit you" and leaving for his mate's house to "chill out . . . for a few hours" until *she* was "all right" again. Reflecting on the incident and what he had said to his mum, Steve explained, "I wouldn't hit her like, but I'll say it."

Since he had recently accumulated a catalogue of convictions for a range of offences, including assaults, thefts, drug-dealing, burglary, and vehicle crimes—"just stupid stuff"—Steve's mother's anger began to seem more comprehensible, while his own claim to have stayed out of trouble since primary school became increasingly incredible. True enough, many of his convictions were for crimes of a relatively trivial nature: sharing drugs with friends, stealing a parrot from someone's house, and assaults stemming from arguments or "just messing about" with other young people he knew out on the streets. A physical assault on an Asian shopkeeper was more difficult to depict in these terms, although charges against Steve were eventually dropped at court. His account of the incident was that he had had the "munchies" and, unaware that his friends were "robbing" drinks from the fridge, was in the shop to buy something to eat. The shopkeeper had tried to stop Steve's friends leaving and, thinking that he was in on it too, had grabbed or punched Steve before he could make himself scarce. Steve had responded to this by hitting the shopkeeper "on the head with a can" before "fill[ing] him in up the corner". Steve's Youth Offending Team worker had referred him to us because of the potentially racist nature of this assault, even though Steve himself insisted he was not a "racist". He knew, and was known by, the local shopkeepers, including the victim of this attack, and reported that everything was "sound . . . sell them stereos and stuff . . . get cheap food off them". Moreover, he claimed to have "always" got on well with black people, "black" being a term he used also to refer to "Asian" people. He explained that his best mate was "black", as, indeed, were "most people" in his year at high school. Steve also claimed to be "safe" with "everyone" in two of Stoke's most ethnically mixed neighbourhoods. His mum worked in a sorting office in one of these areas—"They all know me mum . . . they are all safe with me mum"—while his sister and nan lived in the other: "When I go up there, I speak to them all . . . so [I'm] safe with them all really."

Nevertheless, Steve's attitudes towards people he identified as "Kosovans"—"It's just like 'Kosovans' I don't like . . . come over here and get benefits and don't work or nothing"—suggested a more complex attitude to "race". Initially, it seemed that exceptions could also be made here; a "Kosovan lad" on the same mechanics course as Steve turned out to be the only one of his fellow students with whom he could have a "laugh" and smoke skunk. Asked about this "Kosovan" in a second conversation two weeks after we first spoke to him, however, Steve corrected the interviewer, insisting that this "lad" was actually a "Paki". This change of ethnic categorization appeared to be connected to the story Steve also told about three fights he had had with "Kosovan" men within the last six months. The first of these happened while Steve had been remanded in custody for a week and feared falling victim to the violence he had been warned to expect while locked up. Steve had been playing pool when three "Kosovans" came up to him, grabbed his cue, claimed that they "owned" the table, and then hit him when he grabbed the cue back. As there were three of them, Steve had done nothing at the time, but the next day he had attacked one of them with a plug-filled sock, after which "they got took off that wing". "Everyone" else remanded to Steve's landing was "safe" with him after that. The second altercation had begun when a "Kosovan" friend of the owner of a takeaway had been served ahead of Steve. His protests to the owner dismissed, Steve had invited the queue jumper to step outside. Once outside, Steve hit the man, who had then run off. None of the other workers or customers had dared to intervene because, as Steve explained, "Those people know me and they know if they start. . . [saying] 'Get off him' . . . I'll turn on them." The third fight had taken place on Steve's estate, where he believed a lot of benefit-claiming "Kosovans" lived, and involved three complete strangers staring at Steve as he walked past. Steve's "what you looking at?" challenge had been met with an incomprehensible reply: "They started mumbling loads of shit in their language." Assuming that "they must have been saying something" about him, Steve thought "fuck this" and went up and "whacked" one of them. A mate of Steve's who happened to be passing immediately came to assist him by attacking another of the "Kosovans", whereupon the third ran off, leaving Steve to continue "filling in" the man he had just "whacked".

Steve, persecutory anxiety, and projective identification

In Steve, we have an example of someone who could, from one perspective, be regarded as a relatively persistent racially motivated offender. With four incidents involving the harassment of eight ethnic minority men in the space of just six months, anyone charged with working with Steve could have been forgiven for assuming that his violence was primarily, if not wholly, motivated by racism. As with so many of the explanations provided by offenders involved in such incidents, Steve's own answer to such a charge— that he was not a "racist"—was liable to prove more baffling than illuminating to anyone given the task of challenging his offending behaviour. Having grown up with black and Asian friends, and being so closely identified with a mother who worked with black and Asian people, Steve's claim that he was not a racist, and was generally "safe" with people of different ethnic backgrounds, could not be easily dismissed. His use of the term "Paki" to differentiate someone he liked from the "Kosovans", whom he disliked, certainly complicated matters, at least if one's starting point is the assumption that many of those who hear themselves described in such terms are liable to take offence, and that Steve's own experiences with Asian friends should have taught him this, if nothing else. On the other hand, if one combines the notion that "race" is an "empty category" into which contradictory attitudes and feelings can be loaded, with a recognition of the extent to which cultural and colour-based racisms have been heavily inflected (if not entirely dislodged), both popularly and politically, by an anti-immigrant xeno-racism, Steve's resolute contempt for "Kosovans"—a potential catch-all term for those who appear neither white-British, black, nor Asian—starts to become fathomable as a paranoid–schizoid defence against persecutory anxiety.

The ordering of Steve's violence provides some valuable clues as to how these persecutory anxieties mutated. In the case of the prison violence, we have Steve, a young man acutely worried about his own safety, taking on those who were seeking to monopolise the pool table. When Steve put the "Kosovans" in their place, all the other prisoners became "safe" with him, enabling Steve to put both his own insecurities behind him and to reimagine himself as the heroic righter of wrongs instead of the bully many adults in his neighbourhood perceived him to be. In the takeaway, however, Steve's response to the injustice of someone jumping the queue served only to reinforce the stigma of being the neighbourhood bully, nobody intervening lest an out-of-control Steve turn on them, too. Finally, we have the completely unprovoked attack on the three "Kosovans" talking in their own language. Steve's paranoia seeped through his account here, suggesting that he did not feel "safe" with them even before they started to feel—quite justifiably—unsafe with him. While Steve could not understand what the three "Kosovans" were saying, he felt so psychologically threatened by their looks and incomprehensible words that he chose to defend himself by "filling them in".

Filling people in, had, as Steve's life story revealed, become his customary response to feelings of persecution since infancy. Steve's use of this expression to describe his frequent use of violence to overwhelm others also hinted at his penchant for the application of force as a means of rectifying what he perceived as other people's misperceptions about him. So, Steve "filled in" the "fat guy" at primary school who called him a "prick", his mate who compounded the offence when Steve returned from suspension, and the Asian shopkeeper who accused him of stealing. And Steve did much the same to the seven "Kosovans" who, by muscling him off the pool table, pushing in front of him, and looking at him in a peculiar way, suggested that they had misjudged him in a way that caused him offence. That the provocations needed to summon a violent response became increasingly trifling—from the shopkeeper's accusations of theft to unwarranted claims over a pool table, to favouritism in the takeaway and, finally, to unwelcome glances and incomprehensible talk—hints at the significance of some form of projective identification. To Steve, the more he attacked them, the more menacing the Kosovan "others" began to appear. Against this background, Steve's explanation that "Kosovans" take "our" benefits without working felt like something of an after-thought, an attempt to gloss his actions with the legitimacy provided by popular stereotypes of the undeserving asylum seeker. On the other hand, the contrast between the unemployed, benefit-claiming "Kosovans" of Steve's imaginings and his own parents—who, whatever their failings, worked and were consistently portrayed by Steve as affirming his sense of belonging—provides clues as to why it was so important for him to define himself as "safe" with everyone despite the overwhelming evidence to the contrary.

Whether his father's disappearance from his life was in some way to blame for Steve becoming one of the "wild" children who "terrorized" the locality is impossible to know. It is certainly possible that his father's absence contributed to the enduring potency of Steve's *reputation* as the "bastard of Basford Green"; many people's *mothers* probably regarding Steve as an irredeemably unpleasant young man—and bad influence on their own children to boot—whose father had not been there to pull him into line. Interestingly, the only disputes Steve actually identified as "ifs" were with the parent who was left to pick up the pieces, his mother. Despite his cockiness, Steve was still highly dependent on her approval. Whether or not he got on with her, the other mums, and his mother's black and Asian co-workers, were critical yardsticks against which Steve assessed his own popularity. Coping with Steve and his wayward behaviour alone while building a new home for them on an unskilled worker's wage must have been difficult enough for Steve's mum even before he was first suspended and then excluded from school as the consequences of his violence and fire-starting began to unfold. For Steve, the realization of how his behaviour had affected his mother must also have been painful. That the fear of him "going at" her had inhibited Steve and his mother from ever talking about how he accrued his reputation as the "bastard of Basford Green" suggests both a failure of "containment" and a troubling emotional experience that became increasingly toxic the more it was avoided. Steve must have wondered whether his mother shared everyone else's assessment of him as the "bastard of Basford Green" or, latterly, whether she, too, regarded him as a "bully" and a "thief" given his lengthening criminal record, refusal to live by her rules, and occasional threats to hit her.

Disturbed by his own threatening behaviour towards his mother, Steve fled to his mate's house to "chill out"—which for him meant drinking and/or using drugs. On his own admission, these habits only exacerbated his touchiness and his willingness to hit people who said the wrong thing to him. In truth, Steve's claim that he could "get on with everyone as long as they get on with me" has to be qualified by his failure either to temper his aggression or to acknowledge that "anyone" who said "anything" he disliked immediately put themselves at risk of being "filled in". However, from Steve's point of view, few of those who were saying things could be legitimately avenged. To attack the "little kids" who called him "gyppo" (itself a racialized term of abuse with a complicated etymology, but more ordinarily associated with being untrustworthy, a thief, and a moral degenerate than a scruffy dresser), the aunts and uncles who called him a bully, or even his mum who, through it all, had kept her assessment of her son to herself, would probably only confirm in everyone's else's mind—as well as in Steve's own—that he was indeed an inveterate bully and a bastard, wholly deserving of the bad "reputation" he had acquired. As friends, family, and neighbours, none of these people could safely be "filled in". But groups of "Kosovan" men—collectively stronger than Steve, from neither white, black, nor Asian communities, and popularly regarded as "illegals" and "benefit cheats"—could, if the circumstances were right, be imagined as legitimate and worthy adversaries. Outnumbered by these foreign bullies and thieves, Steve could soothe his persecutory anxieties by consoling himself with the thought that no one would criticize him for "filling in" "Kosovans". The trouble was that, once the schizoid dimensions of Steve's own thinking came into play, the disturbing notion that he was an unlovable bully and bastard could not be kept out of his consciousness, the staring eyes of three complete strangers enough to remind him of exactly what he suspected everyone's mums were thinking. Ultimately, the dynamics of projective identification meant that Steve's violence exaggerated rather than relieved the persecutory anxieties that motivated it.

Putting perpetrators in perspective

By way of confirmation of Rustin's (2000, p. 87) hypothesis, we could surmise that Steve's attacks on those he perceived to be "Kosovans" were facilitated, psychodynamically, by:

- the "suffusion" of his "thinking processes by intense, unrecognized emotion", as evidenced in his violence and his tendency to retreat into drinking and drug use when things got too upsetting;
- the "confusion between [his]self and object" apparent in his attribution of his own thoughts to his victims;
- a "splitting" of Steve's "self" and "massive projective identification", suggested by his inability to perceive the disjunction between being "safe" with everyone and his reputation among so many people in his neighbourhood as a persistent "bully" and a "bastard";
- a "hatred of [the] reality and truth" of what many people in Basford Green, including his mother, knew about his behaviour and reputation;
- the perennial failure of emotional containment ameliorated by resort to racial categorization and, *in extremis*, to "filling in" anyone who appeared to fall into the elusive category of "Kosovan".

Getting at what motivated Steve's violence would have been much more difficult if our starting point had been that he was either an out-and-out racist in denial, or not really racist at all, since this kind of binary approach would have meshed rather too readily with Steve's own defensive splitting. Seeing through this splitting is essential if we are to transcend the fallacious assumptions which so often dog official responses to racist crime: that perpetrators' prejudices tend to be expressed in "pure and readily available forms"; that racism is clear-cut, "conscious", and, to some extent, a lifestyle choice which can be educated away by correcting misconceptions and inculcating more acceptable ways of talking and behaving (McGhee, 2007, p. 216). Conversely, a culturally-sensitive Kleinian perspective, alert to the unresolved identity conflicts in which offenders' families and communities are implicated, provides a more sophisticated means of grasping how potential perpetrators, who already feel defensive about their own failings, are moved from being comfortably familiar with ethnic diversity into all-consuming paranoid states of racialized hostility. A Kleinian perspective can account, at least in part, for the illusory quality of prejudice in many racially motivated offenders' lives. Because even the most obvious expressions of prejudice tend to have an unconscious dimension, it makes little sense from a Kleinian perspective to talk about "witting" or "overt" and "unwitting" or "unconscious" racism as discrete "types". What tends to be unconscious is not racism *per se*, but the unconscionable conflicts, affects, and feelings of persecution kept out of mind through psychic defence mechanisms that are, in turn, lent weight by the culturally sanctioned resources provided by stereotypy and prejudice.

Projective identification: Steve and the "prime suspects"

Against those who might complain that our thesis rests upon no more than conjecture based on evidence drawn from a single case, we would argue that examples of projective identification also abound in the utterances of the five "prime suspects" in the killing of Stephen Lawrence, and that this single, horrifying case—though only one among many racist murders—has had a disproportionate impact on the way policymakers conceive of racially motivated crime. As we suggested earlier, the role of racism in Stephen Lawrence's murder could have been more adequately theorized. Take, for example, the surveillance videos that Edmund Lawson QC drew to the attention of Jamie Acourt during the Macpherson Inquiry's hearings in late June 1998. The extracts from the soundtrack reproduced in the Inquiry's report include: Luke Knight complaining about British football presenters wanting Cameroon— "a fucking nigger country"—rather than Italy to win a match; Jamie's brother, Neil, asserting "that every nigger should be chopped up . . . and . . . left with nothing but fucking stumps"; and David Norris fantasizing about killing himself having skinned alive, tortured, and set alight a "black cunt" before "blow[ing] their two legs and arms off and say[ing] go on you can swim home now" (Macpherson, 1999, para. 7.33). It was these and other equally disturbing comments that led Lawson and many others to presume that the suspects were, as one journalist put it, "behaving according to type" (*Guardian*, 1999b), thus reinforcing the one-dimensional conceptualization of the "racist other" which continues to inform responses to racist crime in Britain today.

Luke Knight's account of the background to his comments, given to the journalist Martin Bashir, suggests other possible explanations, however. Knight's explanation was that "at that time" he felt that "black people had ruined [his] life" (Marks, 1999), a reaction intended, no doubt, to cast himself in the role of victim, but one which can also be construed as an emotionally charged defence against feelings of persecution arising out of the public sympathy for Stephen Lawrence's parents, Doreen and Neville, and a psychic attack on Stephen himself, imagined as instigator, taunting his killers from beyond the grave. Similarly, we would argue that David Norris's explanation that his suicidal and murderous tirade should be read as the "sign of a depressed young man" is not, from a Kleinian perspective, necessarily at odds with Bashir's reading of these remarks as the "sign of a psychotic racist" (*ibid.*). That Norris and Neil Acourt were later convicted of a racially aggravated assault on an off-duty police officer testifies to the enduring legacy of the fantasies that came to consume some of the suspects in the Lawrence case. But it should not surprise us that a group of teenagers who perceived themselves—much like our interviewee Steve—as quasi-heroic outlaws, but who had become cast in the popular imagination as nothing but dangerous, racist thugs, and might conceivably be consumed by unmentionable feelings of shame and guilt, should find themselves locked into a poisonous spiral of racialized hostility in which they imagined that their own public degradation could be transcended by the sadistic incapacitation of their persecutors, and, ultimately, by their own deaths.

To suggest that the racism of the men suspected of killing Stephen Lawrence might have become even more pronounced in the aftermath of the murder is not to repeat the classic error of labelling theory and to conceive of offenders as untainted and unmotivated until so labelled (cf. Lemert, 1964). Rather, it is to maintain that, if further lessons are to be learnt from the Lawrence case, what really needs to be asked is: how racism became so enmeshed in the consistently aggressive, yet defensively masculine, postures of the "prime suspects"; what was unique and specific about their particular developmental pathways; and whether the *Daily Mail*'s (often too uncritically accepted) assumption that all five young men were as racist and as guilty as each other is really justified. Certainly, all five suspects grew up at a time (the early 1990s) and in a place (Eltham) where many white people saw little connection between their hostility towards the "foreigners" they believed had encroached on their territory and the series of violent racist incidents documented in Chapter Six of the Macpherson Inquiry's report (1999). By their own admission, the five men suspected of attacking Stephen Lawrence—again like our own interviewee, Steve—were both of, and outside, their communities, well known on the Brook Estate (on or near to which four of them lived) as "little bastards" for their anti-social and potentially violent behaviour (Macpherson, 1999, pars. 7.8–11; Marks, 1999). Similarly, all five of them regarded their anti-social behaviour and interest in fighting and knives as just the kinds of "stupid things" sixteen- and seventeen-year-old boys like them did (Marks, 1999). Several of them shared a history of exclusion and failure that could be linked quite directly, if somewhat perversely, to issues of "race". Jamie Acourt had been excluded from school at the age of fourteen for assaulting a black pupil, while his brother Neil and David Norris— already excluded from mainstream schooling by their mid teens— also found themselves expelled from a local youth club they had frequented after the letters "NF" (for National Front) were found daubed on its walls (Pallister, 1999).

Should the guilt of the Lawrence suspects ever be properly established, we will need to ask not only how their early experiences of parenting—David Norris with his fugitive father, the Acourt brothers with their single, and occasionally absent, mother—and social exclusion were connected to their defensively macho, racist outlooks, but also whether the reactions of those who deemed them incorrigible "bastards" contributed in some way to the dynamics of projective identification that turned them into racially motivated murderers. While these questions cannot be answered in the cases of the men suspected of killing Stephen Lawrence, then we—academics, policymakers and practitioners—must look again at the cases of other young people involved in racist incidents and think carefully about the particular anxieties, desires, and misperceptions that lie behind their crimes. Ensuring that the victims of racially aggravated offences receive an appropriate and professional service from the criminal justice system, irrespective of their "colour, culture or ethnic origin" is a critical part of tackling the problem of racially motivated violence and harassment. But that problem is unlikely to go away unless we can find ways of detoxifying the anxieties of young men caught up in spirals of projective identification. If proclaiming such offenders "racist" is a critical part of the justice process, we need also to invest in interventions that enable those so labelled to come to terms with why it is that others perceive them thus; interventions that nurture in them the emotional and cultural resources needed to survive the stigma of being known as a "racially motivated offender". It must be part of our task to alert practitioners and policymakers to the possibility that adopting a one-dimensional approach to the question of motive risks compounding the persecutory feelings that prevent offenders from confronting their own guilt and adopting more tolerant, less defensive mentalities in relation to diversity. This is a challenge to which we return in the next chapter.

CHAPTER FOUR

Racially aggravated offenders and the punishment of hate

"The main justification for specific laws against racially aggravated crime is based on social cohesion. Attacking somebody (verbally or physically) because of their racial identity harms not only the victim but wider circles of people who share that identity, and threatens the stability of mixed communities and the development of a tolerant society. It may be asked how far the criminal law can really be expected to exert a corrective influence on dissonant social relations; at least it offers a symbol of civilised norms, which is not without value. Fortunately, the extreme unbridled racism expressed by some defendants (who often appear mentally unbalanced) dealt with in published cases is not shared by the majority of the public, and on the whole sentences reflect decent revulsion, although they may not do much to change the behaviour in question. Most appellants already have a string of convictions for violent and abusive behaviour. The general deterrence provided by heavier sentences is also open to question. Denunciation is the strongest element in this law, reflected back in the powerful stigma said to be felt by many defendants. But leaving court feeling predominantly stigmatised is not helpful. Research

> connects stigma with anger, alienation, and rejection of the
> tribunal's ethical position. It is likely to encourage recidi-
> vism, unless there is some process to resolve the shame"
>
> (Burney, 2003, p. 35)

Written by one of the authors of a Home Office study of the operation of sections 28–32 of the Crime and Disorder Act 1998 (CDA) (Burney & Rose, 2002), these words reflect the flaws in the logic of "New" Labour's attempt to punish "hate" in the form of racially aggravated crime. As Burney suggests, such crimes result in (often severe) physical and psychological damage to individual victims. They may also affect others who share the victim's "race" or ethnicity. Most important of all, they represent an explicit rejection of the foundational values of a diverse, yet cohesive, society. They are, in effect, an attack on all citizens who subscribe to those values. Because they are such a powerful means of communication, hate crimes have been des-cribed as "message crimes" (Burney & Rose, 2002, p. ix; Iganski, 2002, p. 135; Lawrence, 2002, p. 38). To deal with this uniquely expressive form of offending, advocates of hate crime legislation argue that society needs to send an equally forceful and unambigu-ous message in reply and see the criminal law as an important, if not the only, means of communication. As the Home Office Minister Mike O'Brien told the House of Commons Committee considering what was then the Crime and Disorder Bill:

> The Government are tightly focused on tackling racist crime . . .
> Racial attacks . . . tear a hole in the fabric of our multi-racial society
> and the Government want to send a clear, specific and focused
> message about racial motivation, which is why we included it in the
> Bill. [quoted in Malik, 1999, p. 417]

For Burney (2003, p. 35), however, the criminal law may be valuable as "a symbol of civilised norms", and a means of reflect-ing "decent revulsion" through the imposition of appropriate punishment, but it cannot be expected to have much impact on the behaviour of society at large, and may even have a counter-productive effect on individual offenders. As Burney explains, while "denunciation" is the law's "strongest element", the "anger" and "alienation" produced in the stigmatized offender may lead to recidivism rather than reform, and to more rather than less racially aggravated offending (*ibid.*).

This chapter sets out to build on—and, in some respects, to revise—Burney's argument. We begin by tracing the legislative antecedents of the CDA on both sides of the Atlantic Ocean and the specific context within which it was implemented in England and Wales. We then go on to consider the main provisions of the Act and how they have been interpreted by the courts, paying particular attention to the difficulties they have encountered in using the anti-hate crime provisions of the CDA to understand the motivation of those charged with racially aggravated offences. As a result of these difficulties, and the relatively trivial nature of many of the cases that come before even the higher courts, we argue that the message sent out by the CDA in response to "hate crime" is neither clear nor unambiguous. We then go on to disentangle how the messages sent out by the Act were received by some of the people we spoke to in North Staffordshire. We conclude by suggesting that, however well-intentioned it may have been in its conception, the CDA is based on a perilously naïve understanding of the ways in which meanings become attributed to "race" in otherwise mundane confrontational situations, and the processes through which the denunciatory messages sent out by legislators become subverted even while those on the receiving end of those messages perceive themselves to be identifying with them (Dixon & Gadd, 2006).

Hate crime: a history

American origins

The origins of anti-hate crime legislation in the United States can be traced back to the success of the civil rights movement in the 1960s and effective lobbying at county level during the 1970s (Jenness, 2004). The first nationally significant piece of legislation only came a decade or so later, when President George Bush Senior signed the Hate Crime Statistics Act into federal law in 1990. As Valerie Jenness and her colleagues (Grattet & Jenness, 2001; Jenness

& Broad, 1997) have shown, hate crime was put on to the legislative agenda largely through the efforts of radical social movements involving black people, peace activists, women, gays, lesbians, and people with disabilities working together with the markedly more conservative victims' rights lobby under the aegis of the "Coalition on Hate Crime Prevention". The Hate Crime Statistics Act was followed in 1994 by a federal Hate Crime Sentencing Enhancement Act, reinforced at state level by similar legislation dating back, in some cases, to the 1980s. However, in the process of ensuring that statistics on certain types of (usually racially motivated) hate crime were collected, and that those convicted of such offences were sentenced more severely, the original coalition of interest groups fell apart. Thus, for example, neither the federal Hate Crime Statistics Act nor the Sentencing Enhancement Act covered offences involving domestic violence. The scope of the anti-hate crime laws in force in the USA today varies from jurisdiction to jurisdiction (Lawrence, 2002; Perry, 2001). Virtually all laws cover race and/or ethnicity and many also include religion. Sexual orientation and/or gender are covered in some jurisdictions, but relatively few include either age or disability.

The sudden popularity of legislation permitting, if not requiring, sentencers to be more severe on those convicted of "hate", or, to use the more measured language favoured by legal scholars such as Lawrence (1999, 2002), "bias-motivated" crime, has not gone unchallenged even in a country that was (and still is) the most punitive in the Western world. The most comprehensive and sustained critique of the concept of hate crime, and of the fashion for attempting to control it other than by means of the ordinary criminal law, has come from James Jacobs (1998, 2002; Jacobs & Potter, 1998). Apart from doubting the empirical evidence adduced to support the claim that America is suffering a hate crime epidemic, and questioning whether the recent rash of legislation has had any discernible impact on either the incidence or severity of hate crime, Jacobs has argued that—far from binding up the wounds of American society and affirming the nation's commitments to pluralism and diversity—hate crime laws depend on divisive constructions of identity, and have led to "charges about double standards and hypocrisy in the way that some crimes and not others are labelled" (Jacobs, 2002, p. 484). Our findings offer some support to Jacobs' observation about the essentializing tendencies inherent in hate crime laws. But they also suggest that the introduction of anti-hate crime legislation in England and Wales in the form of the CDA may encourage those involved in this type of offending to believe that that they are not so much hate crime perpetrators as the unfortunate victims of law enforcement agencies biased in favour of minority ethnic groups.

"Hate crime" comes to Britain

The history of British attempts to outlaw hate in the interests of better "race relations" dates back some forty years to the Race Relations Act 1965, and the amendment of the Public Order Act 1936 to create a new offence of "incitement to commit racial hatred" (Malik, 1999, p. 414). However, it was not until the late 1990s that the term "hate crime" came into popular usage in the UK. It was also during this period that the incoming "New" Labour government moved to create a new class of racially aggravated offences carrying enhanced sentences, including higher fines and longer periods of imprisonment. The creation of these offences by the Crime and Disorder Act 1998 (CDA or "the Act") was, as McLaughlin (2002, p. 497) has observed, ". . . an important part of the ongoing process of identifying and articulating the values, sensibilities and ground rules of vibrant, multicultural societies, including the public recognition and affirmation of the right to be different".

So, when, seven years on from the CDA, the second Blair government published a comprehensive new strategy on increasing race equality and community cohesion, *Improving Opportunity, Strengthening Society*, shortly before the May 2005 general election, it promised to "step up our work to further reduce racially motivated offending", among other things by ensuring that racially (and religiously) aggravated offences are vigorously prosecuted and—"tough on crime, tough on the causes of crime"—helping to address "the underlying drivers of racist behaviour" (Home Office, 2005, pp. 49–50, pars. 22 and 24). Significantly, these statements are contained in a chapter on "building community cohesion", which also talks about the need for an "inclusive sense of Britishness", the essential elements of which are "respect for others and the rule of law", "tolerance", and "mutual obligations between citizens" (*ibid.*, p. 42, pars. 3–4). Apart from "helping to ensure that racism is unacceptable" and "marginalising extremists who stir up hatred", other sections of the chapter are concerned with "helping young people from different communities grow up with a common sense of belonging" and "helping immigrants to integrate into our communities" (*ibid.*, pp. 41–54). Thus, the criminalization of hate by the CDA 1998 has been seen as contributing to the creation of the cohesive communities—and a nation united in its sense of Britishness—that became the leitmotif of "New" Labour rhetoric following the disturbances in northern towns and cities in 2001.

We will return to the broader issue of "community cohesion" in Chapter Six. Suffice to say here that, seen in the wider context of government policy on immigration, asylum, nationality, and criminal justice, the response to the disturbances in Oldham, Burnley, and Bradford in 2001 has been contradictory, even quixotic. So, and only by way of example, since 1998 the criminalization of hate in the CDA has been accompanied by the no less energetic—and arguably more successful—criminalization of those involved in the 2001 "riots" (McGhee, 2003, 2005), the continuing, post-Macpherson manifestation of "state racism" in the use of police powers of stop and search and the reform of the criminal justice system (Bridges, 2001), the growing stridency of "New" Labour's "xeno-racist" (Sivanandan, 2001) rhetoric on immigration and asylum and the increasingly draconian steps taken to reduce the number of people permitted to take refuge in Britain (Kundnani, 2001), and, finally, the promotion of an ostensibly inclusive notion of Britishness that claims to privilege "no one set of cultural values" (Home Office, 2005, p. 42, par. 4) yet, at least in the formulation of the former Home Secretary, David Blunkett (2005), was strengthened by the celebration of a breathtakingly constricted "English identity" more redolent of 1955 than 2005.

Racially aggravated offending in the Crime and Disorder Act 1998

Following the decision of the Court of Appeal three years earlier in the case of *R vs. Ribbans* (a full citation for this and all other cases referred to in this chapter is provided at the end of the chapter), it was already settled law in 1998 that the courts were required to treat proof of racial aggravation as an aggravating factor in sentencing.

This ruling was given legislative backing in what was section 82 of the CDA and is now section 145 of the Criminal Justice Act 2003 (CJA, 2003). But this was not enough for the new government. Hence, sections 29–32 of the Act provide for higher maximum penalties to be imposed where the prosecution can prove that one of a number of "basic offences" involving assault, criminal damage to property, harassment, and public disorder has been racially aggravated. Thus, in the leading case of *R vs. Kelly and Donnelly*, the Court of Appeal approved a two-stage approach to sentencing racially aggravated offences, whereby the judge should clearly distinguish between that part of the sentence appropriate to the "basic" offence and the amount by which the sentence was being enhanced to take account of racial aggravation. The Court also identified a number of factors "seriously aggravating the racial element". These included evidence that the offence had been planned, that the offender was a member of a group promoting racist activities, or that the offence formed part of a pattern of racist offending (par. 65). Adopting this approach in the case before it, the Court decided that sentences of eighteen months' imprisonment would be appropriate for "basic" offences of assault occasioning actual bodily harm involving the use of a biro pen and a bottle as weapons, while a further nine months was sufficient enhancement for racial aggravation that was not "at the top of the scale" (par. 76).

Critical to all the new offences created by sections 29–32, and, indeed, to racial aggravation for the purpose of section 145 of the CJA 2003 as well, are the definitions of racial aggravation contained in section 28(1) of the CDA. This states that an offence is racially aggravated if:

(a)   at the time of committing the offence, or immediately before or after doing so, the offender demonstrates towards the victim of the offence hostility based on the victim's membership (or presumed membership) of a racial group; or

(b)   the offence is motivated (wholly or partly) by hostility towards members of a racial group based on their membership of that group.

Three further subsections expand on key aspects of this definition. Subsection 28(2) makes it clear that, in subsection 28(1)(a), "membership" in relation to a racial group "includes association with members of that group", while "presumed" means "presumed by the offender". Section 28(3)(b) establishes that it is "immaterial for the purposes of either paragraph (a) or (b) of subsection (1) whether or not the offender's hostility is also based, to any extent, on . . . any other factor not mentioned in that paragraph". Finally, subsection 28(4) explains that a "racial group" means "a group of persons defined by reference to race, colour, nationality (including citizenship) or ethnic or national origins".

Punishing "hate": the law in action

The first point that needs to be made about the CDA as a means of "building community cohesion", making racism "unacceptable" and "marginalising extremists", as *Improving Opportunity, Strengthening Society* would have it, is that some of the "basic" offences listed in sections 29–32 of the Act—common assault and disorderly behaviour contrary to section 5 of the Public Order Act 1986 are the two obvious examples—are relatively trivial and, even when racially aggravated, do not attract very severe sentences. Section 29(3)(a), for example, provides that, on summary conviction for an offence of racially aggravated common assault under section 29(1)(c), a person is liable to imprisonment for a term not exceeding six months, to a fine not exceeding the statutory maximum, or to both. On summary conviction for a racially aggravated offence under section 31(1)(c) involving behaviour likely to cause harassment, alarm, or distress, a person may be fined but not imprisoned (section 31(5)). Thus, though it is important not to underestimate the impact of apparently minor infractions on the victims, it is evident from the CDA that this kind of low-level racially aggravated offending is not to be regarded as especially serious.

A second point to note about the case law takes us back to the conception of "hate crimes" as "message crimes" and the readiness with which the courts have shared the view of those who, like Iganski (2002, 2008) and O'Brien (quoted in Malik, 1999, p. 417), believe that the law has an important communicative role. This is illustrated very clearly in *R vs. Saunders*, one of the first cases on sections 28–32 of the CDA to come before the higher courts. Giving the judgement of the Court of Appeal in *Saunders*, Lord Justice Rose had this to say about the part that the criminal law has to play in countering the evils of racism:

> One of the most important lessons of this century, as it nears its end, is that racism must not be allowed to flourish. The message must be received and understood in every corner of our society . . . that racism is evil. It cannot coexist with justice and fairness. It is incompatible with democratic civilisation. The courts must do all they can, in accordance with Parliament's recently expressed intention, to convey that message clearly, by the sentences which they pass in relation to racially aggravated offences. Those who indulge in racially aggravated violence must expect to be punished severely, in order to discourage the repetition of that behaviour by them or others. [pp. 74–75]

And here, eight years later, is Baroness Hale of Richmond, giving judgement in what was then the highest court in the land, the House of Lords, in *R vs. Rogers*:

> The mischiefs attacked by the aggravated versions of these offences are racism and xenophobia. Their essence is the denial of equal respect and dignity to people who are seen as "other". This is more hurtful, damaging and disrespectful to the victims than the simple versions of these offences. It is also more damaging to the community as a whole, by denying acceptance to members of certain groups not for their own sake but for the sake of something they can do nothing about. [par. 12]

A third and final point which needs to be made before we go on to consider some of the case law in more detail is that, by creating new racially aggravated offences under sections 29–32, and defining racial aggravation in the way that it does in section 28(1)(b), the CDA has compelled the courts to investigate the motivation of offenders, not as they are accustomed to doing (and continue to do under section 145 of the CJA 2003) when it comes to sentencing offenders, but as an integral part of establishing their guilt in the first place. Lord Justice Maurice Kay remarked on the novelty of this development in *DPP vs. Green* (par. 27) when he observed that "The search for a motive can be elusive and complex. That is why the establishment of criminal liability does not generally require it".

Bearing these three points in mind (the relative triviality of much of the behaviour covered by sections 29–32 of the CDA, the commitment of the judiciary to using the law to send out a clear message about the evils of racism, and the novelty of requiring the courts to investigate the motivation of offenders in deciding whether a racially aggravated offence has been committed), we turn now to look in more detail at some of the cases which have been decided under the CDA. What follows is by no means a comprehensive survey, and the cases we discuss have been selected to illustrate how the message sent out by the CDA has been distorted by difficulties in making sense of the definition of "racial aggravation" contained in section 28(1) and in dealing with questions of motivation in cases which frequently involve nothing more serious than disorderly or threatening behaviour or relatively minor assaults.

Racial hostility: demonstrated or motivating?

The most immediate problem presented to the courts by section 28(1) has been the distinction between offences under paragraph (a), where the offender has "demonstrated" racial hostility either during or immediately before or after committing the "basic" offence, and those under paragraph (b), where the offence has been wholly or partly motivated by such hostility. In *DPP vs. Woods*, for example, the defendant had been drinking and punched a man in the head after calling him a "black bastard". The victim was working as a door supervisor at a pub in Hull at the time and had refused entry to one of the defendant's friends. The magistrates who first heard the case found that Woods' hostility was

> ... borne out of a frustration and annoyance as a result of his companion being denied entry to the premises, and whilst he may have intended to cause offence by the words, this was not "hostility based on the victim's membership . . . of a racial group". [par. 6]

The magistrates also found that Woods' frame of mind was such that he would have abused anyone in the victim's shoes "by reference to an obvious physical characteristic had that individual happened to possess one" (*ibid.*). Mr Justice Maurice Kay, sitting in the High Court, did not share their views: section 28(3) made it clear that it was "immaterial" that Woods may have had some reason unrelated to race for calling the victim a "black bastard" and section 28(1)(a)

> ... was not intended to apply only to those cases in which the offender is motivated solely, or even mainly, by racial malevolence. It is designed to extend to cases which may have a racially neutral gravamen but in the course of which there is demonstrated towards the victim hostility based on the victim's membership of a racial group. [*ibid.*, par. 12]

By using racially abusive language immediately before assaulting the victim, the defendant had demonstrated racial hostility within the meaning of section 28(1)(a). There was, therefore, no need to investigate the motives for the assault and it was irrelevant that the punch might have been prompted by anger at what had happened to his friend rather than any underlying "racial malevolence".

Perhaps the most widely cited judicial analysis of the difference between the two paragraphs has been provided by Lord Justice May in *RG, LT vs. DPP*, a case heard some two years after *Woods* in 2004. The defendants were accused of being involved in harassing and assaulting members of a Somali family, and the timing of certain incidents was critical to the case against them. In remarks cited with evident approval by Lord Justice Auld in the later case of *DPP vs. M*, Lord Justice May said that, though there "may be cases where facts are capable of being found on the evidence which bring the case within both [paragraphs]" (par. 23), there was a clear distinction to be drawn between the two limbs of section 28(1). Paragraph 28(1)(a) requires proof not of the "offender's state of mind", but of what he or she "did or said so as to demonstrate racial hostility towards the victim" (par. 13). Section 28(1)(b), on the other hand, is "concerned with the defendant's motivation" and, therefore, with his or her "state of mind, because motive is necessarily a state of mind" (par. 14). What this line of cases establishes, then, is that the only connection between the "basic offence" of harassment, assault, or whatever it may be and the demonstration of racial hostility needed for section 28(1)(a) is a rough concurrence in time (and, therefore, in most instances, in place). Once this has been established, no further enquiry needs to be made into the defendant's "state of mind" and whether his or her behaviour was *motivated* by racial hostility. Only when there is no evidence of any concurrence between a demonstration of hostility and a "basic" offence does the question of motivation under section 28(1)(b) arise.

Three recent cases involving racially aggravated public order offences contrary to section 5 of the Public Order Act 1986 and section 31(1)(c) of the CDA are examples of the relatively trivial nature of much of the behaviour that has come to the attention of the higher courts, and of the very different results that interpretation of the two paragraphs, 28(1)(a) and (b) may produce. In *DPP vs. Howard*, the defendant had chanted, "I'd rather be a Paki than a cop, I'd rather be a Paki than a cop" at two off-duty police officers to whom he happened to live next door. Since neither of the officers was Pakistani, Lord Justice Moses found that there was no question of section 28(1)(a) being satisfied (par. 6). However, the suggestion that "a police officer is even worse than someone who is not worthy of respect" was capable of "showing hostility to members of the Pakistani race" and, thus, of demonstrating that "the *motivation for the offence* is in part hostility towards a racial group" within the meaning of section 28(1)(b) (par. 9, original emphasis). It was irrelevant for the purposes of section 28(1)(b) whether the targets of the abuse were themselves members of the racial group to which hostility had been exhibited (*ibid.*). In other words, what mattered under section 28(1)(b) were the attitudes and feelings of the defendant betrayed by the offensive implication of worthlessness contained in the words of the chant and the significance of those feelings in prompting it. In the event, Lord Justice Moses concluded that, on the evidence before him, the defendant's "sole motivation for shouting these repellent remarks" was not hostility towards Pakistanis, but towards his neighbours as police officers (par. 10):

> The use of racially offensive language may in the circumstances provide evidence of the offence, but if it was not in any way the motivation for that offence then there can be no conviction pursuant to section 28(1)(b). [*ibid.*, par. 13]

None of this is to say that the decision to chant "I'd rather be a Paki than a cop" as a means of taunting his neighbours was not consistent with the defendant being hostile towards people of Pakistani

origin, merely that its use on the occasion in question was not motivated by such feelings.

Similar reasoning was used by Lord Justice Richards in R vs.
Dykes, where the defendant had referred to a doctor who had
treated him as either a "lying fucking Paki bastard" or a "fucking
Paki doctor" in the course of angry protests at being asked to leave
a hospital reception area where he had been allowed to sleep
overnight. Since the doctor had gone off duty at the time of the incident and was no longer on the premises, there was no concurrence
between the threatening behaviour used by the defendant over a
period of between twenty and thirty minutes and the racial hostility displayed in the words he used to refer to the absent doctor.
Thus, as the court put it, there was "no question" of subsection 1(a)
being "engaged" (par. 13). Nor was it certain that the magistrates
who first heard the case would have found that the defendant's
threatening behaviour had been even partly motivated by racial
hostility as required by subsection 1(b) (par. 23). It was unfortunate
that the magistrates had not applied their minds to that subsection,
but it was possible that, even had they done so, they would have
found that the offence had been "motivated by something quite
different, namely annoyance at being removed from the hospital
when he wanted to sleep on" (ibid.).

The contrast between these two cases and the decision in the
third, Johnson vs. DPP, could not be sharper. In this case, the defendant, who was described as "a black male", approached two white
parking attendants—one male, one female—whom he thought
were about to ticket his car and told them, "This is our patch not
yours"; "leave us alone, you're always picking on us. Leave the car
alone"; "leave us alone, why don't you get up Dore with your white
aunties and uncles" (pars. 4 and 6). Giving the judgement of the
Queen's Bench Divisional Court, Lord Justice Richards held that the
words used by the defendant were capable of demonstrating racial
hostility for the purposes of section 28(1)(a). As "a black person
addressing two white people", he was ". . . presenting the matter in
racial terms by reference to colour. He was telling the parking attendants to leave the black community alone, to get out of the black
area where they were and to go to white areas . . ." (par. 11).

Referring to the decision in Howard, but ignoring the fact that it
was concerned with questions of motivation germane to section

28(1)(b), he noted that there might be cases where words are used which are "capable of demonstrating racial hostility" but where "it is found as a fact that there was no racial hostility demonstrated at all" (par. 12). In this instance, however, the Crown Court had had a "proper evidential basis" for finding that the defendant's hostility was "at least in part, racial hostility" (par. 13).

"Real racists" and racially aggravated offenders

Burney and Rose's (2002) research for the Home Office found that, even if they admit to using racially abusive language, many defendants accused of racially aggravated offences strongly object to being labelled as "racists" and often deploy "friends and relatives from ethnic minorities . . . as character witnesses" (Burney, 2003, p. 32). This suggests that what matters for people accused of racially aggravated offences is the implication that they are what we may term "real racists" rather than ordinary people who, in certain circumstances, may be disorderly or violent and use language which the law regards as evidence of racial hostility. What the cases we have reviewed suggest is that the CDA may, as Brennan (1999, p. 23) argued, be too blunt an instrument to enable the courts to discriminate between the run-of-the-mill offender who "may well throw a punch and call the victim a name" but lacks a "racist state of mind", and someone with greater sophistication who "targets the victim whilst making sure that no evidence of racial intent is exhibited". Indeed, as we have seen, where a case of "demonstrated" racial hostility under section 28(1)(a) can be made out, the courts are not interested in exploring the defendant's state of mind at all, and the question of motivation simply does not arise. Although, as Lord Justice Simon Brown said in *DPP vs. Pal*, it is always necessary for the prosecution to prove that the defendant has demonstrated racial hostility, "the use of racially abusive insults will ordinarily . . . be found sufficient for that purpose" (par. 16). Thus, in *R vs. White*, the court was not concerned with why the defendant, a man born in the West Indies who self-identified as African, had responded to accusations by a bus conductress originally from Sierra Leone that he had attempted to steal from a fellow passenger by calling her an "African bitch". The fact that he had used these words, and been aggressive and abusive towards her in other ways besides, was sufficient for the purposes of section 28(1)(a).

Only rarely have the courts been tempted to acknowledge the complexity of the relationship between racism and the kind of abusive, threatening, sometimes violent, behaviour which leads to a conviction for a racially aggravated offence. And only rarely do attempts to avoid the "racist" label to which so many defendants object receive a sympathetic hearing from the judiciary. So, in *DPP vs. Green*, a defendant who had repeatedly abused a police officer "of Asian appearance", calling him, among other things, a "Paki cunt" and a "black bastard Paki" was not helped by evidence that she had also called another officer "a white cunt" (pars. 3 and 22). Neither was the court impressed by her best friend—"a woman described as black"—giving evidence that the defendant "had no racist tendencies", nor by the fact that she herself had "children of mixed ethnic origin" (par. 4). Though Green was both inebriated and generally resentful of police activity, the CDA was "intended to deal with the offender who, sober, has no racist thoughts but, drink-fuelled, articulates them" (par. 24). Mrs Justice Rafferty said that, under section 28(1)(a), the defendant's "disposition" at the time of the offence was "irrelevant" (par. 16); Lord Justice Maurice Kay said that Green could not deflect the attention of the court away from what she said "to some underlying grievance or perceived grievance which caused [her] to say it" (par. 27). Her acquittal by magistrates on a charge of the racially aggravated use of threatening words and behaviour contrary to section 5 of the Public Order Act 1986 and sections 28 and 31 of the CDA was quashed and the case remitted to them with a direction to convict (par. 25).

One case in which the court did take note of evidence suggesting that the defendant, despite the use of racially abusive language was neither a "real racist" nor a racially aggravated offender was *DPP vs. Pal*. The facts were unusual in that the Asian defendant was charged with a racially aggravated common assault on a school caretaker "of Asian appearance" whom he had called "a white man's arse licker" and a "brown Englishman". The prosecution argued that these words amounted to an accusation that, in asking the defendant and three associates to leave a community centre, the victim was betraying his, and the defendant's, "racial group" by doing white people's bidding (par. 10). Alternatively, it was argued, these words displayed the defendant's hostility towards "the white race and hostility towards [the victim] simply on the basis of his association with them" (par. 12). Lord Justice Simon Brown found neither of these arguments convincing. The defendant was not demonstrating hostility "towards Asians", but towards the victim's conduct; "not racism, but resentment" (par. 11). It was also "unreal" to suggest, on the facts, that the defendant was "anti white men", not least because "[h]e had after all been in a group with two of them just before the incident occurred" (par. 13). There was, therefore, no evidence that the assault, involving a push and a kick, had been racially aggravated (par. 17).

Attorney-General's Reference No 78 of 2006 provides a rare example of a court making the kind of distinction between a person who commits a racially aggravated offence and a "real racist", which Burney and Rose (2002) suggest is of such pressing concern to many defendants. The case involved the "one-punch manslaughter" (par. 15) of a man of "mixed race and Asian appearance" (par. 3) outside a pub, and the Court of Appeal was called upon to determine whether the (white) defendant's sentence had included sufficient "uplift" to reflect the racially aggravated nature of the offence under section 145 of the CJA 2003. The Court was not satisfied that this was the case, and increased the sentence imposed by the judge in the Crown Court from two years and three months to three years and three months, including an "uplift" of nine months "to reflect the racial element" (par. 23). In the course of his judgement, Lord Justice Tuckey noted that the judge had been satisfied that "the offender was not racist deep down but liberated by drink and in anger he had used the first objectionable terms he could think of to hurt his victim" (par. 13). The Lord Justice expressed no direct opinion on either the validity or the significance of this finding, but doubted whether the judge had given due consideration to the racial hostility demonstrated by the defendant "before, during and after the commission of the offence" (par. 21). Though not "racially motivated", the unprovoked, drunken, and ultimately fatal assault had been accompanied by "deeply offensive racial comments" towards the victim before, during and after commission of an offence which was "clearly racially aggravated within the meaning of section 28(1)(a) of the 1998 Act" (pars. 21–22).

Reviewing these cases, it is difficult to make out any very clear or consistent message. Some, but not all, of the behaviour is relatively trivial and involves people—frequently from minority ethnic groups—coming into conflict with those in a position of some authority, whether they are police officers, parking attendants, or bus conductresses. Unless compelled to do so by the absence of any demonstration of racial hostility sufficient to bring the behaviour within the parameters of section 28(1)(a), courts unaccustomed to deciding questions of motivation in establishing whether an offence has been committed have shown little interest in pursuing such matters under section 28(1)(b). As a result, their understanding of racism and how it relates to the behaviour that has led to the defendant being charged with the "basic" offence remains superficial at best. For all practical purposes, "racism" is seen as a social evil reflected in the abusive outbursts and criminal behaviour of the minority of individuals who commit racially aggravated offences. And, however much they may resent the label, the individuals found guilty of committing such offences are routinely defined, at least by implication, as "racists". If the purpose of the CDA, and the intention of the courts in using its provisions to punish racially aggravated offenders more severely, is to send out a clear, unambiguous message about the evils of racism by identifying and penalizing "those who commit acts of violence and harassment against minorities out of a deliberate and conscious hatred based on their membership of a racial group" (Malik, 1999, p. 423), the cases we have examined suggest that it has not been a great success. Given this uncertainty in the message being sent out by the CDA and the courts, the next section of this chapter goes on to consider how that message is being received, using data we collected during the course of our research in North Staffordshire.

Getting the message? Reception and interpretation

In order to make sense of how the message of the CDA is received and interpreted in practice, we need to cut through the ambiguities evident in the decided cases. So, taking up the hints provided in the judgements of Lord Justice Rose in *Saunders* and Baroness Hale in *Rogers*, referred to earlier, and drawing on Iganski's (1999) helpful dissection of the reasons for making hate a crime, it is possible to make out two possible messages and three potential, but not necessarily mutually exclusive, audiences. The first of the messages contained in the CDA is concerned with deterring future offending, the other with denouncing past wrongdoing. And the possible audiences are made up of individual offenders, the general public (including victims and their communities as well as those at risk of offending), and, finally, the individuals and institutions that make up the criminal justice system. The nature of our research and the data it has generated mean that we will have more to say about some of these message–audience combinations than others, but we will, at least, touch on all the more plausible possibilities in what remains of this chapter.

Impetus for the criminal justice system

The first message–audience combination we want to consider here is the possibility that the racially aggravated offences introduced by the CDA might, in Iganski's (1999, p. 390) words, provide the agencies involved in the criminal justice system with "not only the means, but also the impetus, for a more effective response to [racially aggravated] incidents". In fact, as he went on to suggest in his conclusion, Iganski (*ibid.*, p. 393) believed that the invigorating effects on the criminal justice system of the special denunciation of racially aggravated offending implied by the creation of the new offences might prove the legislation's most valuable and enduring legacy. Now, it seems to us that, even if the CDA has encouraged the police and the rest of the justice system to take racially aggravated offending (more) seriously, it is hard to justify using the criminal law to send a hortatory message to institutions and individuals that have been charged with enforcing it but, by implication, are failing to do so. The difficulty here is that, in practice, this message–audience combination operates only by further criminalizing people who are already seriously disadvantaged in a number of ways, not least by virtue of their previous contacts with the criminal justice system.

Let us use our own data to illustrate the point. The first thing that needs to be said is that, taking our sample of fifteen perpetrators as a whole, criminal justice outcomes in the form of a conviction for one or more racially aggravated offences were poor indicators of racist attitudes: some of the least racist interviewees had convictions for racially aggravated crimes; some of the most racist had none. If the criminal justice system has indeed been sensitized to racially aggravated crime by the CDA, its response to these legislative promptings seems distinctly arbitrary. Of the eight interviewees who had been charged with a racially aggravated offence, five were white, but three came from minority backgrounds. And of these three, one, a young man of Pakistani descent we called Shahid, had been found guilty of a racially aggravated public order offence in the course of a confrontation with the police; a second, a young man from a Bangladeshi family (Kamron), had been convicted of assaulting a fellow pupil at a local school whom he suspected of writing racist graffiti on a wall; and the third, a lesbian woman (Emma) in her late twenties of mixed heritage (she identified her nationality as "Afro-Caribbean") had committed a number of racially aggravated offences after exchanging a series of racial and sexual insults with a Pakistani shopkeeper. Apart from having to put up with routine abuse about her sexuality, Emma's many problems included a history of mental illness, self-harm, and alcohol abuse, while Kamron, against whom charges of racial aggravation had eventually been dropped after he had spent eight months in custody awaiting trial, was a regular cocaine user. Many of the five white interviewees charged with a racially aggravated offence had similar problems to their minority ethnic counterparts. Thus, Alan, a man in his late thirties, had experienced a number of psychotic episodes over several years and claimed to have no recollection of assaulting and racially abusing an Asian taxi driver as a result of his illness. Carl, meanwhile, though only twenty-five, was a chronic alcoholic who had been drinking since the age of twelve and had got into trouble after calling a policewoman a "dyke" and a "black bitch" in the course of a drunken scuffle with her and seven other officers. Carl's drinking had brought him into adversarial contact with the police on numerous previous occasions, and he felt a deep sense of resentment at the way in which he had been (as he saw it) falsely accused and unjustly convicted of crimes in the past.

The picture that emerges from our research is that the anti-hate crime provisions of the CDA may be used against (often multiply) disadvantaged people, including individuals from minority ethnic backgrounds. Indeed, on occasions, as the experiences of Shahid and Carl suggested, charges of racial aggravation may be used as a resource by the police in dealing with particularly troublesome individuals who, for various reasons, fall into the category of "police property" (Lee, 1981). Though the information about individual defendants is limited, the case law reviewed earlier includes examples of the CDA being used in what may well have been very similar circumstances to those in which Shahid and Carl found themselves. Take, for example, the cases of *Johnson vs. DPP*, in which the black defendant told two white parking attendants to leave his car alone and get out of what he saw as a black neighbourhood in Sheffield, and *DPP vs. Green*, where the intoxicated and angry Patricia Green launched a volley of abuse at an Asian police officer and a similarly offensive insult at his white colleague. Similar data to our own has also been collected by Burney and Rose (2002) and by Ray, Smith, and Wastell (2003b), and leads us to wonder whether the further criminalization of already disadvantaged and marginalized people is too high a price to pay for *creating the impression* that the criminal justice system is taking "race equality" seriously, particularly in the absence of conclusive evidence that the incidence of hate crime has fallen since the 1998 Act came into force.

Specific and general deterrence

The second and third message–audience combinations considered by Iganski (1999, pp. 387–388) were emphasized in the judgement of Lord Justice Rose in *R vs. Saunders*, and concern the specific (or individual) and general deterrent effects of providing enhanced sentences for racially aggravated offences. As Iganski notes, the critical factor here is the *marginal* deterrent effect of the amount by which the sentence for the "basic" offence is enhanced following a finding that it was racially aggravated. Taking the case of *Kelly and Donnelly* we discussed earlier as an example, the deterrent effect of the CDA thus inheres not in the total sentences of twenty-seven months' imprisonment imposed on the defendants for the racially aggravated assaults they had committed, but in the *additional* nine months they were given over and above the eighteen-month sentences that would have been imposed for the "basic" offence. For reasons to do with the theory and practice of specific and general deterrence, ably summarized by Ashworth (1998, pp. 44–52), Iganski is surely right to be sceptical about the likely deterrent effects of such marginal increases in sentence severity on either the individuals who receive them, or on the public at large, the vast majority of whom are not assiduous readers of the law reports, are likely to have little grasp of what the "going rate" or tariff for "basic offences" of assault might be, and are, therefore, unable to appreciate the effect of any enhancement on the overall sentence received. We share Iganski's scepticism, and only add a few observations about general deterrence here because, as the following extracts show, some of the participants in our focus group of young offenders had strong opinions about the way in which racism was used and interpreted by people from minority ethnic groups and the police as gatekeepers to the criminal justice system.

In the first extract, the dominant and most articulate member of the group, a seventeen-year-old we called Ben, complained that people he described as "Pakis" get away with racially abusing white people like him in circumstances in which, if he were to use similar language, he would be in trouble with the law.

Ben: The police don't see it as racism if they call us "white boys", you know what I mean? Or "homeboy" . . . or whatever . . .

Luke: . . . or "redneck" . . .

Ben: Yeah . . . "redneck". But if we go around . . . say I walked up there now and I saw a Paki . . . they'd be after you [. . .] and I said, "Oi, Paki", they could get me done for racism, mate, or slander, or whatever they wanted [to] do, mate. But if they come up to me and they're like, "Oh, white boy, redneck", and all this, like, you just see it as an offence, but you wouldn't go out and ring the police would you? But even if the police heard 'em saying that they wouldn't do nothing. I been there before, mate, when the police have heard them calling me "white boy" and that, and I've never said nothing back because I know I can get in trouble for it. But it's one rule for one and one for another.

Later in the discussion, Ben explained why he was always getting involved in fights with "mates, associates, friends", but tried to avoid confrontations with "Pakis" for fear of violent retribution from their friends:

Ben: ... I never fight a Paki. That's for the simple reason that, if I beat one, then the rest are going to come. [...] What I say is, if they come to me, then they're in my space at the end of the day ...

Gary: ... if you hit fucking one, that's it ...

Ben: ... but if they don't come to me, I don't go looking for trouble with them.

Dale: They all come looking for you, man.

Ben: [...] I don't like 'em because then you are going to have a lot of shit on your head ...

Gary: You hit one, that's it, mate ... fucking ....

Ben: Do you know what I mean? If it's shit hits the fan, you're going to got covered then, aren't you? If you don't go looking for it ... but if they come to you, then you do what you can.

This second extract indicates that, although Ben made no attempt to disguise his dislike of "Pakis", he was also astute enough to recognize that the kind of drink and/or drug-fuelled violence he routinely used in gaining and retaining the respect of his "mates" could get him into serious trouble if deployed against people who could count on their own kind to exact swift and painful revenge and, unlike Ben's white associates, would have little compunction in involving the police. Taken together, these extracts suggest that Ben was deterred from acting on his dislike for "Pakis" at least in part because of the ease with which "they" could represent a confrontation as "racist" and the seriousness with which he believed such allegations would be viewed by the criminal justice system. However, the extent to which the deterrent effect of the prospect of official sanction was the result, either direct or indirect (via its impact on the police), of the sentence enhancement provisions of the CDA, is hard to estimate. For our part, we suspect that Ben's wariness stemmed not from any fears about receiving a more severe sentence if convicted of a racially aggravated offence, but from his own persecutory anxieties and the kind of system effects that

Ashworth (1998, p. 51) attributes to the existence of the "institution of legal punishment", reinforced by a vague, but not unrealistic (Burney, 2003), awareness of heightened police sensitivity to "racist incidents" in the wake of the report of the Macpherson Inquiry (1999).

Denunciation effects

The third set of message–audience combinations we want to consider here relates to what Iganski (1999, p. 388) and McGhee (2005, p. 8) describe as the "declaratory value of legislation", such as the 1998 Act. For many commentators, the criminal law is perhaps uniquely capable of delineating the boundaries of tolerable behaviour (Hare, 1997, p. 417). Anti-hate crime laws also reflect the stress placed on "legal forms of regulation and integration" as the basis for modern, pluralistic social orders according to both the Durkheimian and Weberian traditions in social theory (Ray & Smith, 2001, p. 206). Thus, as the Association of Chief Police Officers put it in their response to a Home Office consultation document on what became sections 28–32 of the CDA:

> The legislative changes will do much to reinforce the seriousness with which the vast majority of members of our society view crime and conduct motivated by racial hatred. It will send out important messages to perpetrators and victims alike, that racist violence and harassment will not be tolerated and that positive action will be taken where this is exhibited. [quoted in Iganski, 1999, p. 389]

The extent to which the CDA speaks to the victims of racially aggravated crime was beyond the scope of our research, but it is important to point out that, as we have seen, its provisions are a distinctly double-edged sword, and it cannot be assumed that the victims of racially aggravated crime will always come from "previously subordinated or marginalized groups" (McLaughlin, 2002, p. 497) and the perpetrators from among the ranks of the dominant and the powerful. What Jenness (2002, pp. 24–25) calls the "norm of sameness" means that, in Britain as in the USA:

> Hate crime laws are written in a way that elides the historical basis and meaning of such crimes by translating specific categories of

persons (such as Blacks, Jews, gays and lesbians, Mexicans, etc.) into all-encompassing and seemingly neutral categories (such as race, religion, sexual orientation and national origin).

In other words, the CDA, like most other anti-hate crime legislation, denounces racially aggravated offending without fear or favour and may be used with equal facility against minorities as against the majority, those who suffer from the exercise of hegemonic power as well as its bearers, Kamron, Shahid, Emma, and the black defendants in *R vs. White* and *Johnson vs. DPP*, as well as committed white supremacists.

But what of the denunciatory effects of the CDA on our focus group of young offenders? Writing shortly after the Act had become law, Malik (1999, p. 423) argued that it was "particularly important that the new racially aggravated offences should reflect attitudes and meanings which are likely to find support in the wider community, and especially the communities where racist crime occurs".

The evidence from our focus groups with young people in North Staffordshire, reflected in the following extracts from a discussion with a group of young offenders undergoing a programme of intensive supervision and surveillance (ISSP) run by a voluntary sector service provider in Stoke-on-Trent, suggests that there may be some important disjunctures in the way in which behaviour is interpreted and evaluated by the state, the law, and the courts on the one hand, and by young people from what are sometimes called "perpetrator communities" on the other.

We chose to explore focus group participants' reactions to racially aggravated offending by discussing a case reported in Stoke-on-Trent's local daily newspaper, the *Sentinel*. In most groups, the participants read an extract from the story for themselves. In the young offenders group, however, one of us (BD) read it out loud. The story, headlined "Brothers jailed for race attacks", reported that three men aged twenty-two, twenty-nine, and thirty-two from deprived, and almost exclusively white, neighbourhoods on the outskirts of Newcastle-under-Lyme had been imprisoned for carrying out two racially aggravated assaults. All three were reported to have been drinking before the two younger ones, Sean and Joseph, "racially assaulted and occasioned actual bodily harm to a black student from Keele University, who was waiting for a taxi with his white girlfriend" in the foyer of a local multiplex cinema. They had then been joined by their elder brother, Roy, in attacking, and inflicting grievous bodily harm on, a "fifty-year-old Turkish man" in the car park of a nearby nightclub. According to the newspaper report, Sean and Joseph had been "imprisoned for a total of four years each", while Roy "received an eighteen month sentence". No mention was made of whether and, if so, by how much, any or all of these sentences had been increased above the level that would have been imposed for the "basic" offences to reflect the racially aggravated nature of the assaults.

The way in which participants reacted to this story has to be understood in the wider context of their own experiences of inter-ethnic violence. We have already seen how (and why) one of the young men, Ben, claimed that he would "never fight a Paki", unless "they" came to him and he had no alternative but to defend himself and his "space". One of the other young men, fourteen-year-old Danny, recounted how, only the previous evening, he had been chased by "a load of Pakis" who objected to him wearing his England-branded baseball cap. Asked why he was wearing it, he had ignored the questioners and "just carried on walking". At this, Gary, aged seventeen and the only serious challenger to Ben's dominance of the group, intervened to say that he would "run" for nobody. If he had been in Danny's position, he would have gone, "Fuck you, Punjabi", and stood his ground. When he boasted that he could take on "fifty of them", punching, biting, and "duffing them up", Ben was dismissive: "That's impossible that is."

Later in the discussion, Dale, also aged seventeen, talked about a similar but much more serious incident. He said that he had been "jumped", racially abused (he had been called a "dirty white bastard"), kicked, and then stabbed "by a bunch of fucking Pakis" in an inner city neighbourhood in Stoke-on-Trent well known for having a high proportion of Pakistani residents. Asked by one of the researchers what had happened after this incident and whether he had gone to the police, Dale's reply was drowned out by the following exchange, which illustrates the group's lack of confidence in the police and their view of "Pakis" as an homogenous, impenetrable mass, indistinguishable in speech, smell, and diet.

> Gary: Why go to the police? They're only going to fucking deny it, aren't they?

Ben: 'Cos they all look the same, you can't . . .

Gary: They all look the same and they all fucking smell the same.
        They all talk the same . . . do you know what I mean? . . .
        They all eat the same fucking shit, so they're all going to
        look the same, aren't they?

A third incident involved both Luke and the police, and was to
end with him appearing in court for racially aggravated public
order offences within days of the discussion. Initially, Luke presented the incident at a filling station near his home as beginning with
an unprovoked attack on a "mate" of his by "three Asians" armed
with "metal bars and everything". He had come to his friend's
assistance and managed to drag two of the Asians away. Only later
in Luke's account did it emerge that his friend had been attacked
after "robbing" the filling station shop. Reflecting on what had
happened, Luke was aggrieved that the police had come looking
for him. The robbery was "nothing to do" with him. All he had
done was go to the aid of a "mate" outnumbered by three well-
armed assailants. What we were given then was a very partial, and
almost certainly self-interested, account of a chain of events
sparked off by Luke's "mate", in which evidence of racial motivation beyond the mere fact that the protagonists were from different
ethnic groups was strikingly (possibly deliberately) absent, but also
in which the police and the courts were seen as unjustly criminalizing Luke's actions in defending a friend in the direst need.

A final point to note from all three of these stories, and from
Ben's personal risk-avoidance strategy, is that people described as
"Pakis" were seen as the real or potential source of danger, as well
as the object of Ben and Gary's crude racism. Precisely who was
covered by this term—for Gary it included Iraqis and Afghans as
well as people with some connection to Pakistan itself—was not
entirely clear. What was evident was that "Pakis" represented not
only the antithesis of the participants' own sense of Englishness,
but also a sharp contrast with "niggers" and "half-castes", who,
despite the disparaging language, participants saw as coming from
England and belonging in places like Manchester and Stoke-on-
Trent. The significance of this construction of English identity in
relation to a distinctively "Paki" rather than African or African-
Caribbean "other" will become evident in a moment.

Returning to the story of the three brothers, we can see how both personal experiences and particular constructions of identity interfere with the message conveyed by anti-hate crime legislation. Ben, as usual, attempted to set the agenda for the discussion by maintaining a running commentary on the story as it unfolded. He had three contrasting reactions to the newspaper's account, reflecting his nuanced understanding of the "other" as an acceptable target for violence. When the brothers' jailing for as yet unspecified "racially aggravated assaults" was mentioned, his reaction was to say, "Good on them". To the revelation that the black student from Keele had suffered actual bodily harm, Ben merely repeated "ABH". Finally, when the attack on the Turkish man was mentioned, he very visibly clenched his fist as if celebrating a goal by his favourite football team. To judge by these contrasting reactions, Ben's first reading of the story was not that the brothers' violent racism had been appropriately denounced, but that they had done something to be applauded, at least in so far as the attack on the "Paki", or passably "Paki"-like, Turkish man was concerned. At this stage, Ben's reaction seemed to be governed by his particular identification of the "other".

Once the story had been completed, Luke—always the most reluctant participant—led an attempt to bring the discussion to a close by arguing that the incident had nothing to do with any of them, and that they did not want to know anything more about it either. Dale agreed that it was old news, but added that the brothers "shouldn't have fucking jumped [the student] for fuck all". Ben merely rehearsed his earlier opinions about not "looking for trouble", but accepting it if it happened to come his way. He, too, had said all he needed to say. Only after calculating that there was little chance of staff at the ISSP centre allowing them to go home for the evening did the participants agree to continue the discussion. When they did resume, their reading of the story became increasingly subtle.

One issue had been raised by Luke immediately after the researcher had finished reading the story, and concerned the veracity of the newspaper's report of the case. Although Ben was prepared to accept that the local paper was more credible than, say, the "Daily Sport", he found its account improbably one-sided: "[T]here's always two sides to a story, and there isn't two sides to that story." A second, and closely related issue was the apparently random nature of the assaults. If the attack on the black student had indeed been unprovoked, Luke, Ben, Dale, and the otherwise almost totally silent Lenny were unanimous in their incomprehension of why the brothers had "jumped" him. Notwithstanding his own impending court appearance, Luke was also convinced that, in the absence of any provocation, the two younger men deserved their four-year sentences, and he could not understand why the third brother had been treated so leniently; although he had not been directly involved in assaulting the student, he had prevented him from running away. In the case of the Keele student, the only conceivable provocation that any of them could come up with was the fact that he had a white girlfriend. Ben, however, was quick to dismiss this as any excuse for such a violent attack. A more plausible and, in the case of the Turkish man, a more likely, explanation was that the brothers' attack had been a response to some provocation that had gone unreported in the newspaper's account of the incident. Inspired by Ben's reservations about the one-sidedness of the *Sentinel's* account, Gary suggested that the "Asian guy might have gone, 'Oh, you fucking wankers'". Dale thought that he could have given them "a funny look", which, in Ben's view, was "all that it takes when you're pissed up", as he assumed, with some justification, that the brothers may well have been.

To the participants in our young offenders' group, the punishment of the three brothers under the terms of the CDA was only deserved in so far as the attacks on the black student and the Turkish man were inexplicable. And they were seen as inexplicable only if the local newspaper's account was credible on the critical issue of provocation. And, finally, even though the *Sentinel's* story gave no hint that either of the attacks were provoked, participants were not convinced that the Turkish man, as the more obvious representative of the dangerous "other", had not done something that might have justified three white men—sensitized by alcohol to the merest hint of disrespect—resorting to physical violence. Thus, the message of the CDA, communicated through the pages of a local newspaper, was affected not only by the perceived reliability of the medium, but also by the constructions of "self" and "other" adopted by those who heard it, and by the listeners' own experience of similar incidents and the reaction of the criminal justice system to them. As the talk that took place in our focus group discussion suggests, the clear message of denunciation contained in the CDA may be interpreted in highly idiosyncratic and unpredictable ways.

Conclusion: reimagining the racially aggravated offender

Critics of the anti-hate crime provisions of the CDA, such as Bridges (2001) and Bourne (2002), have argued that there has always been enough law to deal with racial violence and harassment; what has been lacking is the willingness to use it. Writing four years after the CDA was passed, Bourne (2002, p. 85) flatly rejected the idea that legislation "advocated by the professionalised race lobby has brought black people any closer to justice". Unconvinced of either its necessity or its utility, Bridges (2001, p. 72) concluded that the legislation "is at best misguided" and "at worst may never [have] had more than a symbolic political purpose". We have some sympathy with these views, particularly when the CDA is set in the wider context of "New" Labour policies on immigration, asylum, and nationality, and in the light of the reaction of the criminal justice system to the disturbances in Oldham, Burnley, and Bradford in 2001, and some of the more socially divisive tactics used to deal with the threat of Islamic extremism since the bombings in London on 7 July 2005. At the time of writing, for example, it is being reported in the *Guardian* that discussions are taking place in Whitehall about a new strategy for tackling Islamic extremism. Known as "Contest 2", critics claim that adoption of the strategy will lead to "thousands more British Muslims being labelled as extremists" for holding views on a range of social and political issues deemed to "clash with what the government defines as shared British values" (Dodd, 2009).

Attractive though this line of criticism is, we want to concentrate here on the failure of the courts to gain more than the most superficial understanding of what brings people to abuse and assault their fellow citizens in circumstances where "race" seems, in Rustin's (2000) terms, to be no more than an empty container for a myriad of other frustrations, and racist epithets serve as a defence against a sudden, profoundly unsettling loss of control. What emerges from the case law is a stubbornly one-dimensional view of the racially aggravated offender condemned as racist by virtue of words or actions construed as either demonstrating racial hostility, or establishing that his or her behaviour was motivated by it, under the terms of section 28(1), but which may equally plausibly be interpreted as attempts to legitimize shameful expressions of unguarded hostility prompted by reactions to attitudes attributed to a racialized "other". When behaviour is shorn of its social and biographical context in this way, it is hardly surprising that, as Burney and Rose (2002, p. 91) found, so many offenders resent being branded as racist and will go to great lengths to resist it. Where we disagree with Burney in the passage we quoted at the beginning of this chapter is in seeing "extreme and unbridled racism" in all (even most) of the cases to come before the courts, and in feeling confident that the "majority of the public" would feel "decent revulsion" at the defendant's behaviour. On the contrary, the evidence from our focus group of young offenders (confirmed by our discussions with other groups of young people in North Staffordshire) suggests that, even when considerable violence is used and there is little reason to doubt that an attack was almost wholly motivated by racial hostility within the meaning of section 28(1)(b), people from the communities from which offenders are drawn are likely to react in much more complex and contradictory ways than Burney believes. Hence, it is perfectly possible for some people—like the streetwise young offenders we interviewed—to identify closely with the denunciatory messages of hate crime law, while at the same time perceiving themselves to be the innocent victims of attacks perpetrated by minority ethnic groups who benefit from the enduring biases of criminal justice professionals.

Consequently, if we are to make sense of the behaviour of racially aggravated offenders, and to understand the reactions of bystanders like the participants in our focus group, we need to go behind the abuse, the punches, the kicks, and the easy condonation of violent racism to uncover motivations and frames of meaning buried much more deeply in the fabric of our society and the biographies of individuals than the courts, constrained by the arid language of the CDA, have been prepared to go. Until we are able to do that, and to provide ways of both recognizing and containing the anger and resentments which lie behind the behaviour dealt with by the courts, but only fleetingly noticed by them, Burney is right to argue that denouncing offenders as racists and stigmatizing them as social outcasts is likely to make matters worse rather than better. In the meantime, and rather more prosaically, political, judicial, and academic supporters of anti-hate crime legislation have to accept that the deterrent and denunciatory messages that sections 28–32 of the CDA were intended to send are being communicated in a form of legal code which obscures their meaning, transmitted by media which lack either popularity (in the case of the law reports) or credibility and received by significant numbers of people whose social circumstances and personal biographies make it improbable that they will interpret the messages as intended, let alone act on them appropriately.

Statutes cited

Crime and Disorder Act 1998
Criminal Justice Act 2003
Public Order Act 1936
Public Order Act 1986
Race Relations Act 1965

Cases cited

Attorney-General's Reference No. 78 of 2006 [2006] EWCA Crim 2793.
DPP vs. Green [2004] EWHC 1225.
DPP vs. Howard [2008] EWHC 509 (Admin).
DPP vs. M [2004] 1 WLR 2758.
DPP vs. Pal [2000] Crim LR 756.
DPP vs. Woods [2002] EWHC 85 (Admin).
Johnson vs. DPP [2008] EWHC 509 (Admin).
R vs. Aylett [2006] 1 Cr App R (S.) 34.
R vs. Dykes [2008] EWHC 2775 (Admin).
R vs. Kelly and Donnelly [2001] 2 Cr App R (S) 73.
R vs. Ribbans (1995) Cr App R (S) 698.
R vs. Saunders [2000] 2 Cr App R (S.) 71.
RG, LT vs. DPP [2004] EWHC 183 (Admin).

CHAPTER FIVE

The unconscious attractions of far right politics

"Only a psychology which utilizes the concept of unconscious forces can penetrate the confusing rationalizations we are confronted with in analysing either an individual or a culture. A great number of apparently insoluble problems disappear at once if we decide to give up the notion that the motives by which people *believe* themselves to be motivated are necessarily the ones which actually drive them to act, feel, and think as they do"

(Fromm, 2001, p. 118: original emphasis)

"The complexity of working-class consciousness demands of the listener a fresh theory to explain what he is hearing, a theory that ... involves speculation and generalization far beyond the boundaries of the conversations themselves"

(Sennett & Cobb, 1993, p. 10)

B etween 2001 and 2006, the British National Party (BNP), hitherto widely regarded as too extreme to pose a serious threat to the established political parties, registered a series of striking and well-publicized electoral gains in local elections across England. Commentators have tended to explain this phenomenon as the result of a successful rebranding of the party under the leadership of Nick Griffin, the failure of "New" Labour to live up to the expectations of white working-class voters, and sustained scaremongering about immigration by the BNP and its sympathizers, with which mainstream politicians and the media have, to varying degrees, colluded. Drawing upon survey data, our own focus group material, and the biography of a BNP activist we interviewed in the course of our research in North Staffordshire, this chapter reconsiders this argument, showing that, while it is not without merit, it tends to oversimplify the relationship between anti-immigrant attitudes and class, underplay the role of unconscious fantasies in sustaining support for the BNP, and overlook the hidden psychological injuries, born out of biographically specific experiences, that lure some individuals into embattled, authoritarian-sounding, but, none the less, complex and contradictory racist mentalities. Our exploration of how working class voters *thought* and *felt* about the BNP in the early 2000s leads us to the conclusion that the appeal of the far right party has to be understood, at least in part, in terms of unconscious emotional needs that are inflected by, but not reducible to, the limitations of contemporary "third way" politics (Giddens, 1998) and what Sennett and Cobb (1993) memorably described as the "hidden injuries of class".

The British National Party resurgent

Following his election as national chairman of the BNP in 1999, Nick Griffin, a Cambridge law graduate and former National Front organizer, strove to widen the electoral appeal of his party. His predecessor, John Tyndall, had managed to mobilize modest levels of electoral support among white people in the east end of London embittered by the Docklands and Canary Wharf developments (Ware & Back, 2002). But where Tyndall's long association with neo-Nazism had proved an electoral liability to the BNP, Griffin set out to create a public image for the party that might appeal more consistently to white working-class voters in the Midlands and the North of England, for whom "things" had not—in the words of the party's catchy campaign song—"got better" since "New" Labour's landslide victory in the general election of 1997. So, Griffin distanced the BNP from Nazism and the National Front and ordered campaigning about the repatriation of British-born non-whites off-limits among the party's membership (Copsey, 2004). After 1999, the BNP focused its efforts on blaming a host of social and economic problems on the dispersal of asylum seekers to the rapidly deindustrializing towns and cities of the North and Midlands. Then, following the terrorist attacks on New York in 2001 and London in 2005, the BNP sought to capitalize on public concerns about "terror" by declaring that the Islamic faith posed a fundamental threat to established British values and characterizing its British adherents as an insidious but militant minority gaining ground day-by-day as soft-touch multi-culturalists pandered to the whims of increasingly assertive and powerful minorities.

Prevented by the first-past-the-post system from winning seats in the House of Commons, the BNP began the new millennium by concentrating on establishing itself as a credible contender in local elections. By May 2003, the Party held a smattering of seats on English local councils in Yorkshire (Calderdale) and the West Midlands (Dudley and Stoke-on-Trent), as well as in Broxbourne, in the commuter belt north of London. More noteworthy, however, were the inroads the BNP had made in the Lancashire mill town of Burnley, where it became the main opposition party after eight of its candidates were elected to office. A year later, the BNP increased the number of councils on which it held more than a single seat to include Bradford (four), Calderdale (three), Epping Forest (three), and Stoke-on-Trent (two). It was also represented by lone councillors in Broxbourne, Kirklees, and Sandwell. Renewed competition from the UK Independence Party (UKIP) appeared to dilute support for the BNP in the May 2005 general election, but, with the departure of the high-profile former Labour MP and television presenter Robert Kilroy-Silk from UKIP, the BNP again increased its strength in local government from twenty councillors to fifty-two in the local elections of May 2006. Of these new seats, twelve were won in the outer east London Borough of Barking and Dagenham. The party also gained three seats in Epping Forest, Sandwell, and Stoke-on-Trent, two in Burnley and Kirklees, and single seats in Bradford, Havering, Solihull, Redditch, Redbridge, Pendle, and

Leeds. Only in 2007 did the BNP's political advance begin to stall when, despite fielding 750 candidates, the party made a net gain of just two seats in the May local elections, winning ten seats but losing eight.

Protest, disillusionment and the white working class

In *Contemporary British Fascism*, Copsey (2004, p. 148) attributed the BNP's electoral successes to Griffin's management of "the message" that the BNP had become "a credible modernised and legitimate constitutional party" and to the crowding of the middle ground of British politics associated with "New" Labour's movement towards the centre. By way of evidence, Copsey (*ibid.*, p. 141) highlighted how, in April 2002,

> Labour Home Secretary David Blunkett urged the mainstream parties to fight the BNP head on. But this did not mean ignoring immigration as an electoral issue. On the contrary, against the backdrop of the ongoing controversy surrounding the Sangatte refugee camp in France and the second reading of the new Nationality, Immigration and Asylum Bill . . . Blunkett chose to occupy the BNP's ground . . . [H]e borrowed from Thatcher's 1978 phrase book and declared that the children of asylum seekers were swamping Britain's schools. But if Thatcher's comments had helped undercut support for the extreme right over two decades earlier, then Blunkett's copycat manoeuvre had the opposite effect . . .[:] it gave the British National Party further legitimacy.

Even before the BNP came knocking on their doors, Copsey argued, many voters already considered "bogus asylum seekers", unassimilated minorities, and British Muslims—whether "fundamentalist" or otherwise—objects for legitimate political concern. Meanwhile, the reluctance of mainstream party candidates to undertake old-fashioned doorstep canvassing enabled the BNP to present itself as the *only* party that genuinely cared about these issues. A new cadre of local BNP candidates, much less enamoured of neo-Nazism than the party's long-serving organizers, offered year-round "helping hands" to local people with a view to garnering their support in subsequent local elections (*ibid.*, p. 137). In this way, the BNP presented itself to white working-class voters as a party of "ordinary", "decent", and "hard-working" people, many of whom considered themselves to have been taken for granted by "New" Labour during the party's second term in office.

Although there are differences of emphasis between commentators writing broadly from the perspective of the intellectual left, few critical observers have disagreed with Copsey's (2004) diagnosis that the change in the BNP's fortunes owed much to a combination of disillusionment, racism, and frustration at the absence of viable political alternatives to the mainstream, and increasingly indistinguishable, political parties. Writing in the aftermath of the BNP's early successes in the local elections of 2002, the broadsheet columnist Gary Younge (2002) began by framing his analysis in terms of the "narrative of the empire" that informs so much political debate in the UK, but ultimately explained the BNP's emergence as an electoral force as a gesture of protest against the centrist politics of "New" Labour.

> When British politicians talk about immigration they are really talking about race ... The meaning of the word immigration, in Britain, is not confined to the movement of people in and out of the country. We are not talking demography but demonisation ... The BNP understands this only too well ... The Labour Party understands this too. Blair used to like to say that disaffected Labour voters only had one choice—between him and the Tories. At the last election they showed him they could go to the pub rather than the polls; yesterday they showed him they had another option—extremism. [Younge, 2002]

Likewise, the writer and anti-fascist campaigner, Nick Lowles, cautioned that

> A vote for the BNP is still a protest vote... [M]any of those who voted BNP, particularly the more affluent ones, would quickly switch their support to a more respectable right-wing alternative if it offered a more populist and right-wing agenda. [Lowles, 2002, cited in Renton, 2003, p. 82]

On the question of what had made BNP voters so disgruntled, opinion was more divided. Some commentators, like the historian David Renton, were inclined to blame a media-induced hysteria:

[T]he press coverage of the [asylum seeker] issue entered a new
moral universe. The very poorest people in Britain were accused of
thieving from the rest. Racist violence intensified in a Britain
"under attack". The public was fed malicious, intentional lies . . .
The hysteria prompted government action which, in turn, gave
credence to the hysteria . . . [Renton, 2003, p. 78]

But the weight of opinion pointed to the development of an
acute sense of betrayal among the white working class. The television producer and journalist Michael Collins, for example, argued
that, since the publication of the Macpherson report into the murder of Stephen Lawrence (Macpherson, 1999), the white working
class have been caricatured by intellectuals as "xenophobic, thick,
illiterate, parochial", despite having shouldered most of the social
and economic burden imposed by accommodating the least self-
sufficient of Britain's new migrants (Collins, 2004, p. 8). Likewise,
Jackie Long (2008), summarizing the findings of a poll conducted as
part of the BBC's "White Season", concluded that, "many white
people . . . are ill at ease. Marginalised. Angry. And ignored".
Turning to the findings themselves, she reported that "77% of working class people in the poll" believed that "the British population is
expected to fit in with new immigrants rather than the other way
round", while "88% of white working class people questioned . . .
felt it was difficult to criticise immigration without being labelled a
racist" (ibid.). As we mentioned in Chapter One, sociologist Ray
and his colleagues (2004) came to similar conclusions about the
working-class white populations living in deindustrializing towns
like Oldham, Burnley, and Stoke, many of whom are said to feel a
deep sense of shame at their exclusion from the cosmopolitan
lifestyles enjoyed by those living in larger and more prosperous
conurbations; feelings that they are only prepared to acknowledge
implicitly through racism.

Surveying the evidence: protest, conflicted mindsets, and mixed messages

The evidence supporting these arguments, however, is rather more
mixed than most of these commentators acknowledge. First, BNP

voters are not necessarily as preoccupied with immigration as is often assumed. As the Joseph Rowntree Charitable Trust's (JRCT) (2004) study, *539 Voters' Views*, revealed, BNP supporters were indeed more likely to identify immigration and asylum as a concern than voters for mainstream parties. But, it was also the case that fewer than one in five BNP voters referred to immigration and asylum as the main reason for supporting the party (*ibid.*, p. 30). Based on exit polls conducted in Burnley, Oldham, and Calderdale during three local council by-elections held in the autumn of 2003, the JRCT's study found that only one in ten BNP voters said that their vote had been cast tactically, suggesting "a protest against either the Labour Government or the local council's neglect of their area" (*ibid.*, p. 34). While the study found that all voters had trouble differentiating between the policies of the mainstream parties, BNP supporters were more likely than others to have mixed feelings about "their" party. They were more likely than the supporters of other parties to claim that the BNP "closely represented" their views. Yet, as Table 1 shows, they were also more likely than non-BNP voters to have considered voting for another party.

Second, it is not especially clear that hostility towards immigrants is the preserve of people in the lower socio-economic groups. In fact, the Populus survey on which *Newsnight* drew in making its claims about white working-class anger revealed little difference between socio-economic groups ABC1 and C2DE on the two measures to which Long referred in her report (Populus, 2008).

Table 1.   Party voters considered voting for in by-elections.

Party voted for in the by-election	Party considered voting for							
	Labour	BNP	Lib Dem	Con	Ind	None	All	Total
Labour		4	18	11	0	65	1	100
BNP	13		21	37	0	29	0	100
Liberal Democrat	25	5		29	0	39	2	100
Conservative	15	15	0		0	54	15	100
Independent	33	0	17	50		0	0	100
All voters	11	4	13	22		49	2	100

Source: JRCT, 2004, p. 29, Table 13.

Indeed, the poll found middle-class respondents to be marginally *more* likely than working-class people to worry about being perceived as "racist" (see statement 8 in Table 2, below) and only slightly more inclined to agree that the "British population were expected to fit in with immigrants rather than the other way round" (statement 11). Generally speaking, anti-immigrant attitudes were only *a little* more prominent among socio-economic groups C2DE

Table 2.   Percentage of Populus survey respondents agreeing with statement by socio-economic group.

Statement	Percentage of socio-economic group ABC1 who agreed	Percentage of socio-economic group C2DE who agreed
1. Nobody speaks out for people like me in Britain today	46	58
2. The government seems more interested in helping those who break the rules than rewarding people who work hard and play by the rules	75	84
3. In the last ten years my life in Britain has got worse	20	32
4. In the last ten years law and order in Britain has got worse	66	71
5. The NHS should only treat those born or brought up in the UK or who have paid into the system	55	61
6. Benefits should be restricted to thosewho have been born or brought up in the UK	53	64
7. There is no respect for authority like the police, teachers, and parents any more	89	92
8. You can't criticize the amount of immigration or how individual immigrants conduct themselves these days without being labelled a racist	78	76

(continued)

Table 2. (*continued*)

Statement	Percentage of socio-economic group ABC1 who agreed	Percentage of socio-economic group C2DE who agreed
9. It is not immigration I object to, but uncontrolled immigration	88	88
10. People who have made a contribution to this society are being ignored or pushed aside by new immigrants who just take what they want and offer nothing in return	54	71
11. These days the British population is expected to fit in with new immigrants rather than the other way round	74	77
12. Immigration has changed the character of the area I live in for the better	33	25
13. New immigrants to Britain make less of an effort to fit in than those who first arrived in this country a generation ago	62	74
14. Most immigrants to Britain end up fitting in here if they're given sufficient time to do so	76	71

Source: Populus (2008).

than ABC1s. A clear majority of both groups asserted that immigrants ultimately "end up fitting in" (statement 14), although more working-class than middle-class respondents believed that recent immigrants made less effort to "fit in" than earlier generations (statement 13). The most striking differences between the attitudes of C2DEs and ABC1s were to do with the formers' feelings of disenfranchisement (statement 1) and a sense that the needs of people who (presumably like them) have made a contribution to British society are being ignored in favour of newcomers (statement 10).

A third important point is that the messages people receive about immigration in Britain tend to be very contradictory. For example, a study commissioned by the Information Centre about Asylum and Refugees (ICAR) found that, while many of the most popular daily newspapers continue to run negative stories about asylum seekers, this coverage is increasingly offset by the willingness of regional and local newspapers to print human interest pieces which attack politicians for the way in which they have framed the immigration debate (Smart, Grimshaw, McDowell, & Crosland, 2007). Using a content analysis of over 2000 articles reported in the British press in 2005, the ICAR study discovered that around 10% of news stories about refugees and asylum seekers referred to their contribution to the arts, while around 22% focused on the plight of individual asylum seekers. Predictably, stories about asylum seekers and crime (17%) or asylum policy generally (62%) were found to be more numerous, but there was a relatively even balance between stories suggesting that Britain had lost control of its borders (47%) and those which implied that the tone of contemporary political discourse about asylum seekers was shameful (42%). Readers are able, therefore, to exercise a degree of choice over the kind of story they choose to read (and/ or believe), with those who see regional or local papers more likely to come across stories which humanize the refugee/asylum-seeking experience than readers whose only source is the national press.

Finally, much the same can also be said about the messages people receive about the BNP. Anti-fascist campaigners have consistently claimed, often without much empirical support, that racially motivated offending increases in areas targeted by the BNP. References to the criminal track records of its members, including that of David Copeland, the BNP activist convicted of carrying out a series of nail bombings in ethnically mixed areas of London in 1999, are often made to enhance the plausibility of this claim. Such coverage undoubtedly makes many people think twice about what they know for sure about the BNP, but it may also lead some to make a clear distinction between their own anti-immigrant attitudes and the unapologetic, blatant racism they assume to be the preserve of racist thugs. In our own research, for example, we encountered a group of relatively affluent and well-educated neighbourhood watch activists who were deeply troubled about the way in which some groups of immigrants seemed to be taking advantage of Britain and refusing to integrate. But, however much they feared what one of the participants, sixty-three-year-old Ralph, described as a "time bomb" waiting to go off "in some deprived areas", they had scant sympathy for the BNP, whom they perceived as proletarian "rabble-rousers" and "football hooligans". Conversely, those who are more closely acquainted with new BNP activists may not be so easily persuaded by anti-racist campaigns that seek to tar all members of the party with the same neo-Nazi and criminal brushes (Figure 1).

In Burnley in 2003, for example, BNP candidate Luke Smith was elected in spite of being banned for life from Burnley Football Club and having well-publicized convictions for violence. Similarly, Doug Smith, a new and politically inexperienced BNP candidate in Stoke-on-Trent, secured 23% of the vote in his ward despite local and national newspapers running stories exposing his violent

Figure 1. Left: *Unite Against Fascism* 2005 election campaign leaflet, reprinted with kind permission of uaf.org.uk; Right: *Searchlight's* online "Stop the BNP" campaign, reprinted with kind permission of *Searchlight*.

criminal career. The following year, not long after Burnley BNP councillor Maureen Stowe had defected to Labour, claiming that she had been "conned", the BBC's undercover documentary, *The Secret Agent*, exposed a group of BNP activists rejoicing in the violence visited upon minority ethnic groups. In the news coverage that followed, members of the BNP were depicted by the media as a poisonous fascist presence, "brutes in suits" (*The Economist*, 2004) or, as *The Sun* memorably put it, "Bloody Nasty People". Yet, as the BNP was to discover, much of this negative publicity could be turned to its advantage. Having streamed *The Secret Agent* (BBC, 2004) on its website as evidence of the conspiracy against it, the BNP made its most significant electoral inroads in May 2006, not long after Griffin and another senior member of the BNP, Mark Collett, had been acquitted of charges against them arising out of the original television exposé (Norfolk, 2006). After being retried later the same year on further charges on which the jury had been unable to agree, Griffin welcomed his acquittal as "a victory for free speech" and claimed that his party had become "an icon of resistance to the forcibly imposed multi-cultural experiment which has failed" (BBC News Channel, 2006).

What all of this tells us is that, while it is possible to interpret support for the BNP as a racialized protest against the political mainstream by disillusioned and angry members of the white working class, distinguishing causes from effects is not easy, not least because the differences in attitudes between classes are relatively slight. Not all white working-class voters are hostile to immigrants, not all BNP voters are preoccupied with immigration, and few BNP voters see their support for the party purely as a means of registering a "protest". What needs to be understood now, therefore, is how people make sense of the contradictory messages they hear about both immigration and the BNP, and how individual understandings of these matters are formed in interaction with others. In the rest of this chapter, we attempt to do this by analysing data from two extended biographical interviews we conducted with a local BNP activist in Stoke-on-Trent and three of the discussions we facilitated among groups of white working-class voters in the area, in one of which the BNP activist was a particularly vocal participant.

Fighting talk and "giving the BNP a try"

When we asked focus groups of people living in Stoke-on-Trent how they thought the BNP had won over a large section of the local electorate, the notion of a protest vote often featured in people's answers, but it was rarely the whole story. With "New" Labour seen to have failed to repair the damage done by successive Conservative governments, almost everyone we spoke to could see why people were giving the BNP "a try", even if they themselves would never do so. From this point of view, a vote for the BNP in local elections was treated as a low risk option; unlikely to unsettle the balance of power nationally, it was seen as a way of sending a timely warning to elected representatives that the voters could not be taken for granted. However, as the following exchanges between middle-aged members of a residents' association reveal, these preliminary rationalizations for the BNP's popularity tended to be eclipsed by more emotionally charged reactions as the discussion gained momentum and participants became less guarded.

Ron: People are disillusioned with what the government are doing . . .

Pat: So they do think "Give somebody else a try".

Ron: They don't think they're being, er, listened to . . . and when the BNP come across—they come across very well I think . . . I wouldn't vote for them—I'll be honest with you there—but it's an alternative that people will listen to because it looks like they're representing their views.

Pat: In an area like this that's gone down the nick, I think people are looking for an alternative, aren't they?

Lilly: Well they've tried everything else here . . . They've tried . . . the Labour Party . . . for years and years, and people aren't very happy with it . . . They are looking for an alternative.

Martin: Well, same as . . . same as Enoch Powell said in 1930 . . . He says get the troop ships at Liverpool dock . . . so he must be racist . . . and then, er, send 'em all back because they'll over . . . overrun the country. And, as it happened, they are doing.

Nigel: See ... there's no doubt about it, Tony Blair's lied to this
country. He's lied. He's lied over mass, mass weapons
... in Iraq ... Don't forget, this government helped out
Saddam Hussein to gas the Kurds in 1970, so how they
can turn around now and link ... the Nazis to the BNP is
beyond me ... We have nothing to do with Nazi Germany
... so I wish people would not ... class all BNP members
as National Front ... Nick Griffin broke away ... If
anybody's convicted of race attack in the BNP, they will
be thrown out. If they're not thrown out, I'll be walking
away. But the propaganda is disgraceful against the BNP.
I am standing up. [Thumps table.] I am defending my
culture. I will never, ever allow any other ethnic member
of any country, of any religion, to attack my culture. If my
culture offends them ... I find that offensive ... I've got
no respect for other cultures that attack my culture ...

While Ron, Pat, and Lilly said they would not vote BNP themselves, they could all identify with the disillusionment with Labour
that was widely felt by the residents of the former mining community in which they lived. They all wanted to protest against a
government that no longer listened to people like them, and could
all appreciate why their neighbours might be "looking for an alternative" that might "represent" their views more effectively. Yet, as
we learnt from Martin and Nigel who, as a local BNP activist, was
trying to offer this alternative, supporters of the BNP might be looking for more than an opportunity to express their dissatisfaction
with "New" Labour nationally or protest about their treatment by
its local representatives. Although confusing to the point of impene-
trability, Martin's intervention, with its anachronistic reference to
Enoch Powell and its images of "troop ships at Liverpool dock" and
a country being "overrun" by foreigners, was, none the less, revealing, since it so clearly associated support for the BNP with the need
for authoritative intervention to deal with the threat posed by
uncontrolled mass immigration. Nigel's defence of the BNP was
also couched in the language of war, and consisted of a series of
imaginative leaps from Blair's "lies" about weapons of mass destruction in Iraq to his hypocrisy in associating the BNP and its
leader with the Nazi perpetrators of the Holocaust when the British
government had condoned the Iraqi dictator's use of gas against

the Kurds, and then on to his (Nigel's) own commitment (as a supporter of the BNP) to defending his culture against those "other ethnic member[s]" who seek to attack it. Unless the government stopped "allowing" people to "attack" it, Nigel feared that his "culture" would be lost forever; "I won't have one left . . . I won't have one left", he went on to insist.

As the next extract, taken from a discussion involving members of a parent and toddler group in the same neighbourhood as the residents' association, indicates, it was this kind of embattled mentality that enabled some to overlook the accusations of criminality and violence levelled against the BNP and its members.

Helen: . . . it made me laugh when Tony Blair said anyone who came in before '98 can legally stay. They could have come in yesterday for all he knows . . .

Carol: You don't know how many there is actually in this country.

Helen: There's got to be more of them than there is of us. Get rid of him, get rid of Tony Blair . . . Bring back Thatcher . . . or the BNP. I admit it . . . I voted BNP. I admit it.

Emma: He needs go, Tony Blair. Honest. I could go down there and just punch his lights out. [Laughter]

Gina: . . . get Maggie Thatcher back.

BD: Why is it do you think the BNP have become more popular in the city?

Helen: They know what people want . . . They know they want 'em out . . .

Fiona: They scare me.

Carol: I mean I will, I will say I voted for 'em and I won't deny it. I have, and I'll vote for 'em this time . . .

Helen: I voted for 'em . . .

Beth: . . . all my family did . . .

Carol: I mean how many. . . They've just shut three post offices where, where I used to live . . . which were owned by white people, and there's one here and one at the top that are owned by Pakis. They're still open.

In this discussion, the women's perception that people like them were being asked to accommodate a potentially overwhelming influx of asylum seekers called for and justified the kind of aggressive response that a vote for the BNP seemed to represent. Because there were too "many" of them to count; because there were now "more of them than there is of us"; because "they" could "have come in yesterday" for all anyone knows, and because they could end up running post offices when shops "owned by white people" have had to shut down, a vote for the only party that "knows what people want" had become imperative. If the BNP were able to deliver a political, if not a physical, "punch" in the face to Tony Blair, the man who had been letting countless asylum seekers in since 1998, the women would know that their objections to being outnumbered in their own country had finally registered. But they were also aware that supporting the BNP was not quite the same as supporting any other party. So Helen had to "admit" to voting for them while Carol chose not to "deny it". Beth and Fiona went further, explaining why they regarded the BNP as being too "bad press", "full on", and "scary" to attract their support. Beth did not want to be known as a "racist at all" and would never vote for the BNP, even though the rest of her family had done so, and in spite of Helen and Carol proceeding to accuse her of "not caring what happens to this country". In sum, participants' support for the far right in this group was only superficially unanimous.

Similar disagreements also arose among a group of young men and women on a training programme for the long-term unemployed. Participants in this third group came from all over Stoke-on-Trent, but we spoke to them at the programme's base, located in a part of the city no more than a couple of miles from the former mining community from which participants in the first two groups were drawn. In the following extract, one of the older members of the group, Trevor, talked about how only the BNP (or the National Front) can stop "the Pakis" from taking advantage of Britain—if necessary by violent means. The two young women then joined him in fantasizing about this prospect and the impact it might have on both the country and the lives of people like them.

> Trevor: Everybody's . . . saying . . . the Pakis have taken our country for a cunt . . . And nobody else has . . . had the balls to say it . . .

Julie: Apart from the BNP.

Trevor: . . . you know, because they're afraid of being sued or
            beaten up . . . The BNP and the National Front don't give
            a flying fuck . . .

Julie: Which is right though.

Trevor: "We'll say what we like. If you don't like it . . . we'll intro-
            duce you to an iron bar."

Lisa: [clapping triumphantly] . . . you feel like you can't have
            an opinion.

Trevor: If you, if you stood BNP . . . in power tomorrow, right,
            you'll watch 'em all leave and see how much room we've
            got . . .

Julie: And no fucker would be on the dole.

Trevor: No one in this country is going to be homeless. No one in
            this country is going to be starving . . .

Yet, despite the group's collective indulgence of Trevor's desire
to witness the physical intimidation of the "Pakis" they blamed for
their own misfortunes, Lisa went on to "play devil's advocate",
asking the group to reflect on whether they were merely being
"racist". Eventually, Julie, too, confessed that she disagreed with
Trevor. She was "very grateful" to an Asian doctor who had assured
her that she was "on the mend" after she had a miscarriage, and,
therefore, could not really look forward to a (mythical) day when
all Asian people would be forced out of the country by the BNP.
Julie's change of heart was something that Trevor found particularly hard to accept, perhaps because their racism was in some
senses both a product and a symbol of their mutual dependency.
As a victim of rape (something she disclosed during the course
of the discussion), Julie had good reason to be wary of sexually
predatory men, even if her assumptions about the inherent aggres-
siveness of Asians were unambiguously racist. In response to her
apparent vulnerability, Trevor often acted as Julie's chaperone-
cum-minder on drunken nights out, when her outspokenness tended to cause offence to the Asian taxi drivers on whom they relied
to get home. Having been "stabbed" by a "Paki" as a teenager and

denied an opportunity to "fight for his country" because of a disability, Trevor's own admission that he "loved" fighting, together with his preoccupation with tackling those "Pakis" who had "taken our country for a cunt", suggested to us that his identifications with the BNP and the National Front, together with the feelings of embattlement which seemed to underlie them, were complexly connected to these apparently traumatic biographical experiences.

Similar things, we discovered, could also be said about the sources of some of the differences of opinion that emerged among participants in the other two groups discussed earlier in this chapter. In the mothers' group, for example, Helen, one of the BNPs most vocal supporters, expressed her sympathy for a friend of her brother's (and a fellow BNP supporter) who had got into trouble with the police despite "not even throwing a punch" in a fight in which he was implicated. And while she did not make a connection between this and her own experiences, she, too, had recently attracted opprobrium from her fellow supermarket workers after attempting to assault an Asian customer who had had the temerity to wear an England football shirt. In the residents' association group, by contrast, Lilly and Pat's studiously neutral accounts of why other people were giving the BNP "a try" appeared to owe something to their identifications with people on the receiving end of prejudice and harassment. Pat was opposed to all kinds of bullying, racist or otherwise, because her children's lives had been "made hell" by homophobic taunting, while Lilly was visibly upset when she recalled how, arriving in 1950s Liverpool from Ireland, her family had searched for accommodation only to be greeted by notices warning that "Irish need not apply". Placed in this social context, one has to wonder not at why working-class support for the BNP remains as patchy and ephemeral, as our focus groups suggest, but how it is that a politically engaged, deeply moral man like Nigel—no less committed to his fellow residents than Lilly and Pat—can become so trenchant in his support for a party notorious for its racism and so insensitive to the feelings of those intimidated by its very existence as an organized political force. As we will now explain, only when we had the opportunity to study Nigel's life history did we begin to understand how this could happen.

A pen portrait of Nigel

Asked at the end of the focus group discussion we documented earlier if he was interested in taking part in some life history research that would "explore the links between his personal experiences and his politics", Nigel readily agreed. Invited to actually tell his life story a couple of weeks later, tears soon welled up in Nigel's eyes as he explained (figures in [brackets] indicate a pause timed in seconds):

"Me childhood . . . I didn't exactly have a . . . Looking back, I was unhappy as a child. I used to spend a lot of time coal picking . . . I remember me dad was working sometimes and sometimes he was unemployed. We were poor but we all stuck together but, ur, I think I missed out on a lot of things but me dad used to . . . Me dad was pretty hard on me personally like. And me mum was always very protective and, ur, I never forget the first time that ur . . . All the local school children used to talk about the discothèque . . . [M]e mum finally let me go one day. Me dad was working in the mines at the time and he went away on Friday for a two-week holiday to the miners' homes . . . And the Monday come [3] and, ur [4], me mother finally let me go to this discothèque [4]. I was really looking forward to it [4]. I think I was about fifteen . . . [4] I went to the discotheque [becoming breathless] . . . [15] When I got [6], when I got back home [crying] me mother, me mother had died. She died upstairs in the bed. So it's just something I can't ever forget really. I was so excited at going out and to get a shock like that, and then you know, it was a big shock for me . . ."

Sharing a council house with a large family of pot bank and pit workers, times were very hard during Nigel's youth. His sometimes-employed, sometimes-unemployed father and housewife mother raised nine children, of whom Nigel was the seventh, in a three bed-roomed property they shared with Nigel's grandmother. As a child, so much of Nigel's time out of school was spent running errands and picking coal that he had few friends. Although he likened himself and his siblings to "scavengers", the young Nigel had enjoyed aspects of the coal picking: he would clean the drivers' tractor cabs and in return they would give him free lifts and tip him off as to where they would be dumping the fresh slag so that he could tell his dad. His father would treat himself to a drink down the pub on the money Nigel made, but on his return he would sometimes beat Nigel for no apparent reason. Nigel could still remember the terrible nightmares he used to have as a child, associated in his account with his dad bringing a hot water bottle up to him and two of his three brothers squashed together in one bed, and how these nightmares had caused him to attempt to jump out of the bedroom window one night, believing that his sister was being assaulted in the garden. By the age of eight, Nigel was so miserable that he had contemplated ending his life by walking under a neighbour's car.

After school, Nigel would often be sent to the butcher's shop to buy food for the family's "workers", but at mealtimes he would have to sit waiting "like a dog", begging his older siblings to leave something on their plate for him to eat. His mum also fell foul of her husband's temper from time to time, but she did her best to protect Nigel, reminding him to keep quiet and sending him to bed when his dad returned from the pub. Not knowing why his father had treated him like this still troubled Nigel: "I don't know why he kept picking on me . . . I don't know if I was a cheeky kid." Difficult though things had been while his mother was alive, Nigel's memories of events after her death were particularly painful. When his father returned prematurely from his holiday on being told of his wife's sudden death, he had offered Nigel no sympathy, only the accusation that he, Nigel, had in some way been the cause of it: "He said, 'Is this you?' [3], meaning is it me that's caused me mum to, you know. That really hurt. 'Is this you? Carrying on?' That's all he said . . . No hug."

Soon after this, Nigel's girlfriend fell pregnant. Forced by his father to choose between living at home and supporting his girlfriend, Nigel fulfilled his "moral duty" and moved out. Despite his father's unreasonableness in denying the couple use of a "spare" room made vacant by his grandmother's death and some of his brothers leaving home, Nigel's filial feelings for his father remained unshaken: "I still respected me dad because he was me dad and, looking back, it must have been hard for him."

Having left home, Nigel and his girlfriend moved to rented accommodation where an Asian landlord exploited the young couple's predicament, insisting that Nigel clean the house every day for a pound a week. The other (Asian) men who lived in the house "always used to come in late at night because they'd been working on the pot banks . . . cooking their curries . . . and talking loud". Unsurprisingly, Nigel didn't recall this experience with any fondness: "I've lived with them as well Dave . . . and they treated me like shit." Evicted by their landlord after refusing to do any more cleaning, Nigel and his girlfriend's relationship became strained and the first two children they had together were taken into care. Nigel "couldn't handle" this, "was crying all the time", still thinking about his mum, and ended up taking an overdose. Eventually, the couple had two more children, but the relationship remained unstable and erupted in violence on at least one occasion when Nigel's girlfriend humiliated him by trying to "be clever in front of people". Several years later, and despite his girlfriend's pleading, Nigel left her and married another woman, Mary, a devout Catholic.

The "total opposite" of his "common law wife", Mary was "supportive", "very placid", had "not got a big mouth", and was no "gold-digger": she "liked the simple things in life". Mary had been willing to adopt Nigel's first two daughters, but social services had insisted he hand over all rights to them when they were taken into care. Nigel began sobbing again as he recounted how he told the social worker that he would ". . . never sign nothing . . . and when my children [10] come looking, I'll look them straight in the eye with honesty and say that [4] it wasn't me."

Nigel and Mary eventually went on to have four children of their own together.

Although he had no religious convictions himself, Nigel regarded being "good" as something rather sacred: "I just simply believe you can be good without going to church . . . I just simply believe there is no life after death. I never will. I don't still believe it."

In spite of his own lack of faith, all four children he had had with his wife had been "christened as Catholics", were regular church-goers, and "are all well educated and . . . trying to build a life for themselves and put something back into this country"—a country Nigel was later to refer to as a "Christian country" in the context of an extended polemic about the "dangers" of unrestrained immigration. Throughout their marriage, it was Mary who had been the "real breadwinner". Indeed, while Nigel had taken many semi-skilled jobs over the years, he had never held any of them down for long. A combination of his sometimes explosive temper, recurring back pain, and poor mental health had led to him either being dismissed from, and/or walking off, a succession of jobs. "Although I tried to forget the past," he explained, "you can never forget the past. It still comes up from time to time." At one point, Nigel had left a job in a local mine, claiming "I cried at work . . . I can't sing when she's there, I can't sing . . . I think it stems back to the memories of my mum"; even "walking round a shop . . . listening to the Christmas songs" could "upset" him. It was as if he wished he had faith, or at least a belief in life after death, as this might have allowed him to come to terms with his mother's death.

Aged thirty-eight, Nigel finally broke down in front of his wife's health visitor and was referred to psychiatric services. Prescribed medication for "chronic depression", Nigel preferred to tell people, "I'm out of work. I don't say I'm ill." Rather than do nothing, he had taken to campaigning tirelessly about local issues, trying to "put something back" into his community. Earlier manifestations of this public spiritedness had involved him breaking a world record in snooker to raise money for charity when he was still in his twenties. Later, in his thirties, it had meant leading a campaign to introduce traffic calming measures to stop children "being killed or run over". Then, in his forties, Nigel had taken to lobbying the council until they cleaned up residents' gardens and children's play areas. Although he feared that the strain of all this campaigning would put him in "an early grave", Nigel consoled himself with the thought that his children would at least be able to say that their "dad did something . . . They can walk away from this estate and say, 'My dad's done that, and my dad's done that, and my dad's done that'".

As he approached middle age, life had got no easier for Nigel. Pregnant for a fifth time, his wife had miscarried, leaving the couple with feelings of "emptiness", only made worse by their inability to pay for a funeral for their still-born child. Then, after a long period of illness, during the course of which Nigel had struggled to raise the funds needed to buy his father an electric wheelchair, the old man had died. To Nigel's great distress, his eldest brother had instructed the funeral directors not to bring the body into the house after the bit of money "for everyone" that their father had promised failed to materialize. Similar issues again came to the fore a couple of years later, when this brother, too, died (of throat cancer). On this occasion, Nigel had been unable to afford a wreath, and was appalled when his brother's partner insisted on burying her husband in "a right grotty hole" miles away from where the rest of his family lived. The sadness Nigel felt about this and his many other painful memories had "spoilt" days out for his children more than once. When his family worried about him, Nigel told them to "just leave" him "alone". But when he was alone, for example in his caravan, something he described as getting away from the "rat race" and being with his "own kind", his "own community", he struggled "to get to grips" with himself.

More recently, when Nigel's two estranged daughters had "come looking" for him, he had found himself unable to get back "the bonding" that had been so painfully broken when they had been taken into care. One of the girls had broken off all contact with Nigel after he described her husband as a "cagey drug-dealer" and a threat to his "family". Nigel blamed his former partner—"now going with a coloured chap"—for telling "lies" and suggested that she was "poisoning" his grandchildren's minds against him. Then another of Nigel's daughters was turned down for a "budgeting loan" she had applied for from the council. In his biographical interviews, Nigel explained that it was this turn of events and not, as he had stated in the focus group, the Blair government's policies on immigration and Iraq that had prompted him to join the BNP. Forced to beg and borrow from his family to raise the deposit for privately rented accommodation for one daughter and her children, and distanced once again from another, Nigel described this as "one of the lowest times" in his life—"embarrassing and . . . shocking":

> "I felt as if . . . the country has let us down badly. My daughter's worked for nine years . . . The only time she has ever asked the government for any help, help she would be paying back, they turns us down. And that is when I joined the BNP."

However, as his subsequent rationalization was to reveal, Nigel's decision to join the BNP was not so straightforwardly linked to this one event as he sometimes implied. Somehow, the council's recent refusal to give his daughter a "budgeting loan" had become conflated in his mind with the day, some thirty years earlier, when his first two daughters had been put up for adoption:

> "It's because I've been there and I care . . . I feel for them because I been that side. You know it comes from the heart, Dave. Like I said, they took me children away, me grandchildren away. That's when I got involved."

Perhaps because of this conflation of experiences, when he was asked a question that caused him to reflect on the differences between his childhood memories of his father and his own children's experiences of him, Nigel's commitment to the BNP began to falter.

> "All I believe is try to make sure that, er, I don't affect my kids like he affected me. I still loved him, Dave. I still had respect for him. [4] I'd never let anybody harm him. [4] But the scars that are left are there, Dave. I mean I have to be truthful to myself, Dave, as passionate as I may be . . . underneath, underneath, I know that . . . if I was elected as a councillor, I couldn't, wouldn't sleep for weeks . . . knowing that they're [other councillors] betraying and telling lies. People only see one side of me, Dave, but underneath I'm heartbroken . . ."

Having acknowledged this during the course of his interview, Nigel subsequently withdrew as a BNP candidate in the forthcoming local elections, bringing two years of campaigning on its behalf to an abrupt and, given his impassioned—if intensely embattled—defence of the party when we first met him at the focus group discussion, somewhat unexpected end.

When the personal becomes political: Nigel's story

In one sense there is nothing particularly unique about Nigel's recollections of his childhood. Seabrook's (1982, p. 27) collection of oral histories, *Working-class Childhood*, contains many similar tales and is a testament to "the violence, not only of industrial life, but of war, disease and early death, that expressed itself in the way [working-class] children were brought up within the family". It is no revelation that the family lives of post-war industrial workers in cities like Stoke could be extremely bleak. The hardships of manual labour and the downturns in working men's fortunes and health meant that loyal Labour men—men like Nigel's father—were not always easy to live with, especially in crowded conditions. Some fathers, like Nigel's, got drunk and depressed and needed respite, leaving their families behind to holiday alone. Domestic abuse and child neglect were not uncommon, even if they were rarely discussed openly. Many families struggled to make ends meet, saving what little food they had for the family's "workers". And, whatever their shortcomings as fathers and husbands, the authority of male breadwinners *had* to be, and was, respected in order to maintain the appearance of respectable working-class family life.

Tellingly, however, Seabrook notes that the "cruel conditions in which the old working class lived made people turn to each other for consolation" (*ibid.*, p. 33). Children "recognize[d] the harsh conjuncture of the family discipline and the world which shaped it. They knew their parents had no choice" (*ibid.*, p. 26). Nigel, on the other hand, while no less aware of just how "hard" times had been for his parents, suspected, even if he struggled to say so, that his father had had a choice. Nigel could not understand why his father had treated him so harshly as a child, hence, the rhetorical questions about whether he really was such a "cheeky kid", nor, in Nigel's youth, why the older man had been so unwilling to let the mother of his unborn grandchild live in the family home. Even if poverty justified the scavenging for coal and food, it could not explain his father's uncaring contempt for him. This contempt had eaten away at Nigel, causing him nightmares he could still remember forty years on. When, at the age of fifteen, his mother— the one person who had protected him from his father—died, Nigel was devastated. To be accused of causing her death by a father who offered him no word or gesture of sympathy left him with a sense of persecution that seemed never to have left him. Lacking any religious conviction and unable to believe in an afterlife, unlike the "Asian community" of whom he was so critical, Nigel had never come to terms with his parents' deaths. He talked about them as if they were still alive and was unable to function at work when he remembered his mother: "I can't sing when she's there."

By his own account, Nigel had failed in so many ways to prove himself as a worker, a provider, a father, and a husband, prompting uncomfortable memories of his father's low expectations of him and his unfortunate tendency to confirm them. Being "treated like shit" by the Asian landlord who took him in after his father had refused to allow him and his pregnant partner to stay in the family home had provided an enduring emotional hook upon which Nigel could hang his anguish at the loss of his mother and rejection by his father. The "Asian community", "ethnic members", and Muslims had, over many years, become repositories for his crippling self-doubts, his Asian landlord and fellow lodgers—"I've lived with *them*"—assumed to be representative of a wider population he imagined to be destroying his "culture". That so many of the personal tragedies of his adult life were compounded by financial hardship—the shame of not being able to bury a still-born child, of having to beg and borrow money to look after sick relatives, pay for funerals, and support children and grandchildren when they became homeless—fuelled Nigel's hostility towards the "immigrants" he perceived to be immune from the misfortunes of his "own kind". He often cried inexplicably, and preferred to tell people he was out of work rather than confront his chronic depression. He tried hard to respect his dad because he was "dad", even though he must have been aware, if only unconsciously, how devastating the psychological damage his father had caused him really was.

While telling his story, Nigel reflected that he might not have had so many children—eight in total, plus one still-born—had his father treated him differently. Placed alongside his desire to make lasting changes to his community, we took this as revelatory of the extent to which so much of what Nigel did was motivated by an unconscious desire not to repeat his father's mistakes and to make good his own shortcomings as a parent and a provider. As Sennett and Cobb (1993) have observed, the kind of self-sacrifice evident in Nigel's account is a common manifestation of the *Hidden Injuries of Class*.

Working-class fathers . . . see the whole point of sacrificing for their children to be that their children *will* become unlike themselves . . . [H]is sacrifice does not end in his own life the social conditions that have made him feel open to shame, prey to feelings of inadequacy. To call the pressure working-class fathers put on their kids "authoritarian" is misleading in that the father doesn't ask the child to take the parents' lives as a model, but as a warning. [Sennett & Cobb, 1993, p. 128]

Part of what sustained Nigel's community activism—including his support for the BNP—was a desire for his children to be able to say that their father had done something to improve things for the next generation. Nigel, of course, had particular reasons for wanting his children to be able to say this, having long anticipated the day when his first two children would come "looking" for him, presenting an opportunity to set the record straight by telling them that he was not to blame for their estrangement. When, in the event, things turned out differently, Nigel was forced to confront the pain of the original loss once again, and his response to his daughters was so defensive that his own careless words cost him the chance of "getting the bonding back". Unable to admit this to himself, he blamed his ex-partner's "poisoning" and "lies" (or uncomfortable truths?) for his daughters' rapid loss of interest in rebuilding their relationships with him.

When one of Nigel's younger daughters failed to secure a "budgeting loan", the unexpected reverse became conflated in his mind with the day, almost three decades earlier, when social services had taken his first two children away. Publicly, he saw this as all of a piece with the wider attacks on "his" family and culture, being mounted by untrustworthy political elites. Privately, however, the story he told had more to do with his inability to help his children in their hours of need and the damage this did to his fragile sense of self-worth. It is not hard to see how the BNP's views on conspiring Islamists, the unsettling homogeneity of "the Asian community", Tony Blair's lies, and the threat of unfettered migration resonated with Nigel's persecutory sensibilities at this time. But it is also impossible to explain *why these came to matter so much to him* without taking into account his inability to forget—rid from his conscious awareness—an excruciatingly painful, inescapably humiliating past. No wonder Nigel perceived his entire way of life to be under attack. And no wonder, either, that he admired the renegade Nick Griffin, someone who had admitted to making mistakes but claimed to have put his past behind him and to be standing up for those beleaguered white men who have a habit of offending people whenever they speak their minds. But if "standing up", "defending", and "breaking away" were what he idolized about Griffin, Nigel himself was occasionally capable of less embattled responses. Faced with the risk he ran of alienating his own children—just as he had been estranged from his own father—and aware of the opportunity he had to avoid making the same mistake, it became possible for Nigel to direct his resentment towards the hating parts of himself. Somehow, this evoked in him a desire to "be truthful", to face up to how "heartbroken" he was "underneath", below the surface of the defensive racism that had fostered his enthusiasm for the BNP.

Conclusions: personal problems and political fantasies

What can we conclude from Nigel's story and the stories many of our focus group participants told us about their reasons for supporting—or not supporting—the BNP? As we have shown in this chapter, the appeal of the BNP cannot be explained solely in terms of class-based resentments, protest votes, media-induced hysteria, and/or the failings of "New" Labour. These factors are not unimportant, but their explanatory power is limited by their inability to account for the range of individual reactions to the BNP we encountered and for the way in which the party has been able to appeal to voters, notwithstanding the obloquy heaped on it by anti-fascist campaigners, mainstream politicians, and the tabloid media alike. Just as the promise that "things can only get better" encouraged voters to put their faith in "New" Labour back in 1997, so the "new" BNP became invested, in some white working-class voters' minds, with fantastical qualities quite at odds with its chances of delivering any kind of tangible change. The BNP's ability to position itself as a political outlaw has enabled voters to imagine its candidates as folk heroes, transgressing social and political convention and, if need be, the law, to right wrongs, to give Blair a bloody nose, and to intimidate the asylum seekers and "Pakis" so easily made the scapegoats for a range of social problems and personal issues.

However, if we are to make sense of why it is that some voters have been lured towards a party that can deliver so little, we have, as Fromm once advised, to give up on the notion that people are motivated solely by the forces they believe themselves to be motivated by. Instead, we must look beyond their words for sentiments buried in metaphor, contradiction, and defensive gestures, and be prepared to interpret the hidden meanings that lie behind people's public explanations for their actions. The relevance of class cannot be understood unless, as Sennett and Cobb (1993, p. 10) suggest, we move beyond the boundaries of what is either said or sayable. But we also need to reconsider exactly what it is about class that is important to this kind of analysis. When we focus only on attitudinal differences between broad socio-economic groups, we lose sight of the many fears, losses, and grievances that get compounded and conflated with each other to cause the imperceptible psychological wounds which Sennett and Cobb conceptualize as the hidden injuries of class.

Of course, such injuries are as gendered and racialized as they are class-ridden. But, that said, our view is that it is these hidden psychological injuries which give rise to the defensive embattlement that underpins support for the BNP and gives meaning to the apocalyptical clichés—"last straw", "last resort", "desperate times and desperate measures"—on which people rely to explain why they vote for a party with a track record of bigotry, violence, and extremism. Where we would depart from the more sophisticated sociological readings of this phenomenon is in our insistence that the way in which these injuries are thought about by particular individuals—and, indeed, whether these injuries are properly thought about by them at all—matters a great deal. Hence, it makes a difference that some individuals, like Lilly and Pat in our residents' association group, are able to identify with the fear of harassment felt by minority ethnic groups because of their own experiences of victimization. It also matters that some people, despite their investments in the most vitriolic forms of prejudice, are, like Julie, able to perceive how ludicrous racist fantasies are when measured up against their actual experiences of people from ethnic minority groups. Within this context, what we need to understand more fully is how it is that other individuals, like Helen, Trevor and Nigel, become so locked into racist mindsets that the similarities between themselves and those they hate become imperceptible, while the individuals concerned become so afraid of measuring their opinions against their own or other people's experiences that they lose touch with reality. Nigel's story is particularly instructive here, since it reveals how people suffering the most acute emotional pain can come to depend on extremist politics to cope with their own inner turmoil. It may also help us to explain why those who desperately need to forget their pasts may be particularly susceptible to the fantasy that an ethnically purer future will somehow make them feel better. For us, cases like Nigel's reveal not only how artificial the divide between the personal and the political can be, as feminist campaigners have long argued, but also how dangerous and unmanageable the personal can become when politicized in such a way that the biographically mediated meanings which inform it are beyond the conscious awareness of the individual and invisible to those with whom he or she comes into contact. Instead of seeking to exploit it for their own ends, mainstream politicians need to find ways of getting behind and understanding the sources of the embattled defensiveness on which the BNP has fed in place like Stoke-on-Trent. To assist this work, our academic analyses need to focus on how alternative identifications can be opened up for those whose hatred of others protects them from feelings of self-hatred. These are issues that the next three chapters attempt to address.

CHAPTER SIX

Rethinking community cohesion

*Community cohesion: progressive policy,
or part of the problem?*

Between 2001 and 2010, "community cohesion" became a
centrepiece of "New" Labour policy-making that dislodged
the older agendas of multi-culturalism, anti-racism, and "race
relations" (Denham, 2002, 2006). Yet, as a number of academic
commentators have remarked, it is not clear exactly what is meant
by "community cohesion" (Alexander, 2004; Burnett, 2004; McGhee,
2003; Werbner, 2005; Worley, 2005). Many of the early policy
pronouncements failed to define the term altogether. Eventually,
cohesive communities were described in the Home Office (2004,
p. 1) document, *Strength in Diversity: towards a Community Cohesion
and Race Equality Strategy*, as the cornerstone of a "successful
integrated society that celebrates strength in its diversity". Even
in this document, however, details were scarce. In her preface to
what was "not a conventional Government consultation document
and deliberately so", the then Parliamentary Under Secretary for
Race Equality, Community Policy and Civil renewal, Fiona
MacTaggart MP, explained that the Home Office had "not set out

specific proposals which could close down options and risk narrowing the debate". The intention was, rather, to provide a framework for "honest and robust debate" (*ibid.*). Two years later, the incoming Communities Secretary, Ruth Kelly echoed these sentiments and called for a "new and honest" debate about "race in Britain", adding that it was "'not racist' to voice concerns about immigration and asylum" (Younge, 2006). Taking up this suggestion, the *Guardian's* Gary Younge (*ibid.*) pointed out that

> Any candid discussion of race, immigration and asylum that was not racist would not just acknowledge fear and prejudice but challenge them both. Since ministers are not able to do that about ethnic minorities, maybe they should start off with a subject with which they are more familiar. Let's have an open and honest discussion about white people.

Younge's suspicions soon proved correct: the political agenda was never as open as MacTaggart and Kelly implied. The debate the government wanted to have about "why we need a Government wide community and race equality strategy"—the question asked in the title of the first chapter in *Strength in Diversity*—already assumed a central problematic:

> In many areas, the diversity within and between communities has been a source of rich cultural interactions, but in other areas segregation has led to fear and conflict, which has been exacerbated by political extremists who capitalise on insecurities to promote their own narrow objectives. Structural inequalities and the legacy of discrimination have resulted in whole groups that are effectively left behind, with young people failing to share in the opportunities that should be available to all, which in turn fuels their disengagement from mainstream society and creates pathways to extremism. [Home Office, 2004, p. 5]

Like so much of the rhetoric surrounding community cohesion, this formulation raised as many questions as it answered. What exactly are the causal relationships between the various social phenomena identified here? Which group or groups of young people fail to "share in the opportunities that should be available to all"? What, precisely, is it that fuels the "extremism" to which the Home Office refers? "Structural inequalities" and the "legacy of discrimination" were mentioned, but it was "segregation" that was assumed to have led to "fear and conflict"; why?

Two influential reports, both published in 2001, legitimized this focus on segregation, even if they failed to justify it empirically. First, Cantle (2001) attributed the 2001 riots in northern English mill towns to what he saw as the proliferation of ethnically distinct "parallel lives".

> Separate educational arrangements, community and voluntary bodies, employment, places of worship, language, social and cultural networks, means that many communities operate on the basis of a series of parallel lives. These lives often do not seem to touch at any point, let alone overlap and promote any meaningful interchanges. [Cantle, 2001, p. 9]

Competitive tendering for regeneration grants, Cantle suggested, had turned the disadvantaged against each other, while greater parental choice in education and the advent of increasingly mono-cultural schools had reduced the amount of contact between adults and children of different ethnic groups. Against a backcloth of racialized suspicion and hostility, Cantle argued, people living in relative poverty were rarely offered reasonable guarantees of security by the police, prompting the more marginalized residents of the former mill towns to "look backwards" for "some form of identity", either "to some supposedly halcyon days of a mono-cultural society", or, alternatively, "to their country of origin" (ibid.).

Then, in his report, *Community Pride, Not Prejudice*, Lord Ouseley (2001, p. 3) called for "immediate action to initiate change to end racial *self-segregation* and cultural divisiveness" (our emphasis). Too many people, he suggested, were in the "grip" of "fear" (ibid., p. 1), frightened of

> ... talking openly and honestly about problems, either within their communities or across different cultural communities, because of possible repercussions, recriminations and victimization ... of leading and managing effective change because of possible public and media criticism ... of challenging wrong-doing because of being labelled "racist" ... of crime [and] of confronting the gang culture, the illegal drugs trade and the growing racial intolerance, harassment and abuse that exists. [ibid.]

Ultimately, the terms of public debate became less measured, slipping rapidly from "segregation" to "self-segregation" and from the protests of particular young men in particular places to racialized generalizations about "crime" and "gang" culture. When those who did not speak English in public, refused to swear allegiance to the flag, or "forced" arranged marriages on their children were publicly criticized for failing to "integrate" (most notably by Trevor Phillips, the then Chair of the Commission for Racial Equality and latterly of the Equality and Human Rights Commission which replaced it, in his "sleepwalking to segregation" seminars), the dangers inherent in the kind of honest talking recommended by Kelly, MacTaggart, and Ousley became all too apparent. Invited to speak their minds, politicians and members of the public alike blamed both "insular" minority ethnic groups and "political correctness" for the perennial problems of white racism and urban disorder (Worley, 2005). The 2005 terrorist attacks on London only made matters worse, with a succession of senior ministers adding to the clamour. With John Reid talking about "fanaticism" and "no-go areas", Jack Straw calling on veiled women to think about the impact of their attire on community relations, and Hazel Blears pleading with the nation not to "tiptoe" around the issues of Islam and integration, it was hardly surprising that sections of the press felt able to turn what was supposed to be an "honest and robust debate" about the causes of urban unrest and what should be done about them, about community cohesion and race equality, into an inflammatory and speculative tirade against "soft" liberal reformers and those, mainly Islamic, minorities deemed unwilling to assimilate.

From realist critique to subjective engagement

Consequently, little attention was paid to those academic commentators who cautioned against inferring "ethnic" and/or "self" segregation from the concentration of ethnic groups in certain localities (Dobbs, Green, & Zealey, 2006; Ratcliffe, 2004). Be that as it may, their research shows that the concentration of certain minority ethnic groups in particular residential areas has rarely been a matter of freely chosen "self-segregation". Even before the government's own dispersal policy began to dictate where asylum seekers were accommodated, patterns of settlement in Britain have long been shaped by factors beyond the control of new arrivals. Poverty, unemployment, the workings of the private and public sector property markets and the cost of borrowing, the availability of much-needed support services, and experiences of racism and discrimination all help to explain why, from the 1960s onwards, first generation migrants often "chose" to live in close proximity to minority ethnic communities facing similar challenges (Werbner, 2005; Webster, 2003). By way of contrast, the children and grandchildren of these migrants have a wider range of opportunities available to them, a different set of aspirations to their elders, and are often much keener than the general population to move away from neighbourhoods in which their own ethnic group predominates (Simpson, 2004).

More scathing still in his criticism of the community cohesion agenda was Burnett (2004, p. 8) who described it as a form of "class criminalisation", an "instrument to be forcibly inserted into areas characterised by structural economic deprivation", and "a thinly veiled attempt to control those non-white communities designated a risk to 'Britishness' because of their resistance to even more informal control". Burnett argued that, despite the seemingly neutral language used in government policy documents, the rhetoric of community cohesion involved a double standard. The violence of white communities was construed as "representative of the frustration and instability" felt by impoverished working-class people, while the violence of angry and desperate Asian youth was treated as "representative of inherent Asian criminality", of "their unwillingness to accept the national morality of 'law and order'" (ibid., p. 9). White racists were regarded as "extremists", a minority who were not like ordinary whites, whereas those members of the Asian community who participated in the riots were perceived as "normal" examples of " . . . an audacious criminal community" (ibid., pp. 6–7). As Bagguley and Hussain's (2008) empirically rich analysis of how an ethnically homogenous crowd was created by the actions of the police and subsequent media reporting, such assumptions about the "Asian rioters" who took to the streets of northern towns in 2001 simply cannot be justified. While "New" Labour encouraged communities in general to take action against those whose behaviour offended them, many of the young Asian men who took a stand against far right activism and violent racists received punitive deterrent sentences (McGhee, 2003, 2005). Indeed, if one returns to the substance of what people said to the inquiry teams that went into those towns where violence did erupt, as opposed to the policy responses to the teams' reports, it becomes much easier to appreciate how some young Asian men—many of whom had not been trouble with the law before and had tried in the early stages of the disturbances to stop the conflict from escalating—ultimately came to regard taking the law into their own hands as a justifiable response to the situation in which they found themselves.

In Burnley, for example, many of the white people who contacted the inquiry team did not differentiate those of South Asian ancestry from more recent "immigrants". Neither group were thought to "belong" in the town: both were assumed to be the ill-deserving beneficiaries of preferential treatment from the police, health care providers, and the local authority. Lord (Tony) Clarke (2001), the Burnley review team's chair, decided not to publish the most racist responses his team elicited, but what he did publish was revealing enough. Some white adult householders wrote to the team claiming that their "whole life and culture [was] under threat" and that they were suffering "a silent invasion" (ibid., p. 47). Others believed that the "Asian population [were] either unwilling or too lazy to learn our language, thereby making themselves unemployable" (ibid., p. 51), and that "the minorities get money to move" (ibid., p. 58). Indeed, the Inquiry was told that its own Task Force was largely made up of the groups who caused the problems in the first place, "left wingers and liberals (who allowed immigration against the wishes of the majority) and the immigrants themselves" (ibid., p. 22). Similar responses were forthcoming in Oldham, where Lord Ritchie's panel were shocked by what appeared to be "almost casually racist language on the lips of many white Oldhamers for whom 'Paki' is not only the acceptable term for Asians but the normal term used" (Ritchie, 2001, p. 4). Against this background, it is scarcely surprising that the young Asian men living in Oldham and Burnley were not just angered by the extremists who were intimidating them and their families. What really infuriated them was the fact that these extremists appeared to have the tacit support of many local white people, and that neither the police nor other official bodies seemed willing to challenge those inciting or condoning hatred against them.

Similar dynamics to those identified in Bradford, Burnley, and Oldham appeared to us to be in play in Stoke-on-Trent during this period. Like these northern towns and cities, Stoke experienced escalating tension between young Asians and the police during the summer of 2001. These tensions culminated on 14 July in what the national press reported as a "riot" in the Cobridge area of the city, home to most of its British Asian population (Bamber & Syal, 2001; Dodd, 2001). Many of the people we spoke to in the city three years later—public officials, community activists and young Asian people alike—contested this description, but subsequent events followed a pattern not dissimilar to that which unfolded elsewhere, and, two years after the "riot", the city was awarded Community Cohesion "Pathfinder" status following a now-standard process of "competitive bidding" (Home Office, 2003). However, since mayoral elections held in the same year as the Cobridge "riot", the city witnessed a steady growth in support for the BNP, with between a fifth and two-fifths of voters now supporting the party in wards where it puts up candidates.

In the previous chapter, we looked at the unconscious attractions that the far right may hold for people in places like Stoke-on-Trent. Here, we want to make sense of developments since the events in Cobridge on 14 July 2001, in the wider context of the so-called community cohesion agenda, by concentrating on discussions we held with a group of young Muslim men of Pakistani descent who attended a local youth club, elderly white members of a working men's club, and a group of professionals from local government and the third sector involved in implementing community cohesion initiatives across North Staffordshire. What we hope to be able to show here is that the nature of the relationships between different sections of the population living in deindustrializing towns like Stoke-on-Trent cannot be adequately understood without taking into account the underlying structure of the thinking that informs each section's perception of the others. We show that it is possible to see clear *parallels* in the defensive ways in which white working-class people, South Asian youth, and local community cohesion professionals think about each other. We argue that how these *parallel patterns of thinking* are responded to, both within communities and by politicians and policymakers from outside, determines whether people are able to identify with the personal tragedies, fears, and grievances of those from different social groups living in close proximity to them.

Taking the initiative? Young Asian men's experiences of community cohesion

Tariq (aged eighteen), Omar, (seventeen), Ali (seventeen), Imran (sixteen), and Mohammed (fifteen) were five British Muslim boys of Pakistani descent who had lived in Stoke-on-Trent all their lives. Unlike those depicted in *Strength in Diversity*, these young men were not disengaged from the political mainstream. Actively involved in local community cohesion initiatives, knowledgeable about world affairs and sensitive to the connections between global events and local politics, their levels of civic engagement were far greater than our own. Some of the group claimed to have been present during the confrontation with the police in Cobridge on the evening of 14 July 2001. But, like many of those who took part in the disturbances in other northern towns that summer (Webster, 2003), these young men did not see the "riot" as the expression of some inherent criminality, but as a justifiable response to rumours that the BNP were planning a march through the area and the failure of the police to protect their neighbourhoods from the provocations of far right activists. From the perspective of these young men, the relatively minor confrontation with the police that followed was not due to a lack of community cohesion. On the contrary, they insisted that it was a manifestation of it: a gesture of solidarity which transcended ethnic divisions and expressed their multi-ethnic community's rejection of racism and opposition to the emergence of the BNP as a viable electoral force in Stoke-on-Trent. This was Imran's memory of the supposedly Asian "riot":

> "Debbie ... that big [white] woman, yeah, from the estate ... she went on the frontline with a bandanna on her face going, 'Allah'. ... [W]hite, Asian, black people in Cobridge ... come together. Because at the end of the day we live in a community where all types ... I tell you straight ... truthfully, there are white people and black people on my street ... I treat them like I treat my own

family. .... 'Cos they, they're our family really, if you think about it, your neighbourhood is ..." [Imran]

"Family" clearly mattered a great deal to Imran, and he could not understand why the "nice old [white] woman" down his road had no family to support her: "Her family most probably left her because she's old ... Anything could happen to that woman ... If you don't look after your parents, tomorrow, bro ... what goes around comes around."

Omar agreed. The disdain shown by white people towards the elderly manifest in television commercials and comedy shows was deeply distasteful, and evidence of the lack of loyalty to family to be found amongst many white Britons. From Imran, Ali, and Omar's perspectives, if there was a lack of cohesion anywhere it was within the family structure of the white community. Why, they asked us, did white women come to their neighbourhood to prostitute themselves, why did white people leave syringes and condoms in their streets where "little kids" could find them, and why did they let their dogs "shit" in the park or, as some of the group suspected, do so themselves?

After the disturbances of 2001, Tariq, Omar, Ali, Imran, and Mohammed had helped to prepare a bid for a Single Regeneration Budget (SRB) grant to provide a football pitch in their local park. They also entered a team for a football tournament intended to promote community cohesion in the city. Sadly, neither of these attempts to respond to the community cohesion agenda had lived up to the teenagers' expectations. The application for SRB funding failed to generate enough money to lay the synthetic turf pitch they had hoped for, while the "friendly" football tournament exposed them to racial abuse and physical danger. Facing defeat from younger Asian players they regarded as "shit", one member of a local white team had started calling his opponents "Pakis" and "black bastards". At full time the Asian boys retaliated by "battering" the abuser and his friends, only to find themselves "caged" in by the police and subjected to more racist abuse:

Imran: They could have terrorized us all ... We were just
            surrounded in, in a circle... People trying to come
            ... just punching. We had to fight for our lives ...

Mohammed: Like going in a war. It was war.

For Tariq, Omar, Ali, Imran, and Mohammed, their experience of being "caged" in and abused in this way could not be disconnected from their many other experiences of racism, direct and indirect, first and second hand. These included: persistent bullying in school and their teachers' failures to deal with it; the harassment of Tariq's father—a "practising" Muslim—by the police in the wake of 11 September 2001; popular support in Stoke-on-Trent for the BNP; the death of Gareth Myatt, a local boy of mixed heritage who suffocated as he was being restrained by workers at a privately-run secure unit for young offenders; the racist murder of Stephen Lawrence; the death of an African-Caribbean man, Christopher Alder, in police custody in Hull; George Bush's and Tony Blair's rationalizations for the so-called "War on Terror". The cumulative impact of these experiences generated some deeply ambivalent responses among these young men. Aggrieved by the injustice of it all, Imran's initial reaction was more ironic than angry: "You see, and all this is supposed to be community cohesion, bringing people in . . . social inclusion not socially excluding." Yet, as the following extract reveals, an underlying bitterness was soon exposed as the boys' contempt for "racist bastards" in Stoke-on-Trent who bring their children up to "hate Pakis" led Omar and Ali on into a sardonic tribute to the elusiveness of Osama bin Laden.

Ali: It's the older members of the community, yeah, brainwashing . . . Like him [Mohammed] . . . he got chucked out school, yeah, for fighting . . . against racist guys. And we sat in a room with 'em, yeah . . . and we said, "Why are you racist?" And they go, "Oh it's cos our olders. That's how they taught us . . . this, that . . .".

Imran: . . . the parents, yeah, racist bastards, yeah, teaching their kids to hate Pakis and that . . . Muslim terrorists.

Omar: You know, like they tell nightmare stories. Guess what they say? "Oh, beware of the curry monster" . . .

Imran: It all boils down to BNP and racist stuff like that . . . The media don't help, yeah. When they start this Abu Hamza business [the radical Muslim cleric, known in the tabloid press as "Hook" because of his prosthetic hands, was much in the news at the time of this discussion] . . . to sell numbers, and make money . . . They show you what they want to show you . . . propaganda, bro. They didn't even tell you, yeah, about the American soldiers that . . . got killed, yeah . . . Oh, they've got Saddam Hussein, but have they told you anything about it . . .

Omar: Where's Bin Laden? I know where Bin Laden is, you know. Big up to Bin Laden.

Ali: [Grabs microphone] You're never finding him. He's in the mountains . . .

Omar: . . . what gives them the right? They got nuclear weapons themselves. Do you get me?

While he was coy about exactly who had done what, Omar went on to suggest that some of the group's participants had taken it upon themselves to challenge the actions of an independent councillor whose well-publicized opposition to a hostel for asylum seekers had been exploited by the BNP. When, in the wake of the Cobridge disturbances of 14 July 2001 and the attacks in New York on 11 September, the councillor had run the Union Jack up a flagpole in a local park near the site of the hostel, members of the group had removed it. From Tariq's point of view, the problem was not that the flag had been put up, but that it had been put up in a place where a flag had never been flown before at a time when the local community had so recently been under threat from the far right, and when Muslims around the world were being so widely vilified. For Imran, the flag-raising only accentuated his own feelings of unease about the influence of far right activism on his doorstep: "When it comes to the BNP, I get angry, man. I get headaches. I can't go to sleep at night." Omar was more candid, sexually explicit, and misogynistic in expressing his disgust: "The BNP, sons of bitches all of 'em. Fuck their mums."

The group became even more agitated when one of them mentioned a child whose picture had appeared on a recent BNP election leaflet, explaining how "his dad" was not a "racist", just an ordinary man who wanted "all these Muslim terrorists out". Infuriated by this, some of the boys claimed to have seen another white boy hung up on the notorious flagpole in an act of retribution for some unknown offence. Details of the incident were sketchy and there was some confusion over the identity of the victim. Heavy hints were dropped about Ali and Imran's involvement in the incident, but Omar, having rejoiced in the unknown boy's brutal humiliation, quickly moved the discussion on from what he seemed to regard as dangerous ground to the safer territory of the origins of the Cobridge "riot":

Ali: If that kid, yeah, that same kid [. . .] come into [the] park. . . . he got hanged on there, right. [Others laugh]

Omar: [Laughing] He did. You see . . . No, that was another kid. Oi, got that. Oi, fuck that. No . . . that's not ready for that. Well, check this, yeah. You know the BNP . . . well that's why the Cobridge riots happened . . .

Later in the discussion, and in marked contrast to the glee with which he recalled this white boy's apparently brutal humiliation, Omar was keen to emphasize the essentially peaceful nature of their faith, even while Ali was reminding the group about the ultimate triumph of Islam:

Omar: They [are] trying to [say] terror, but our religion is all about peace. We want peace. When we greet each other, we say, "Peace be upon you". You get me . . .?

Ali: They know, yeah, they're a threat, yeah, because we've been promised, yeah, that Muslims are going to take over. And no doubt about it.

Mohammed: Yeah, I know. It's true, bro.

Fear and nostalgia: elderly white people's responses to ethnic diversity

As we shall see in a moment, the nine elderly members of an (exclusively white) working men's club we spoke to were no less preoccupied with the flag in a local park than the young Asian men using the youth centre two or three miles away. Aged between sixty-eight and eighty-two, and having lived in Stoke for most, if not all, of their lives, these elderly people felt a deep connection to "the Potteries", despite the steep decline in the area's fortunes. They had fond memories of what the local area had once been like: "heaven", a "lovely village" with busy canals and "pot banks", helpful neighbours, immaculately swept streets, and a lively social life. This nostalgia for the lost world of their youth contrasted sharply with their somewhat dystopian view of the present:

Rita: I wouldn't want to live anywhere else because I was born and bred here. But it isn't the, the place itself, it's the people that are coming into it. I mean we've had foreigners, we've had . . . I mean Bert's had 'em next door to him and I don't agree with it . . . They don't speak our language. They don't like [to] eat [what] we do. So I don't think they ought to be here . . .

Janet: D'you think it's all their fault though? I think that it's these absentee landlords . . . They don't care as long as the DHSS pays their rent . . .

Rita: . . . pays their wages, yeah . . . pays the rent . . .

Audrey: And . . . among these people, there's no such thing as overcrowding because they take 'em to the ceiling in every room. Nobody knows how many are living in these houses . . . nobody does . . . You don't know who's there, what's there . . . There's women going in . . .

Rita: Like the Pakistans . . . they're all Hussains, aren't they? [Annie: Khans . . .] They're all named Hussain, I mean, they are . . . They're getting away with murder . . .

Annie: Khan . . . Khan.

Valerie: They don't just put the rubbish out, they throw it out . . . throw it over the walls . . . The entries are disgusting . . .

Audrey: It's like living in Beirut.

Valerie: Walk along Taylor Street and you think you're walking in Africa.

For these elderly women, their affection for the neighbourhood in which they had grown up and knew so well was being sorely tested. On the surface, at least, responsibility for its deterioration could be laid, almost literally, at the doors of newcomers, people who were not from "round here", people from Pakistan, Iraq, and Kosovo, people who spoke different languages and had disconcertingly similar "foreign" names.

Not everyone in the group was so pessimistic, however, and Bert, the only man and the only participant who actually lived on Taylor Street, disagreed. With a lifetime of community activism behind him, Bert explained how, when he had to sit outside his house to catch his breath, there "isn't one of those coloured people, or foreigners as we call them, come out without waving their hand and speaking to me, asking, 'Are you all right?'" As for Audrey's worries about women going in and out of a house along the Street (the clear implication was that they were working as prostitutes), Bert had spoken to his next-door neighbours, explained to them that people were trying to "clean up" the area, and threatened to involve the police if the comings and goings continued. The men who lived at the address had apologized and there had been "no further trouble"—proof, Bert argued, that conflicts could usually be resolved when people were approached "in the right manner". Nor was this the limit of Bert's willingness to reach out to his new and unfamiliar neighbours. He told the group how he had helped several of his asylum-seeking neighbours to complete forms and had even lent money to one family who could not afford food for their baby. Echoing Janet's feelings about who was really to blame for the neighbourhood's decline, Bert maintained that he was not "against the immigrants", just the "English people that are running 'em". To many of the women in the group, however, Bert was kind-hearted but gullible. Having let Bert have his say, Mavis and Audrey suggested that he was oblivious to the "cute and manipulative" character of his neighbours. Outnumbered and shouted down, Bert ultimately relented, confessing that he, too, was worried about the apparently uncontrolled fertility of the African women who lived nearby, and that he, like other members of the group, favoured the reintroduction of "corporal punishment" as the only way to bring ill-disciplined youth into line.

Yet, when they returned to what made them feel "ashamed" to live in the neighbourhood they loved so much, the focus of the female group members' attention shifted from ethnic minorities and asylum seekers to a range of other, home-grown "ne'er do wells": people who refused to tax or insure their cars; "drug-ridden" people living on a new estate; rude and ill-disciplined children who had "wrecked" a park but couldn't be smacked; and drug "dealers", "vandals", "burglars", and other "riff-raff" from across the city who had come into the area, but whom the council were unwilling to move on. To this motley collection, the group feared, were soon to be added "all the gyppos"—including "murderers and thieves"—from "Russia" who had been turned away by countries like Australia, New Zealand, and France but to whom Britain was likely to fall prey as the European Union (EU) expanded to the east and opened its external borders. This conflation of "race" and nationality with criminality in the way the group talked about their concerns for the state of their community, and the changes it had undergone since the halcyon days of their youth, prompted one of us (BD, who was facilitating the discussion) to ask where the "riff-raff" who concerned them so much came from. Back came the reply: no, they were not asylum seekers or economic migrants from elsewhere in the EU, but "English" people from outside the area. In truth, then, it was English people with no "respect" for themselves or others who were the principal source of trouble for these elderly white people, even if, in the abstract, ethnic minorities, gypsies, and asylum seekers were a perennial source of worry, their presence a constant reminder of the changes a once "thriving" neighbourhood had undergone.

What made these elderly white people so "bitter", Audrey and Janet explained, was the fact that no one "listened" when they asked the council to clean up the streets and parks, or improve delivery of the public services on which they depended. Like so many Potteries people, most, if not all, members of this focus group had once been Labour Party loyalists. In the past, Rita told us, you could "Put out a donkey [and] it'll go Labour". That this loyalty had been betrayed was enough to convince her that "Enoch [Powell]" was "right"—the foreigners were indeed multiplying and becoming dominant in a country where they did not truly belong. Mavis felt that elderly white people did not want to be "multi-cultural" and could see no reason why being "English" was not the same thing as being "British". The local BNP candidate, for whom many of them had voted, did not, it seems, trouble them with such complexities. A former president of their club, and widely regarded as a "very good bloke", he had clearly identified with many of their concerns. The independent councillor reviled by the young Asian men for flying the Union Jack was also regarded by this group of elderly white people as one of the few "good ones" amongst a mass of anonymous and uncaring elected representatives. According to Rita, the councillor was "wonderful" because "she really worked for this constituency". Then, recollecting the controversy over the flag that had so exercised the young Asian men, Audrey went on:

Audrey: She took a stand over a flagpole, in Cobridge Park ... and she sat all night under this flagpole, right, with her daughter ...

Mavis: It's known as "Paki Park" now ...

Audrey: ... a Pakistani child [came] in with a ... a Jack Russell ... and this little lad sat by [the councillor], with the Jack Russell ... It was nuzzling on to her ... Next thing into the park comes a Paki with a Rottweiler ... The Rottweiler gets the scent of [the councillor] off this dog . .. and that Rottweiler went for that woman and them bloody Pakistanis allowed it to happen ... Am I right, Rita?

Rita: Yeah. Yes. And they pulled the flag down ...

Audrey: ... and they set fire to it. Why should we put up ...? We don't touch anything of theirs. Why should they rip our flag down? We don't damage their mosques but they, they put things on our church doors ...

Rita: They've taken over ...

Audrey: It's all wrong ... they're taking over, and we're not allowing it. If this BNP will stop it, fine ... they'll have my vote.

Mavis: I think that's it ... I think people are tired now ... and they'll, they'll give the BNP a chance ...

Mavis then went on to reveal just why she, in particular, felt "tired" enough to "give the BNP a chance". Her grandson had been bullied at the same school from which Mohammed, one of our group of young Pakistani men, had been excluded for, as Ali put it, "fighting racist guys". When Mavis's son went to collect her grandson from school, they had been "surrounded by about ten Paki lads". Mavis's son had called his two elder sons for backup, and a fight had ensued, culminating in "one of the Pakis" sustaining a cut to his head. After "twelve months of hell" in the courts, Mavis's family were still "sticking together", resolutely denying their guilt, while "the Pakis" continued to "aggravate" her grandson despite having finished their studies and left school. Rita, a sympathetic listener throughout Mavis's account of her family's travails, found it easy to diagnose the problem: "do-gooders" had enabled the "Pakistanis" to "take over".

Professionals' perspectives: liberal "do-gooders", or a beleaguered minority?

But who were these meddling "do-gooders"? The nine public and third sector professionals we interviewed were well aware of the extent to which local people perceived them as meddlesome and misguided. Dismissed as "politically correct" by some and ostracized for advocating a "soft touch" approach to asylum seekers by others, Tessa no longer admitted to strangers that she worked for a local advice agency because of the hostility she had incurred as a consequence. If anything, things were even worse, and more directly threatening, for workers who came from minority ethnic backgrounds. In Gordon's view, the government had actively encouraged a sense of "hysteria" to develop over the issue of "asylum", but the dangers of doing so were clear, as his rhetorical question addressed to a female participant who shared his African Caribbean heritage suggested: "When they've finished with the asylum seekers, as they say, or the Muslims, who's next? Me and you?" (The allusion here was to the regrets expressed by the German theologian Martin Niemöller about the failure of the Protestant churches to oppose Hitler's attacks on Jews, Catholics, and trade unionists, leaving no one to defend him and his co-religionists when the Nazis eventually turned their attention to them.)

As a "race equality" worker, Gordon remarked on how often he came into contact with minority ethnic people who had either Anglicized their names in an effort to fit in, or resigned themselves to the kind of poorly paid and insecure work their parents or grandparents, as first-generation immigrants, had also been forced to accept. Because of the "very covert discrimination" that continued to exist in so many "employment fields", Gordon argued that few workers from black and minority communities had reached positions of sufficient authority in public sector organizations to be able to "make a difference" or inspire younger minority people. Gordon himself had experienced discrimination and described how, despite living in Stoke-on-Trent for forty years, many people—including some of the public sector professionals with whom he worked—still did not regard him as one of them.

Moreover, and irrespective of their ethnic origin, it could be difficult for those charged with promoting community cohesion who worked and, in some cases, lived in Stoke-on-Trent to feel that they "belonged" in the city. Anita, a manager at a local housing association and a former pottery worker, conceded that she sometimes felt "embarrassed" to call herself a "Stokie"—feelings echoed by her co-worker, Grant. Wendy, who worked for the Youth Service, had chosen to live in Stoke for "precisely the reason that people who tend to be well paid move out of the city", while Tessa, who lived outside the city, explained the difficulty of identifying with its residents:

> "They think that they're being terribly oppressed because they're not allowed to call people 'Pakis' any longer. I mean, it just, just needs people in this world to get a little bit more real about what actually damages people's lives."

Changing attitudes in Stoke had felt "like . . . pushing a rock up a mountain" to Tessa, but she was by no means unsympathetic to the plight of a population that had not only lost its industrial base but had also been taken for granted by a civic leadership that had manifestly failed to prepare both them and their city for a post-industrial future. Anita agreed, arguing that many local white people simply felt "so low" that they were unable to perceive the positive changes that regeneration projects were bringing about: "They're so negative about it, because they just don't think it's ever going to happen." Her colleague, Grant, thought that people tended to blame local service providers for their misfortunes because they had no "pride" in themselves or the city any more. Anita, however, stressed that that such negative assessments were not personal:

"They're just judging by the uniform, nothing else." Wendy went further, attributing the electoral success of the BNP in Stoke-on-Trent to people's need to "blame" someone for the city's deterioration. Unfortunately, this success risked making the jobs of those employed to promote community cohesion all the more difficult, as the following exchange about what might happen if the BNP eventually gained real political influence illustrates.

Wendy: What do we do if, on the committees that we work . . . you end up with someone in from the BNP in the chair, or them coming in and saying, you've got to do this? . . . We did talk about resigning.

Tessa: You and I have actually had that conversation . . . Because I think we were talking about if somebody got . . . if one of the elected members got put on our management committee . . .

Wendy: Yeah. What we'd have to do is rely on the political process to challenge . . . if they were asking us to do something racist . . . that we wouldn't do it. We'd go through the tribunal and hope that the system's strong enough . . . It's a hope in Stoke, isn't it ? It's a bit of a hope . . .

Yet, despite receiving hate mail because of her work with asylum seekers, Tessa remained guardedly optimistic:

"I had to go and talk to the pensioners' convention in Stoke about refugees and asylum seekers. And I have to confess my heart sank to my boots . . . I mean I just was really frightened. And, do you know, they were fantastic. You couldn't have asked for a more generous and tolerant [audience] . . . I didn't expect that."

Honesty, defensiveness, and spiralling projections

However ambiguous the empirical support for the existence of the "ethnic segregation" referred to in *Strength in Diversity* may be, there is at least one sense in which the notion of "parallel lives" resonates with the material presented above. This is not the objective sense in which it is used by policymakers in order to criticize the myopia of people assumed to have chosen to live apart from those whose colour and customs are different from their own. Rather, it is the much subtler, subjective sense in which people who share a common cultural interest in matters of justice, public health, and a better quality of life tend to attribute the lack of these things to out-groups who they believe do not share their values. Hence, although they did not realize it, the young Asian men we interviewed shared the concerns of their elderly white neighbours about the state of their local parks and public spaces and the problems of crime, prostitution, and drug use they believed to be rife there. The public and third sector professionals shared the elderly white residents' view that the local Labour Party and its elected leaders had deserted their most loyal supporters. And the idea that some white people's insistence on giving vent to their prejudices—including the tendency to defend their right to use the term "Paki" irrespective of the offence it caused—was troubling for the professionals and the young Asian men alike. These two groups also felt themselves to be unfairly judged by working-class white people. In this respect, then, the idea of "parallel lives" does capture something of the source of conflict in deindustrializing English cities: the *lack of a common awareness of the shared nature of the problems* faced by young and old, working-class service users and middle-class providers, the white majority and members of minority ethnic groups. Instead of setting out to overcome residential segregation, the community cohesion agenda should, perhaps, have been aimed at emphasizing these shared perceptions and common experiences.

Unfortunately, what our focus group discussions illustrate is why debates about communities, crime, race, and difference within a given social group so rarely lead to any sense of shared understanding between that group and others. As Sherwood's (1980) often overlooked analysis of the psychodynamics of racism so ably demonstrated, talk about these subjects is often defensive talk. Through the case study analysis of race talk within a white British, an Indian, and a West Indian family, Sherwood showed how and why people use members of other racial groups as repositories for mental conflicts they consider too disturbing or painful to face.

The groups chosen as repositories are felt to be "safe" in the sense they are unconsciously regarded as fitting receptacles to "hold" the anxiety and contain it. Since racial groups outwardly differ in appearance, the choice of a racial group as repository for unwanted and denied aspects of the self is particularly seductive, because it gives the added advantage of putting wider visible social distance between the person acting to offload denied aspects of his identity and the racial group chosen as a receptacle. [Sherwood, 1980, p. 493]

As the extracts from the group discussions reproduced earlier in this chapter illustrate, the problem was not so much that our respondents were afraid to speak their minds through fear of appearing racist, but that, invited to say what they thought about situations that make them unbearably anxious, many people resort to demonizing discourses which attribute to others the negative qualities they think others are attributing to them. In so doing, they symbolically distance themselves both from the things they feel anxious, embarrassed, or ashamed about—the decline, decay, and illicit behaviour on their doorsteps—and their own inability to do anything about them. Meanwhile, the legitimizing rhetoric of friends, family, and those in positions of political authority enables wider claims to be made about the attacked out-group. In turn, criticisms of specific individuals are generalized as attributes of those imagined to inhabit a radically different value system, who do not live in the "real world", or do their share, who have self-segregated and are, hence, bad and irresponsible citizens. As these projective processes inflict their "humiliating indignities" on others, they arouse "latent vulnerabilities" in the targets of these attacks (ibid., p. 564), prompting them to respond in kind.

This in turn, modifies and affects their unresolved identity conflicts and so leads them in turn to use defence mechanisms also and thus to resort to the misuse of racial groups. This impinges back upon the primary group and begins to promote a further twist to the spiral. [Sherwood, 1980, pp. 496–497; original emphasis]

Ultimately, this counter-defensiveness enables stereotypes to harden as the qualities of the out-group become the focus of even greater "distortion" and of "intensely pejorative imagery", culminating in a spiralling of projective attacks and counter-attacks (ibid., p. 499).

It is these parallels between the spiralling psychodynamic processes that inform white and minority ethnic people's talk about race, crime, and community that need to be better understood by those interested in promoting community cohesion. Consider again why the elderly white people we interviewed spoke so fondly of the "lovely village" they used to inhabit. It is possible to see their nostalgia for a bygone era as being not only about the decline of the pottery industry, but also about the loss of the esteem in which they had once been held. Once active and productive citizens, men and women who had held their families, communities, and industries together, they felt increasingly devalued as economically redundant, politically irrelevant, and a burden to a local authority struggling to deliver adequate services to an expanding range of users. As a result, they were envious of the attention they believed was paid to ethnic minorities and mourned the loss of the reassuring cultural homogeneity institutionalized in the pubs, clubs, and shops they had patronized in their youth. From the perspective of these elderly people, outspoken pride in a particular "Potteries" or "British" way of life provided an important counterweight to the stigma associated with advancing age and growing dependency, a way of imagining that some semblance of the esteem in which they had once been held had survived the destruction of "their" industries and communities.

Something similar can also be said about the stories told by the young Asian men we interviewed. Some of them had taken down the flag flying in a local park because they believed Muslims were being demonized in the name of British patriotism. They claimed a boy had been hanged from the same flagpole to show people that they—as British Muslims—meant business and would not take their demonization lying down. And maybe this is exactly what they did, justifying their violence as a response to the global, national, and local politics of Bush, Blair, and the BNP. But perhaps they also dramatized the story, conflating fantasies about what they had wanted to do with what actually happened, their bravado concealing a painful awareness of their inability to resist the local, national, and international political processes generating the racism and Islamophobia to which they all felt they were subjected. Mohammed's attempts to resist racism at school had resulted in his expulsion. The police had thwarted their challenge to the footballers who had racially abused them. Their protests against the far right had not deterred a sizeable minority of the local electorate from voting for the BNP. Mohammed's reference to "war"—"Like going in a war. It *was war*"—certainly gave a sense of the boys' willingness to meet violence with violence. But his metaphor also hinted at the feelings of persecution they were beginning to experience, a sense of persecution that explained the appeal of Ali's fantasy that one man alone—Osama bin Laden—could defeat their international oppressors, even if the racists, whoever "they" were, continued daily to humiliate so many ordinary Muslims in Britain.

Preventing racist spirals

Sherwood (1980, p. 498) concluded that racist spiralling tends to persist whenever fantasy subsumes reality: when "[a]spects of individuals become inextricably tied up with the racial group and people are unable to test ideas against reality . . . defensive energy keeps the process going". Conversely, some groups manage to avoid getting caught up in racist spiralling. This may be because they do not feel exposed to the kind of threats that give rise to persecutory anxieties, or because they redirect their hostility towards non-racialized groups who are somehow disconnected to the spiralling process. A third possibility is that they are able to contain their feelings of persecution because of their emotional capacities to: ". . . weather dissensions, rows and tensions without the solid undertow of good loving feelings being endangered. They are able to tolerate ambivalence which in turn allows them to tolerate this in others" (*ibid.*, p. 543).

This combination of factors was certainly part of the reason why the professionals we interviewed were not as locked into the kind of spiralling projection evident in the other two groups' discussions. Castigated for their "political correctness" and resented by the communities they were meant to be helping, these public sector professionals had reason to feel harshly criticized. But because they were not as vulnerable to the financial insecurities and the sense of environmental decline experienced by the other groups, they tended not to interpret these criticisms as an attack on their culture, identities, or characteristics. Thus, they were able to use the group discussion to try to understand what motivated those who were hostile towards them, often detoxifying their attacks by rendering them comprehensible, rather than feeling diminished or threatened by them. Even though they were critical of the parochialism of the working class, the maliciousness of the far right, the self-interestedness of senior politicians, and the limited aspirations of minority ethnic groups, the professionals did not succumb to the temptation—characteristic of paranoid–schizoid modes of thinking—of reducing their critics to these faults. Instead, they often appeared to identify with their detractors. So, when Anita explained the group's typecasting as liberal "do-gooders" as a case of being judged only "by their uniforms" and "nothing else", she effectively detoxified the stigmatization that might otherwise have consumed her. She was also able to see similarities between the "lowness" felt by local people and the frustration she and her colleagues experienced. When Gordon talked about his dismay at the compromises some minority ethnic people made to "fit in", he also seemed to be identifying with their discomfort and drawing on his own experiences of discrimination and exclusion. Tessa, too, had been moved when her expectations of the pensioners she had been asked to speak to were confounded by the "fantastic" reception she had received. Perhaps it was for this reason that she, like Wendy, was willing to put her faith in the capacity of the tribunal system to protect them from having to work towards a racially divisive agenda at the behest of a BNP-controlled local authority.

This is not to say that the young Asian men and elderly white people we interviewed were entirely lacking in this capacity to detoxify threats and identify across difference. On the contrary, and in spite of their awareness of the racism older white adults had instilled in some of their classmates at school, Imran and Omar described their elderly white neighbours as part of their "community" and their "families". And, at the end of our discussion with them, all of the boys in the group were eager to know more about what the young white people we had interviewed thought about them. Yet, as the exchanges reproduced above reveal, when the multiple threats posed by Islamophobia, discrimination, and racial harassment were coupled with abuses of police power and far right activism, the anxiety this evoked seemed too great for them to manage—the revelations about the treatment meted out to Tariq's father, a "practising" Muslim, by the police convincing them that the system was loaded against even the most law-abiding members of their community. Invested in both the "peaceful" tenets of his Islamic faith and a street-orientated masculinity in which the physical defence of one's community was valorized, the provocative electioneering of the BNP caused Imran "headaches" and insomnia. Omar, by contrast, was disgusted by the BNP projecting on to them the very sexual and moral degeneracy he and the other boys claimed had "infected" their neighbourhood and local white women. Ultimately, both Omar and Imran "got angry" and indulged Ali—the group's "hard man"—in fantasizing about exacting retribution from a younger white child and eulogizing the essentialized purity of Osama bin Laden.

Much the same could be said of Bert in the elderly white people's group. Picking up on Janet's reluctance to blame asylum seekers for the deterioration in the state of their neighbourhood, Bert revealed a remarkable ability to identify with those struggling in the face of adversity. As mothers and grandmothers, the women round the table could have identified with Bert's selflessness in helping his neighbours fill in forms and lending money to the parents of a hungry child. That a number of them began to confront the fact that it was not so much asylum seekers and foreigners who troubled them, but anti-social white people, suggests that Bert's compassion struck a chord with at least some of these women. But because they had very specific and personal reasons to be aggrieved, Mavis and Rita were either unwilling or unable to imagine any similarities between their own hardships and those endured by "foreigners". Turning their hostility towards Bert, they forced him to resort, somewhat defensively, to more popularly racist assertions. Meanwhile Mavis's contempt for "Pakis" seemed to be very closely connected to her anxieties about the trouble in which the men in her family had found themselves after the fight at her grandson's school. Racist stereotyping was not strictly essential to her vociferous defence of her family's reputation, but, in constructing her son's aggressors as "Pakis", Mavis sought to protect him from any suggestion that he had either instigated the violence or was no better than the people with whom he and his sons had fought. The group tacitly supported her analysis of the incident and its aftermath, but some of its members—such as Bert and Janet—may well have come to rather different conclusions had earlier anxieties been contained rather than exacerbated in the course of the discussion.

Concluding remarks: from community cohesion to the promotion of identification

Where does this leave the community cohesion agenda? As we argued in the first part of this chapter, the parameters within which the community cohesion debate has been conducted up to now have tended to add to the very tensions it was meant to ease. The government's many invitations to talk about community cohesion tacitly assume that discussion inevitably gives rise to shared understanding, that "honest" talk and "meaningful interchanges" are ultimately the same thing, and that, by promoting dialogue, people's lives will begin to "touch" those of other ethnic or cultural groups. However, our data suggests that people who feel themselves to be unfairly judged, derided, or ostracized will have psychological difficulty in perceiving *strength in diversity*, be resistant to being *touched* emotionally by the plight of others, and find it much easier to manage their feelings of persecution by establishing greater social distance between themselves and those whom they deem to be culturally different and morally inferior. This is why many ostensibly law-abiding white people, like our elderly respondents, remain so unshakeably invested in the idea that "Pakis" are "foreigners" and see them as a formless, undifferentiated menace, people who ought to be policed more heavily, or simply sent back to where they came from along with other, more recently arrived asylum-seeking populations. It is probably also why many young Asian men are seduced by the rhetoric of militant Islam, even while they may suspect that the promise of revolution is entirely empty, at least as far as their own lives in Britain's deindustrializing towns are concerned.

Because of this, the many similarities between elderly white working class people and Asian young people—from their common experiences of bureaucratic indifference, to their vulnerability to neglect and victimization and their frustrated hopes for better lives for themselves and their loved ones—slip all too easily from view.

It is disappointing, therefore, that, for all its efforts to tackle the economic deprivations suffered by Britain's most marginalized communities, "New" Labour did so little to draw attention to the experiences and aspirations which the white working class share with minority ethnic youth and new migrant groups. As the broadsheet columnist Polly Toynbee (2006) observed:

> It has been an odd failing that Labour has redistributed more to the poor than any government since the war, but has done it in radar silence, never seeking to persuade, never using it as a flagship boast in elections . . . [I]t takes loud persuasion and repetition of political messages to attract attention.

In the same article, Toynbee goes on to explain how a recent Mori survey discovered that, given a chance to question and debate the issue, those who were "sceptical" about the "existence of real poverty" became willing to "pay more to improve children's lives".

> What shocked them were real examples: the many children who never have a birthday party or go on holiday, cannot afford to go swimming or take a school trip. What struck home was the bleakness of those children's lives compared with the childhoods in their own families. It was heart-warming to watch. [*ibid.*]

In this example, it is possible to see the political promise of a politics of persuasion that places identification with real, as opposed to mythologized, people at its core. Back in 1997, "New" Labour, with its "Third Way" politics dependent on "flexible concepts that can be understood in different ways by different constituencies" seemed capable of delivering on this promise (Levitas, 2004, p. 1). By getting tough on hate crime, "anti-social youth", immigration, extremists, and "self-segregating" minorities, "New" Labour garnered enough support among the "law-abiding" majority to secure three terms in office. But it has never been able to get equally tough on ordinary racists or the causes of racism, because to do so would have undermined the supposedly unifying rhetoric of national identity—Cool Britannia—that made its political reinvention possible (Gilroy, 2004). A decade later, those deemed insufficiently "cool" and/or unconvincingly British became only too aware of the ease with which they could be identified as the source of their own misfortunes, a process which helps to explain much of the anger, outrage, and persecutory thinking we encountered in our focus group interviews in Stoke-on-Trent. If we are to get out of the current impasse, it will be necessary for those charged with doing something about community cohesion to take some risks, to redress the "structural inequalities and legacy of discrimination" once so central to the government's "community and race equality strategy", while at the same time having the courage to see, study, and identify with distress where others see nothing but trouble.

Politicians need, somehow, to capitalize on the capacities—however limited—of people like Bert and Janet, Tariq and Imran to identify with, and care about, those in demonized and demoralized groups, despite the injustices these people have endured. If community cohesion is really to be fostered, the thrust of political intervention must move beyond the obfuscating rhetoric of the "Third Way" and find new methods of empowering people whose response to difference, and the existence of "communities" different from their own, is not limited either to the actualization of racist stereotypes or the kind of self-centred disregard the community cohesion agenda has tended to take as the "norm". It is, in our view, simply not good enough to invite people to speak honestly and openly about their fears and then leave those fears to escalate, uncontained and untempered, into persecutory anxieties. Rather, we must try to assist fearful individuals to come to terms with what fuels their worries and enable them to connect with those who can help them to recognize, however gradually, when such fears are unfounded, fantastical, and/or self-perpetuating. Convincing those who are already trying to do this in their everyday lives—whether as professionals or ordinary members of the public—that the state cares about them too will, in the longer term, be a much more effective way of preventing the reoccurrence of public disorder than scapegoating insularity, attacking political correctness, inventing an illusory sense of nationhood, or ramping up the rhetorics of community cohesion and immigration control.

CHAPTER SEVEN

Zahid Mubarek's murderer: the case of Robert Stewart

"Simple questions unanswered"

"The question was a simple one. Yet it took the Mubarek family six years, an internal prison investigation, a CRE investigation, hearings in the High Court, Court of Appeal, House of Lords and a Public Inquiry to answer it. It was the Public Inquiry, in the end which came closest to answering why it was that a known violent racist was placed in the same cell as Zahid Mubarek on the 21st March 2000 . . . The final report lists more than 180 failings that led to Zahid's tragic death, names and shames certain individuals and makes 88 recommendations for the future . . . It is not fanciful to suggest that the murder of Zahid Mubarek was a wake up call for the prison service in the same way that the murder of Stephen Lawrence was a wake up call for the police force. It is now up to all of us to ensure that both these cases leave the lasting legacy that both families deserve and can be proud of"

(Khan, 2006, p. 5)

"In the weeks and months leading up to March 20, Stewart had been bragging, boasting and daydreaming of this:

nailbombing the Asian communities of Southall and Bradford; doing the same to Brixton and Brick Lane; killing
'Gooks'; bashing 'Pakis'; and bringing death and destruction
to anyone who wasn't like him. Zahid wasn't like him . . .
Like the wind through the trees, Stewart moved invisibly
through the Public Inquiry, and shook everything in it. I . . .
recall reading the very earliest medical and psychiatric
reports of this boy from a troubled home . . . Robert Stewart
was not treated very well. But it would be insulting to
Zahid's parents to suggest that Stewart was a victim like
Zahid so unfortunately became. I don't mourn Robert
Stewart's squandered life as I mourn Zahid's. But I do worry
about it. I worry about the dozens, possibly hundreds, of
Robert Stewarts we're creating all around this country. How
will we recognise them? What does it take to see their hate
and deal with it differently?"

(Dias, 2006, p. 7)

I f the Inquiry into the murder of Zahid Mubarek was as loud a
wake-up call for the prison service as the Macpherson Inquiry
had been for the police, the failure of social scientists in general
and of British criminologists in particular to engage in any depth
with the former must surely tell us something about the poverty of
our disciplines. Leaving aside some largely anecdotal references to
the Inquiry in writing about imprisonment (Bhui, 2008b; Edgar,
2007), criminologists have said almost nothing about the murder of
Zahid Mubarek, either to the media or in their own learned jour-
nals. There may, of course, be many reasons for this, not least criminology's peculiar fascination with police rather than prison culture
and the unprecedented, if belated, media interest in the murder of
Stephen Lawrence. Other possible factors include the lack of
mystery about the Mubarek case—apart from unproven allegations
that prison staff had forced young offenders to take part in "'glad-
iator-style" fights, there was no evidence of corruption. Unlike the
Metropolitan Police in the aftermath of Stephen Lawrence's murder, the Prison Service accepted the blame for Zahid Mubarek's
death. Martin Narey, the then Director General of the Prison
Service, publicly apologized in writing to the Mubarek family, and
no one contested the Inquiry's conclusion that the murder had been

entirely "preventable". Finally, there is the simple fact that Zahid Mubarek's killer was instantly identifiable and was rapidly brought to justice. On the other hand, there are those, like Gilroy (2003), who argue that, since the 1980s, criminology has lost its critical purchase when it comes to racism and that even the best of its scholars lag behind "worthy liberals like Macpherson" (*ibid.*, p. xxviii) in the quality of their analysis. In short, Gilroy believes that too many criminologists do not take racism seriously enough.

However this scholarly indifference to the killing of Zahid Mubarek is explained, it was, in many ways, an even greater tragedy than the murder of Stephen Lawrence. As Suresh Grover, a leading campaigner on behalf of both the Lawrence and Mubarek families has argued:

> In the Lawrence case, the institutional racism in the Metropolitan Police led to a collective failure to prosecute the racist murderers *after* the murder. In the Mubarek case, it was the failures within the prison system *while Zahid was alive* which led to his murder. [Grover, 2006, p. 9, original emphases]

Placed in this context, the criminological silence about Zahid Mubarek's murder has been both depressing and inexcusable.

The report of the Zahid Mubarek Inquiry

Mr Justice Keith's report painstakingly documented the catalogue of failures in the prison service that contributed to Zahid Mubarek's murder, linking a string of "systemic shortcomings" in all of the prison establishments where Robert Stewart had been incarcerated with the "culture of indifference and insensitivity which institutional racism breeds" (Keith, 2006b, p. 4). These shortcomings are too numerous to document here, but included: the many failures to collate and consider evidence of mental disturbance and acute dangerousness in records kept about Robert Stewart's time in prison; a lack of resources and under-investment in a dangerously overburdened prison service; the virulent racism of some prison officers and many prisoners; the absence of viable procedures for prisoners experiencing racial harassment to get their complaints

properly investigated; the lack of a properly administered race relations strategy; overcrowding, enforced cell sharing, and poor
management by prison governors at Feltham. The eighty-eight
steps Keith advocated to rectify these shortcomings included: the
end of enforced cell sharing and the implementation of risk assessment in decisions about cell allocation; much more comprehensive
systems of information sharing and management; the implementation of a "violence reduction strategy" that makes prisoners "think
they have let other prisoners down if they resort to violence" (*ibid.*,
p. 37); mental health screening and routine reviews of prisoners'
emotional well-being; diversity training and the adoption by the
prison service of the Macpherson definition of a racist incident
(*ibid.*, p. 48).

The Inquiry Report was, in many ways, an authoritative blue-
print for change, but, with the steps designed to deal with issues of
discrimination not beginning until recommendation 79, one could
be forgiven for wondering what was meant when Keith claimed
that "racism" remained at "the heart of the Inquiry" (*ibid.*, p. 3).
Equally perplexing is the fact that the conclusions to neither the
concise nor the full version of Keith's report mentioned racism at
all, whether institutional or otherwise. Instead, both documents
asserted that the "focus of the Inquiry" was on "violence in prisons,
specifically attacks by prisoners in their cells" (Keith 2006a, p. 32,
2006b, p. 552). Stylistically, this made the eighty-eight risk-reduc-
tion "steps" that followed seem more self-explanatory (2006b, p. 2),
no doubt enhancing the urgency of the report's prescriptions to
policymaking audiences. More cynically, it may also have appeased
those in the prison service keen to "minimise the cause of institutional racism in Zahid's murder" without being seen to abandon
the issue altogether (Grover, 2006, p. 10). The truth is, however, that,
as Dias (2006), the Mubarek family's barrister, points out in the
second of the quotations with which we began this chapter, Robert
Stewart's racism haunted the Inquiry in ways that were not always
confronted, his hatred an ill-understood and invisible presence that
chilled everything it touched. How Stewart and Mubarek came to
be sharing a cell was quite rightly the principal focus of the Inquiry.
But, as Dias reminds us, we still need to consider some more fundamental questions about how it is that, despite all the reforms generated by the Inquiry into the murder of Stephen Lawrence, this

country continues to produce men like Robert Stewart; and what it would take to "recognise" these people properly, and to "see their hate and deal with it differently" (*ibid.*, p. 7). This chapter attempts to address these questions by applying psychoanalytical insights to the many letters Stewart wrote in prison and the voluminous records and reports placed in the public domain about him during the course of the Mubarek Inquiry.

The murder of Zahid Mubarek

At 3.35 a.m. on 21 March 2000, Zahid Mubarek was in bed— although not necessarily asleep—when his cellmate, Robert Stewart, struck him at least seven times with a dagger he had fashioned earlier that week from the leg of a wooden table. Zahid was serving the last night of a prison sentence imposed for breaching the terms of a community sentence for theft. When Zahid's family were able to visit him in hospital, they saw not the child whose return they had eagerly awaited, but someone whose "abhorrent injuries made him simply unrecognisable—he didn't look human" (Amin, 2006, p. 4). As his uncle remembers, this "otherwise hand-some young man was reduced to a bruised, bloodied, swollen featureless face" (*ibid*). Zahid Mubarek died without regaining consciousness a week later on 4 April 2000. Zahid Mubarek's family's six and a half year struggle to find out why their son was sharing a cell with Robert Stewart began there, as did a concerted effort on the part of the Home Office to avoid answering the Muba-rek family's questions.

Although this was not his primary task, Mr Justice Keith did what he could to explore Stewart's motives for killing Zahid Mubarek (Keith, 2006b, p. 24). After considering 15,000 pages of documents relating to Robert Stewart and the institutions in which he had been held, Keith was unable to identify a "definitive reason" for the attack and contented himself with highlighting a number of possibilities:

> Stewart himself claimed that he did it to get out of Feltham, which was a place he loathed. That resonated with one of his letters in which he had talked of killing his cellmate if that was what was

172 LOSING THE RACE

needed to get him transferred. Maybe it was his ultimate attempt to get on equal terms with Travis [another prisoner with whom Stewart had become friendly], whom he had always looked up to. Maybe it was his virulent racism which made him see Zahid as a target, his prejudice being fuelled by his time at Feltham. Maybe he was re-enacting scenes from *Romper Stomper*. Maybe it was simply that because he had not got bail, he was not going to let a "Paki" like Zahid enjoy his freedom. It could have been a combination of all these factors. And it may be that he had no motive at all. His lack of concern for other people or for the consequences of his actions meant that he was *not constrained by the things which would restrain a normal person*. At his trial, he said that he just felt like attacking Zahid. Perhaps it was as *simple as that*. [*ibid.*, p. 641; our emphases]

For some commentators, it was indeed "as simple as that". Tabloid and broadsheet newspapers alike seemed satisfied with the notion that Stewart was a "violent racist psychopath", frequently citing as evidence a paragraph from what became known as the "extreme measures" letter written on 23 February 2000: "If I don't get bail on the 7th, I'll take extreme measures to get shipped out, kill me padmate if I have to, bleach me sheets and pillowcase white and make a Ku Klux Klan outfit".

Many media accounts of the murder suggested that Stewart, having written a letter in which he asked the recipient if he had seen "dat film, starring me", may have copied the behaviour of Hando, the neo-Nazi lead character in the film *Romper Stomper* (Kelso, 2000; Casciani, 2006a).

The evidence presented to the Inquiry, however, suggests that Stewart's motives were by no means "simple" and that no single explanation for his behaviour will suffice. First, the psychiatrists who interviewed Stewart before and after the murder did not consider the film to have had any causal effect. They could not agree on a diagnosis of psychopathy either, and were not unanimously persuaded that the assault on Mubarek had been racially motivated (see, for example, the report of Professor John Gunn, the Former Chairman of the Faculty of Forensic Psychiatry at the Royal College of Psychiatrists: Gunn, 2004). The balance of opinion favoured the idea that Stewart was not suffering from a diagnosable mental illness, but a "personality disorder", which, while "severe" in his case, did not necessarily differentiate him from the many other young men in British prisons who are similarly afflicted (Keith, 2006b, p. 8). As his solicitor was to observe, what made Stewart stand out as "strange" was how incredibly "difficult to connect with" he was. This lack of "emotion", an "eerie calmness", "almost detachment", had been picked up and commented on earlier in his life by the many mental health specialists with whom he had come into contact during a troubled adolescence (Singh, Jandu, & Passley, 2003, p. 33). Second, while Stewart did write about having to share a cell with a "Paki" whom he regarded—perhaps stereotypically, or perhaps because Mubarek was a convicted thief struggling to come off heroin—as "lazy" and light-fingered, there is no evidence to suggest that he particularly disliked Mubarek or said anything overtly racist to him before or during the lethal assault (*ibid*. pp. 37–39). From Stewart's perspective, he and Mubarek "got on reasonably well" (Nayani, 2000, p. 45). Stewart regarded Mubarek as "alright" and "safe" with him (*ibid*., p. 32; Singh, Jandu, & Passley, 2003, pp. 37–39). He felt he could "talk" to Mubarek (Joseph, 2000, p. 4), probably because, unlike many other prisoners at Feltham, Zahid did not ridicule him. Third, given Stewart's knowledge of the prison system, the notion that he killed Mubarek in order to get "shipped out" of Feltham seems rather implausible. There is good reason to believe that Stewart did want to be transferred back to Hindley (one of the many institutions he had been in before arriving at Feltham) and we know that his friend Maurice Travis had suggested killing his cellmate as a means to this end. But Stewart himself would have realized that, if he was convicted of either the offence for which he was on remand, or any other serious offence, he was unlikely to be returned to Hindley, a relatively small young offenders institution and remand centre which took neither lifers nor prisoners over the age of twenty-one.

Robert Stewart

Having denied that he was a racist during his trial, Stewart's written admission to the Inquiry five years later that "racial prejudice played some part" in his murderous behaviour was potentially revealing. If someone had asked him *what part* prejudice played, we might have learnt a little more about why he did what he did.

Certainly, Stewart's talk about "race" in his letters and in his conversations with Mubarek suggests that, since so many of Stewart's
racist utterances were, from his perspective, about other things;
"racial prejudice" was indeed only "part" of the explanation for
his violence. Moreover, Stewart's disclosures to the psychiatrist
Dr Phillip Joseph (2000, p. 4) suggested that he had experienced the
attack as cathartic in a way that he was not able fully to articulate,
at least in socially acceptable terms. In the end he may have
resorted to the "shipped out" explanation as a way of accounting
for something horrific that were impossible to rationalize: ". . . he
knew what he had done but not why . . . He went on to say the
attack was a bit like wetting the bed. He said, 'I know I am doing
it, but you just carry on until you wake up more'" (ibid., p. 6).

Experienced as an almost involuntary, even warming, release,
bed-wetting usually becomes a source of shame for children as they
find themselves accountable to others with greater self-control (Gau
& Soong, 1999; Morrison, Tappin, & Staines, 2000). A bed-wetter
until he was at least eight years old, Stewart was in good position
to deploy this metaphor in explaining his feelings about the attack
on Zahid Mubarek (Nayani, 2000, p. 7).

Stewart's psychiatric reports hint at a deeply unhappy childhood. His mother had never been able "to be physically affection-
ate towards him", even when he was a "baby she had found it difficult to hug him" (Haddad, 1990). When, at the age of nine, Robert
started stealing, it was discovered that his mother bought him
things instead of showing her affection psychically, and she was
"counselled about the need to make him feel wanted and secure"
(Keith, 2006a, p. 77). With the possible exception of his brother. Ian,
who also spent most of his adolescence in care homes and custody,
there appears to have been no one else willing and able to make the
young Robert feel loved. Stewart was bullied by his ageing father;
a man who beat his sons "badly" and had hit his wife (Kelso, 2000;
Orr, 2000; Singh, Jandu, & Passley, 2003, p. 35;). In infant school,
Stewart was both "top" of his class and the most disruptive pupil
his teachers had to deal with (Judd, 2005). So insecure was he at
school that he scrubbed his own face out of a photograph because
he thought he was "ugly" and attempted to destroy the work of
pupils he thought were cleverer than him (Judd, 2005). The psychiatrist Tony Nayani (2000), who gave expert opinion at the trial,

described Robert Stewart's home life as poverty-stricken and emotionally impoverished. Nayani cited from the report of a psychiatrist who assessed Stewart when he was nine. This psychiatrist discovered a boy who regularly told lies, had no friends, and would scratch himself until he bled (Nayani, 2000, p. 7). As an infant, Stewart broke into his school and flooded it (*ibid.*). Aged ten, he also set fire to the school's noticeboard and a girl's hair. Aged thirteen, on a night when he had run away from home, Stewart set fire to a shop in Middleton near where he used to live (Deo, 2004, p. 2). All things considered, it is hard to believe that his mother was being entirely honest with herself when she claimed that Stewart had been a "happy child" (*ibid.*). Indeed, when social services suggested placing the then fourteen-year-old Robert in care, his mother indicated that she was desperate to "wash her hands" of him (Nayani, 2000, p. 10), as she already had of his brother. And this is precisely what she proceeded to do. When Stewart was hospitalized because of injuries to his face, neither of his parents went to visit him (*ibid.*, p. 14). They did not go to see him when he was in custody either, but never provided any explanation for their unwillingness to do so (*ibid.*, p. 15). Nor did they talk to him about why they had separated (Joseph, 2000, p. 3). Although Robert sometimes claimed not to be "bothered" by them, these parental failures were a perennial source of worry to him (*ibid.*, p. 2).

While he was in custody, Stewart often took out his frustrations on his own body. Much as his teachers had done when, aged thirteen, Stewart had slit his wrists during a science class (Nayani, 2000, p. 9), staff and health workers at Feltham were later to dismiss Stewart's self-harming behaviours—including occasions when he swallowed razor blades and set his cell on fire—as manipulative acts designed to win attention or intimidate others. He signed many of his letters "*Mad* Hatters" (our emphasis) and was known to "talk" to his cell walls (Stewart, 2000, pp. 377, 396, 405). Interestingly, given what has been said about his virulent racism, Stewart had the words "Bob Marley" (Taylor, 2000, p. 6) tattooed on his forearm as well as the letters "R.I.P" on his forehead. Other prisoners interpreted this latter tattoo as a death threat, and some tormented him about it. But it could equally plausibly have signalled Stewart's own psychological need for *peace of mind*, or conveyed a sense in which he continued to feel disturbed by the *loss* of someone or something important to him. He knew he was "crack-ing up" in Feltham (*ibid.*). Three years after Zahid Mubarek's murder, Stewart was to tell a team from the Commission for Racial Equality that someone should have known he was a "time-bomb ready to explode" (Singh, Jandu, & Passley, 2003, p. 12).

As a teenager, Stewart became particularly sensitive about being bullied. After his expulsion from school, Stewart's family had to move because they were being victimized by a gang of youths (Nayani, 2000, p. 16). Soon after this, in Werrington Young Offen-ders Institution (YOI) in Stoke-on-Trent, Stewart threw bleach at a prison officer whom he considered to have "taken" him "for an idiot" (*ibid.*, p. 12). After his release, Stewart joined a gang who, armed and masked, committed a series of robberies. Later, serving time in Stoke Heath YOI, Stewart conspired with Maurice Travis, an old friend from his days in care, to slit the throat of a fellow inmate by the name of Alan Averall whom the pair considered to be "bully-ing", or otherwise "takin [*sic*] the piss" out of them (Various, 2004, p. 1040). In HMP Altcourse, Stewart (by then aged eighteen or nine-teen) stabbed two other prisoners in the face, one of whom he believed had "robbed" all his "stuff" (Nayani, 2000, p. 21). Stewart said he had originally made the weapon he used to kill Mubarek in order to protect himself from the "gangstas" who were bullying him (Stewart, 2000, p. 323). The fear of being bullied often distur-bed his sleep, and had done so again on the night of the murder (Nayani, 2000, p. 38). He wished the black prisoners who tormented him "would shut up" (Stewart, 2000, p. 446).

Gaining sadistic pleasure from anticipating the suffering of others seems to have been another way in which Stewart coped with his inner torment. Asked why he had set fire to a girl's hair during his schooldays, Stewart said he did it "for fun" (Shapiro, 2004, p. 2). In his early teens, "Paki-bashing" became "just some-thing" he and his friends "did" to pass the time, a form of leisure activity akin to kicking a football around (Judd, 2005). Much of the more fantastical racism expressed in Stewart's letters was accom-panied by "Ha" or "Ha, ha" in parentheses, and text annotated in this way included passages in which he mused about the injuries he had inflicted on Zahid Mubarek and others, where he identified with Hitler and Hando, the anti-hero of *Romper Stomper* (Stewart, 2000, p. 435). There was also a peculiarly sexualized quality to much of Stewart's humour, especially his racist joking. While he was in Feltham, Stewart harassed a female prison psychologist with whom he considered himself to be "in love" (Various, 2004, p. 2344). He asked his brother to send her "a wreath and the gas man at 3 o'clock in the mornin'" (Zahid Mubarek Inquiry, 2005), together with some "Ann Summers catalogues" (*ibid.*). Indeed, the offence for which Stewart was on remand at the time of the attack on Mubarek involved the harassment of a thirty-eight-year-old white woman who worked as a chat-line operator and had "mixed race" children. Stewart alleged that she had been "cheeky to his brother" (Taylor, 2000, p. 4). He had written letters to the woman demanding sex, calling her a "nigger loving slag" (Zahid Mubarek Inquiry, 2004), and enclosing some of his pubic hair (Various, 2004, p. 1296). Stewart told the police it that this was just a "joke" (*ibid.*). But after receiving letters suggesting that her children would be murdered, the victim was left feeling "terrified" to leave her own home, "extremely ill" with "depression", and "paranoid" about being followed (*ibid.*).

Stewart himself was not necessarily opposed to mixed race relationships, for he had dated black "girlfriends" before he was sent to prison (Judd, 2005). It was the idea of black or Asian men having sex with white women that particularly repulsed him. For example, he complained to his brother that their younger sister, Karen, was "pregnant to some erm black man" from Moss Side: "rumour has it . . . but the gap will be narrowed out if a jigaboo pops out" (Stewart, 2000, p. 23). Stewart's much cited "extreme measures" letter was also laden with miscegenation fantasies addressed to a female prisoner Stewart regarded as his "girlfriend". How and when their relationship began is not clear, but it seems more than coincidental that prison officers noted marked improvements in Stewart's behaviour—deserving of "some kind of recognition"—in the summer of 1999, shortly after the two of them had started corresponding (Keith, 2006b, p. 12). The relationship between Stewart and this woman had deteriorated by the winter of 1999 and, in the "extreme measures" letter, he begged her for reassurance that she had not left him because of something he had said to her. He said he no longer believed that she had engaged in "interracial Pakistan sex" and hoped she had not "divorced" him because of this "figment" of his "imagination" (Stewart, 2000, pp. 391–393). Yet, despite his conscious awareness of its unreality, Stewart struggled to free himself of this troubling fantasy. In a letter written to Maurice Travis, Stewart downplayed his feelings about this girlfriend. He claimed he was not "arsed" about her, it was she who was "in love wiv" him: "I just have to say, 'I love you' in each script to keep her sweet!" (ibid., p. 373). One might have taken this assertion at face value had Stewart not then gone on to say, ". . . some Paki tried to get fresh wid her in some restaurant in Hyde and she bit his tongue off and smashed a wine glass . . . in his face. I'll kill the Paki bastard if I catch him" (ibid., p. 374).

The woman had, in fact, already explained to Stewart (in a letter dated 13 January 2000) that she had never "even kissed a fuckin' Paki", but this did not settle the dispute between them. In a letter written the day before he killed Mubarek, Stewart wrote to his girlfriend: "I keep thinking I have said somert wrong" (ibid., p. 440). Then, in a desperate attempt to persuade her to resume the relationship, Stewart promised that, should she "forget to write back" he would not "keep harassing" her and "become a 'stalker'" (ibid.).

If Gupta's (2005) reconstruction of what followed is to be believed, Stewart tried to discuss the problems he was having with Mubarek, asking him if he, too, had a girlfriend. When Mubarek said he did not, Stewart explained that he had threatened to "chop off" his girlfriend's "head". Mubarek tried to change the subject and began playing a track by the Notorious BIG. When he asked Stewart what kind of music he liked, Stewart responded, "Not this shit. Not this shit. Not this shit. Look at my fucking house. Look at my fucking car. Look at my fucking birds . . . Jigaboo, gangsta rap shit . . . I hate it" (Gupta, 2005, pp. 79–80).

This kind of offensive language may well have been part of Stewart's standard vocabulary. But given how many times Stewart had covered himself in excrement during his imprisonment and the fact that he reported "feeling pretty shitty" around this time (Nayani, 2000, p. 38), one has to wonder if there was some deeper significance to this scatological tirade, for it was in this context that Stewart wrote, on the eve of the murder, about his intention to

> . . . nail bomb the Asian community of Gt Norbury, St Lumm Road and them areas. Its all about these illegal immigrants getting smuggled in here, Romanian beggars, Pakis, chinks trying to take over the country, and using us to breed ½ casts. [Stewart, 2000, p. 446]

Letters he wrote a week after the assault on Mubarek suggest that Stewart may well have regarded Zahid similarly. After seeing that "two whites" were accompanying the Mubarek family to court, Stewart was eager to know who the "young pretty white girl wiv her mam" was (Stewart, 2000, pp. 308, 472), and encouraged his brother to use some of their tried and tested "phone antics" on his behalf (Society Guardian, 2004).

Miscegenation, melancholia, and motive

There is now a vast literature that draws parallels between contemporary discourses about race, race-mixing, and "cultural hybridity" and the often obsessive concerns about miscegenation that justified some of the world's worst abuses of black and indigenous populations: lynching in the southern states of the USA; apartheid in South Africa; the forced assimilation of Australia's stolen generations; and the disproportionate number of "mixed race" children taken into care in Britain after the Second World War, to mention only the most obvious examples (Hendricks, 2001; Ifekwunigwe, 1998; Kalra, Kaur, & Hutnyk, 2005; Kovel, 1971; McClintock, 1995; Papastergiadis, 1997; Phoenix & Owen, 1996; Rich, 2005; Young, 1995). Despite its theoretical complexity, however, hardly any of this literature explains why a minority of white people in Britain today remain so preoccupied with racial purity, a colonial ideology of little obvious relevance in contemporary society and regarded as crude and anachronistic by most people. Fortunately, Gilroy's (2004) book *After Empire* helps us to address this conundrum.

Gilroy begins by drawing attention to white Britons' "inability to face, never mind actually mourn, the profound change in circumstances and mood that followed the end of Empire and the consequent loss of imperial prestige" this entailed (*ibid.*, p. 98). The British, Gilroy argues, cling neurotically to the mythology of the "great" anti-Nazi war of the 1940s because it keeps potentially unsettling knowledge about their nation's fall from grace at bay. Gilroy suggests that, because there has been no mourning of the empire's passing, because we cannot and will not let it go, a cultural melancholia has set in. The symptoms of this melancholia include a neurotic self-loathing projected out in the form of xenophobia against immigrants with whom we are imagined to be at war, political ambivalence about admitting to the enduring damage done to former colonies by British imperialism, recurring anxieties over the prospect of British subjugation to the neo-colonialist war-mongering of the USA, and an inability to relinquish in its entirety the "race-thinking" that supplied the antonyms and dualisms through which English national identity has historically been defined. While welcoming the emergence of convivial youth multi-cultures in Britain's metropolises, Gilroy notes how some people in Britain have become unconsciously dependent on the "certainties" of "race" to "keep their bearings in a world they experience as increasingly confusing" (*ibid.*, p. 116). It is when these certainties are exposed as false that pathological hatreds are most likely to be unleashed. Today's hatreds, Gilroy explains, arise not, as they did in the heyday of colonialism, "from supposedly reliable anthropological knowledge of the stable identity and predictable difference of the Other", but because "the Other's difference in the commonsense lexicon of alterity" appears impossible to "locate" (*ibid.*, p. 137).

> Different people are hated and feared, but the timely antipathy against them is nothing compared to the hatreds turned towards the greater menace of the half-different and the partially familiar. To have mixed is to have been party to a great civilizational betrayal. Any unsettling traces of the resulting hybridity must therefore be excised from the tidy, bleached out zones of impossibly pure culture. [*ibid.*]

Did Robert Stewart perceive Zahid Mubarek as some kind of "half-different" but "partially familiar" mixer whose otherness could not be located in the "commonsense lexicon of alterity"? Did Mubarek come to symbolize for Stewart "a great civilizational betrayal" whose excision would serve some kind of purifying function, expunging the "shitty" feelings he was experiencing along with the arrival of the smuggled immigrants whose corrupting presence he so feared? We think that there is evidence of this in Stewart's behaviour and writing, but in order to see it one has to engage more fully with the notion of melancholia as it has been conceptualized psychoanalytically.

Freud, Klein, and lost love objects

Freud's own description of the melancholic (1917e) captures Robert Stewart even more precisely than Gilroy's formulation. Freud defined the melancholic as someone who cannot get over an emotional loss, whether it has been caused by death or estrangement, or is the result of being "slighted" or "disappointed" by a significant other. Consumed or "eaten up" by such an unbearable loss, the melancholic cannot love again. Instead of working through their feelings, melancholics swallow them whole in a form that is barely digestible, and do all that they can to prevent them from returning to conscious awareness (Cheng, 2007, p. 138). In keeping the loss down, the melancholic experiences a sense of self-torment. Consciously, the melancholic "is not of the opinion that a change has taken place in him", yet, unconsciously, he "reproaches himself, vilifies himself and expects to be cast out and punished" (Freud, 1917e, p. 246). Although his feelings "of shame *in front of other people* . . . are lacking' (*ibid.*, p. 247, our emphases), he takes "refuge in narcissistic identification", an omnipotent love of the self that finds all difference intolerable, that brings "hate . . . into operation" whenever the other's difference is encountered (*ibid.*, p. 251). Substitutive love objects are sought so that "sadistic satisfaction" can be derived from their "suffering" (*ibid.*). What Freud called "erotic cathexis" is "carried back to the stage of sadism which is nearer to that conflict" (*ibid.*, pp. 251–252) and unbearable feelings of powerlessness are kept at bay by "thoughts of suicide" alternating with "murderous impulses against others" (*ibid.*, p. 252).

One of the most emotionally detached young men the professionals who examined him had ever met, prone to mutilating himself and twice a killer, shameless in his racism, inclined to revel in the suffering of others, and repeatedly involved in sending menacing letters to older women whose sexual attention he craved, Robert Stewart undoubtedly displayed many of the symptoms of pathological melancholia. Why this was so, however, is best explained through the work of Klein and the object relations school for whom Freud's psychodynamic depiction of melancholia provided much inspiration. Describing the difference between *mourning*, when people "withdraw" libido from their love objects (their internal perception of the lost loved one) and displace it on to new objects (new loved ones), and *melancholia*, when libido is instead "withdrawn into the ego", Freud noted how the latter serves:

> ... to establish an *identification* of the ego with the abandoned object. Thus the shadow of the object fell upon the ego, and the latter could henceforth be judged as a special agency, as though it were an object, the forsaken object. [Freud, 1917e, p. 249, original emphasis]

In Kleinian theory, this agentic, forsaken object is typically understood as the child's internalization of an unrelinquished fantasy of its first love object, its mother, whom, it perceives as omnipotent. As we explained in Chapters Two and Three of this book, Klein's (1935, 1945) thesis revolves around the idea that the infant greets those upon whom it is most dependent with an intense mixture of love and hate, envy and gratitude, idealization and denigration. Being able to see its mother as a person in her own right—a whole object—rather than simply an extension of the self requires that the child works through these conflictual emotions, moving between what Klein calls the paranoid–schizoid and depressive positions. The transition demands a form of mourning, involving the resolution of feelings of guilt and depression, because the fantasy of the ideal mother has, if psychologically healthy development is to ensue, somehow to be given up and replaced with a more realistic conception (Klein, 1935, 1940). Relational theorists regard the parents' ability to show to the child that they can withstand its hostile attacks without responding retributively as key to this process. The extent to which the parents are able to withstand the child's hostile attacks shapes the child's capacity to come to terms with its own hostility and aggression. The less it is afraid of its own hostile feelings, the more the child is able to contemplate making reparation for the retribution it has phantasized exacting, and the more it is able to consider life from the perspective of significant others.

We know Robert Stewart's experience of growing up was nowhere near as emotionally enriching as this. His mother had never been able to make him "feel needed" and ultimately wanted to "wash her hands of him". His father's chastisement of his children and their mother was brutal. Robert Stewart's childhood photos reveal him to have been "angelic looking", but Stewart considered himself so "ugly" that he erased his face from one of them (Judd, 2005). He must have felt completely unloved. Klein observed that children who feel unloved struggle to free themselves of persecutory anxieties and are, therefore, prone to intense fear and hatred (Hinshelwood, 1991, p. 142). Unable to mourn the loss of the ideal mother of his phantasies, the unloved child is confused and mixed up, terrified that his hatred will damage those he loves. He may "identify" defensively with the "internal deadness" he unconsciously perceives he has instilled in his mother (*ibid.*, p. 143): the identification of the ego with the abandoned or forsaken object described in Freud's classic essay. Manic defences are liable to be mobilized to fend off the internalized dread to which this identification gives rise. Consequently, badness—often associated among young children with defecation (*ibid.*, p. 162) or, in Stewart's words, "shit"—is constantly attributed to others, who may in turn come to be perceived as repulsive and menacing through the process of "projective identification". This makes it difficult for the unloved child to form new relationships, since other individuals tend to be perceived as unknowable and strange "part-objects" as opposed to complete people. Their very externality—the fact that they see things differently—threatens the unloved child, who responds by trying to possess, control, or destroy all those who appear more emotionally complete than they are (Benjamin, 1998, p. 86). When this spiralling of projective hostility is consistently uncontained, the inner world of the unloved child is experienced by them as "in bits", the extremity of their psychic splitting destroying the capacity to feel (Hinshelwood, 1991, pp. 158–160). Sadistic tendencies are liable to emerge as the retaliatory harm anticipated from those dominated—whether in reality or only in fantasy—is acted out (*ibid.*, p. 408).

Stewart's subjectivity

On all the available evidence, Robert Stewart seems to have been prone to adopting this kind of acutely persecutory, incessantly retributive mentality. His early experiences of an abusive father and a mother who did not want him may well have sown the seeds of his fluctuating identifications with the positions of "victim" and "victimizer". The way he behaved as a person, and the sheer amount of time he spent in closed institutions during his formative years, must have further diminished his chances of encountering other people with whom he could form alternative, less polarized forms of identification. His brother Ian and his friend Maurice Travis, themselves quite disturbed individuals, together with the imprisoned girlfriend he wrote to were among the few people with whom Robert Stewart had any kind of lasting or meaningful relationship. Robert shared his preoccupation with miscegenation and racial purity with his brother, and it seems possible that there were specific developmental reasons for their common interest. Both boys routinely referred to their mother as "Fat Mama" (Judd, 2005), a term synonymous with a genre of sexualized ridicule directed primarily at middle-aged black women by younger black men. One has to wonder how the Stewarts' father justified his violence towards his wife. Did he denigrate her in sexualized and racialized ways? And if so, did his sons identify with their father's aggression towards her?

What we do know is that, in one way or another, a crudely sexualized racism came to facilitate the projective identification through which Stewart dealt with his intensely persecutory anxieties. By imagining himself as the chivalric protector of white women threatened by sexually predatory black and Asian men, Stewart could attribute his vulnerability—his need to be wanted—to the former, while disowning the corrupting, dirty, dangerous, and hostile parts of himself by attributing them to the latter. The chat-line operator Stewart harassed, his sister, and his girlfriend were all perceived by him as *at risk* from those being "smuggled in here" and "using us to breed ½ castes". As a defence against the dread of confronting the emotional deadness of his childhood identifications, the "smuggled in" immigrant reminded Stewart of the permeability of his own mind and the extent to which he was at risk of being both overcome by an identification with a lost loved object that had been so hard to swallow, and attacked by all those persecutors against whom his hostility was directed. Because all of this was negotiated below the level of his conscious awareness, Stewart tended not to perceive himself as a racist. From his perspective, his concern with race was tangential to his absorption with sex, violence, and retribution. He identified, as best he could, with other male bullies—his father, his brother, Maurice Travis—because he felt intensely persecuted. In an unusual moment of self-reflection, he saw something of himself in *Romper Stomper*'s Hando, a character the film's director Geoffrey Wright conceived of as an "intelligent but frightened misfit", self-evidently "rigid" and "brutal", but also, and most significantly, "low" in "self-esteem". Men like him

> ... detest and are terrified of change, because in order to keep up with it, they would have to change themselves. Deep down, they feel that they're not capable of doing this, so they try to hang on to the past by delving into the arcane, ferocious nonsense of the Third Reich. [Smith, 1993]

Deep down, Stewart, too, must have wanted to change, however much this prospect frightened him. No longer a juvenile, the criminal justice system had given up any pretence of being able to settle him back into a law-abiding life. Far away from where he had grown up in Manchester, Stewart was friendless in Feltham. In prison his menacing appearance invited ridicule. He had nightmares. He wrote incessantly. He begged his "girlfriend" to forgive him for implicating her in his vile fantasies of miscegenation. Her loss of interest in him can only have underscored what an unlovable person he had become. Even as he became aware of how outrageous his miscegenation fantasies were, Stewart could not let them go. He felt consumed from within and overwhelmed from without. He tried to talk to his cellmate about his girlfriend, and—remarkably, given how unnerving he found Stewart—Zahid Mubarek tried to listen. We know Stewart saw Mubarek as *both* a "Paki" and someone who was "alright" and "safe" with him. Given that they were both nineteen-year-olds who had been excluded from school with histories of problematic drug use and involvement in car crime, the two of them did have things in common, however convenient it may be to think otherwise. In considering this commonality, Mubarek may also have reminded Stewart of everything he would have liked to have been: good-looking, easy-going, untroubled by a chaotic love life, and about to be returned to a family who missed him and still loved him dearly in spite of his bad behaviour. But Mubarek could not identify with Stewart's murderousness, or contain his pain. He was, in Gilroy's (2004, p. 137) words, "half-different" and "partially familiar", perceived by Stewart as smuggling uncomfortable thoughts into his head, being better than him, judging him, making him feel "shitty", no longer the "safe cellmate" but yet another ethnic "gangsta" reminding him of how insignificant he was. For Stewart, as for many incarcerated killers, murder was

> ... the ultimate act of self-defense, a last resort against ... "losing one's mind", an attempt to ward off psychosis or "going crazy".
> ... It is an attempt to hold off paranoid delusions; the riddling, tormented feeling that one is being spied on, watched, hexed by an evil eye, gossiped about, ridiculed, and accused of possessing character traits that shame-driven men find intolerably shameful ...
> [Gilligan, 2000, pp. 75–76]

By attacking Zahid Mubarek, Robert Stewart protected himself from losing what was left of his mind. Consciously, he knew what he had done, but not why. Unconsciously, Stewart experienced the attack as cathartic because it forced Zahid to feel the tortured inner turmoil with which Stewart himself had to contend. By projecting his hate into Zahid, Stewart prevented himself from acknowledging the menacing misfit he knew others perceived him to be. By physically incapacitating him, Stewart could imagine that Zahid was the trapped and powerless outcast he himself was. By spilling Zahid's blood across his bed, Stewart made his own sheets seem relatively clean, unblemished, *bleached* white (again in Gilroy's (2004, p. 137) terms). By bludgeoning Mubarek's *handsome* face out of all recognition, he was symbolically erasing the "ugly" features of the unloved child he had always been, and the unlovable young man he had become.

Recognition and secure, intersubjective containment

What does it take to see the hate of men like Robert Stewart, to recognize it, and to deal with it differently? In relational psychoanalytic theory, *recognition* involves the "processing of [the] other's psychic material, and its integration in intersubjective expression" (Benjamin, 1998, p. 29). While simply *seeing* the other's hate might involve processing it mentally, *recognition* involves a succession of transformative measures of containment and identification. It involves taking in the other's hate, feeling it, thinking it through, and acknowledging that something similar, if not identical to it exists within ourselves, but without being destroyed or over-whelmed by it. This kind of recognition was something people were increasingly unwilling and unable to contemplate in relation to Robert Stewart. When he was a young child, his parents were largely oblivious to his feelings. Some of his teachers, on the other hand, did notice his hate, but tended to dismiss his behaviour as mere attention-seeking. The psychiatrists and social workers called upon to respond to his behaviour spotted its connection to an acute emotional need to feel wanted, but ultimately failed to do anything about it. While Stewart's parents remained unmoved by his needs, he turned his hate outwards in increasingly volatile ways. The more he did this, the less people noticed the self-loathing behind it. Nobody doubted that the adolescent Stewart was a dangerous manipulator. Everyone perceived him as emotionally detached. Fewer and fewer people were willing and able to reach out to Robert Stewart, to work through his inner turmoil intersubjectively, to identify with his hate and the self-loathing that underpinned it. His brother and Maurice Travis colluded with it, fuelling Robert's bizarre fantasies of purity and danger. Prison officers kept their dis-tance while other prisoners ostracized and tormented him. Before the murder few people, aside from Zahid Mubarek and the girl-friend Stewart wrote to, took the time to listen to Robert. The insti-tutional racism that has bred a culture of indifference and insen-sitivity in prisons made sure that no one thought twice about the consequences of placing Zahid Mubarek in a cell with Robert Stewart. But the pathological hatreds of men like Robert Stewart are not caused primarily by institutional racism. They arise, instead, because of the insensitivity and indifference of many adults to the trauma felt by unloved, abused, and neglected children.

Zahid Mubarek died because of the incapacity of prisons to offer him and Robert Stewart good enough care, because prisons equate "secure containment" not with the emotional labour needed to "hold" and detoxify the troubled inner worlds of so many disturbed young people, but with reducing the immediate risks that prisoners pose to their keepers and the outside world. As Mr Justice Keith ably documented, it was not only Stewart's inner world that was "in bits"; so were the key sources of information about him, dispersed across hundreds of uncollated documents or locked up in the minds of wing staff and fellow prisoners. This is another reason why Stewart's hatred was so hard to recognize. When cut into pieces, his extremism did not always look like racism. His letters to his girlfriend, and to the other women whom he had harassed, appeared to be primarily about sex. His references to "Pakis" and "niggers" did not set him apart from other prisoners and prison officers, who were sometimes "blatant" in their use of racial epithets. Indeed, Stewart's rants about "smuggled in immigrants" are all of a piece with the scaremongering about asylum seekers indulged in by many politicians and the media.

Making sure that prisoners from minority ethnic groups never have to share cells with violent racists is perhaps the simplest way of ensuring that we prevent racist murders *in prison cells*. But sequestering men like Robert Stewart away—away from those who are similarly vulnerable, away from those whom they mistakenly imagine to be to blame for their incomprehensible inner turmoil, and away from those who might conceivably be willing and able to care for them—is only going to fuel the persecutory anxieties and retributive sentiments they express through hatred and violence. If we want to deal with what causes this hate differently, we must be prepared to identify, as best we can, with the ugly, mad, and maddening qualities unloved children attribute to themselves. We must also be willing to help them to detoxify the poisonous mentalities that overwhelm them, and prepared to show them that other sources of identification, however remote, are available. Unless we can find ways to open up these possibilities, both within prisons and within our national culture, the melancholia that makes ethnic intolerance permissible in Britain will remain untouched and unchanged. We should not be allowed to console ourselves that men like Robert Stewart are nothing like us, violent racist psychopaths immune to the things that constrain "normal people". Thinking in these terms only makes it easier for us to reimagine institutional racism as the failure *only* of those very peculiar organizations—such as the police and prison services—dominated by problematic occupational cultures. If the murder of Zahid Mubarek is to generate a lasting legacy of which we can all be proud, we cannot shy away from reflecting on what it is about our national culture, as opposed to the subculture of our prisons, that enables us to be indifferent to minority ethnic groups' experiences of racism and insensitive to the complex emotional needs of uncared for young people, whatever their background may be.

CHAPTER EIGHT

Racism, respect, and recognition

"Give respect Get respect"

What became known as the "respect agenda" first emerged as an idea during the British general election campaign of 2005, which led to the then Prime Minister Tony Blair securing an unprecedented (at least for a leader of the Labour Party) third term in office (Casciani, 2006b). However, it was not until the following January that Blair formally launched this new "agenda", complete with the slogan "Give respect Get respect" and a detailed *Respect Action Plan* running to over forty pages (Respect Task Force, 2006). Less than two years later, *The Times* reported that, following a change in government policy on tackling youth crime, the initiative had been quietly dropped, the thirty-strong "Respect task force" replaced, and its head, "Respect Commissioner" Louise Casey, redeployed to other duties in the Cabinet Office (Ford, 2008). Apart from the fact that it was so early a casualty of the need for Blair's successor, Gordon Brown, to distance himself from at least some of the policies of his predecessor, what is interesting about this initiative is the way in which it interpreted the notion of "respect", and then sought to promote it through a series of actions ranging from "new legislation to tackle poor behaviour in schools" (p. 14) through the "establishment of a National Parenting Academy" (p. 18) to setting up "a national network of intensive family support schemes" (p. 22), developing "a Respect Standard for housing management" by social landlords (p. 27), and a raft of new initiatives under the general rubric of "effective enforcement and community justice" (p. 30) (Respect Task Force, 2006).

In an agenda-setting speech delivered on 10 January 2006, Prime Minister Blair announced that he wanted to debate "anti-social behaviour" and the measures the government were proposing to tackle it, "not at the crude level of 'tough' or 'not tough'; populist or not", but "as a genuine intellectual debate about the nature of liberty in a modern developed society" (Blair, 2006). In doing so, he drew on some familiar "New" Labour rhetoric about pairing "rights" with "responsibilities" and balancing "enforcement measures" with "prevention" (*ibid.*). But he also referred to Hobbes' *Leviathan*, R. H. Tawney, and Richard Sennett in the course of remarks touching on everything from the maintenance of order as the "central question of political theory" (Hobbes) to the relationship between "increasing material inequalities" and a tendency not to observe "the basic courtesies" of everyday life (Sennett). We will return to Sennett's work on respect in a moment, but what exactly did Blair himself understand by this key notion? The answer to this seems to lie in the following passage:

> Respect is a way of describing the very possibility of life in a community. It is about the consideration that others are due. It is about the duty I have to respect the rights that you hold dear. And vice-versa. It is about our reciprocal belonging to a society, the covenant we have with one another. [*ibid.*]

In his foreword to the *Respect Action Plan*, Blair provided a slightly less high-flown account. Intractable problems with the behaviour of "some individuals and families" were attributable to a ". . . lack of respect for values that almost everyone in this country shares—consideration for others, a recognition that we all have responsibilities as well as rights, civility and good manners" (Respect Task Force, 2006, p. 1).

Later, in a short section headed "What is respect?", the Action Plan described respect as "something that people intuitively understand" (*ibid.*, p. 5), yet dependent on the existence of the "common set of values" set out by Blair in his foreword. Finally, the answers provided by some young people to the question "What is respect?" were listed, this among them: "Appreciating someone, even though they're from another country and they're different" (*ibid.*).

The only direct reference in the *Action Plan* to the other "New" Labour "agendas", race equality and community cohesion, with which we have been concerned in previous chapters, was fleeting but illuminating in its ambiguity:

> Ethnic and cultural diversity is a source of strength and dynamism for our society both nationally and locally. But without a shared framework of respect and rules, people can be susceptible to the argument that differences in culture and lifestyle are undermining community cohesion. [*ibid.*]

Diversity, it seems, is good, but only so long as certain values— civility, manners, and an acceptance of responsibilities as well as rights—are both shared and respected. To reject such values is to invite justified criticism and to threaten the development of cohesive communities.

What, therefore, was striking about these formulations was their conception of "respect" as a quality either present or, in some degree, lacking in political, social, and communal relations. What Blair was asking us—or, more specifically, badly behaved school children, anti-social youth, chaotic families, and persistent offenders—to respect were the terms of the social contract, the conditions under which we can call ourselves citizens, and the sense of shared values on which all political communities depend. Absent from all of these definitions—with the exception of the statement made by the anonymous "young person" to whom we will soon return— was any sense, beyond a duty to be civil and well-mannered, of how "respect" is demonstrated in the course of interactions between individuals, or what it means and feels like to be respected (and disrespected) by others. Also missing was any consideration of respect for diversity rather than sameness, plurality rather than unanimity, heterogeneity rather than homogeneity as the basis for "community cohesion".

By way of contrast, in talking about respect as involving an appreciation of otherness and of difference, the young person quoted in

the government's *Action Plan* offered a more sophisticated understanding of respect and its relevance to tackling the very specific
problems of hatred and violence with which we are concerned. In an
attempt to develop such an understanding, the next two sections of
this chapter explore the work of the sociologist Richard Sennett on
respect and the psychoanalyst Jessica Benjamin on recognition. We
then present a case study of one of our interviewees from Stoke-on-
Trent to illustrate how, through the processes of identification and
recognition discussed by Sennett and Benjamin, one man was able to
move beyond the racism, hatefulness, and violence of his youth.

The Formation of Character in an Age of Inequality

Tony Blair's brief comment in his "respect" speech about the "per-
suasiveness" of Richard Sennett's work does the eminent sociologist scant justice, for Sennett's (2003) book, *Respect: the Formation of
Character in an Age of Inequality*, presents a lucid and psychoanalytically informed analysis which goes far beyond the inverse nature
of the relationship between "the basic courtesies" and "material
inequalities". A semi-autobiographical exploration of the unin-
tended consequences of welfare reform, Sennett's book attends to
issues of politics, culture, and personality via an analysis of the
problems which inequality presents to British and American societies. He begins his book by recalling his childhood experiences of
Cabrini Green, a racially mixed housing project close to the centre
of Chicago in the late 1940s. Writing fifty years later, Sennett argues
that public housing schemes like Cabrini challenged their residents'
"sense of self-worth" in two ways: first by placing them in a
demeaning state of "welfare dependency" (a humiliation made
worse for white residents by virtue of the proximity into which they
were brought with African Americans), and, second, by denying
them control over their own lives, by making them "spectators to
their own needs" and by exposing them to "that peculiar lack of
respect which consists of not being seen, not being accounted as full
human beings" (*ibid.*, pp. 12–13). The outcome was both socially
and psychologically damaging:

> Lack of respect, though less aggressive than an outright insult, can
> take an equally wounding form. No insult is offered another

person, but neither is recognition extended; he or she is not *seen*—
as a full human being whose presence matters. [*ibid*, p. 3, original
emphasis]

The youthful and musically gifted Sennett and his social worker
mother soon left Cabrini Green, but—his career as a cellist cut short
by a hand injury—he returned to the project twenty years later as a
"role model" for "the ones left behind" (*ibid.*, p. 32). Now working
as a sociologist, Sennett was struck by the hostile reception given to
one of his fellow mentors, a young Puerto Rican doctor who delivered an uncompromising message of self-improvement, to which
his audience of "ghetto adolescents", "highly sensitive to being
'dissed'", reacted by heckling before falling into a hostile, sullen
silence (*ibid.*, pp. 33–35). Remarking on this response to his colleague's disrespectful behaviour, Sennett observes, "in places
where resources are scarce and approval from the outside world is
lacking, social honor is fragile; it needs to be asserted every day"
(*ibid.*, p. 34).

At much the same time as he was revisiting Chicago, Sennett
was studying the discontents of the white working class in Boston
in an effort to understand how the psychological damage caused by
a lack of recognition of the kind inflicted on his audience in Cabrini
Green by the bullish young doctor creates opportunities for right
wing politicians to mobilize the anger and resentment felt by poor
whites against both the professional and liberal elites above them
in the class structure—and upon whom the poor are dependent in
so many ways—and the poor blacks and migrant workers below
(*ibid.*, p. 45; Sennett & Cobb, 1993). When they were brought
together in groups, white working-class Bostonians who were
otherwise "balanced and open about themselves in relation to
others in the city" began to "indulge in gross racial slurs and jokes,
spurring one another on, railing against the liberal elite and the
media" (*ibid.*, p. 46). Reflecting on this change, Sennett recalls that
the participants in these groups were playing a "zero-sum game of
respect" in which "respect to blacks was denied in order to affirm
one's own worth".

Inequality had translated into doubt of self; that doubt might
be partly relieved by attacking the integrity of others. . . . [T]he

condition of "not being seen" had produced a desire to avenge. Here, then, was one bleak result of the social scarcity of respect. [*ibid*]

Thus, according to Sennett, where there is a lack of respect, when people—whether they are "ghetto adolescents" in Cabrini Green or working-class white Bostonians—are not "seen", potentially destructive codes of honour assume its cultural place. Although it shares the "mutuality" inherent in relationship founded on respect, honour "signals a kind of erasure of social boundaries and distance" and an inability on the part of the individual to see him/herself other than as s/he is seen by others (*ibid.*, p. 55). Its affirmation within a group can also lead to "destructive behaviour towards those who lie beyond the group's boundaries" (*ibid.*).

If, as Sennett argues, social honour represents the negative pole of mutuality, recognition is its opposite. To explain this, he returns to his love of music and the nature of the relationship between a singer and a pianist performing a particularly difficult piece of Schubert. To understand how such a collaboration works, Sennett suggests, it is necessary to appreciate what Mills and Gerth (1953) meant by "character": a person's ability to communicate with others through shared "social instruments", be they "laws, rituals, the media, codes of religious belief, political doctrines" or musical texts (*ibid.*, p. 52).

It is the capacity to engage the larger world . . . which defines a person's character; character can be thought of . . . as the relational side of personality . . . The concert furnishes a positive example of character: treating with respect the need perceived in another when acting together. [*ibid.*, p. 53]

Unlike honour, then, recognition involves a complex relational process. But whence might a more positively mutual and fully "relational" character, less dependent on the denigration of others, emerge? On this question, Sennett derives his answer almost exclusively from the work of the child psychoanalyst Donald Winnicott.

Winnicott interpreted autonomy as the capacity to treat other people as different from oneself; understanding that separation gives both others and oneself autonomy. . . . We commonly think of "autonomy" as the capacity to separate from others, which is a self-referential use of the word. Winnicott describes autonomy as a strength of character based on perceptions of others; that is, it establishes a relationship between people, rather than an isolating difference—the child developing autonomy can see and engage outside himself or herself. [*ibid.*, pp. 120–121]

As Winnicott's (1958) analyses were famously to reveal, the "good enough" parent facilitates their child's separation from them, not by asserting absolute difference, but by encouraging a process of differentiation that keeps both sameness and difference in play. Once the parent's autonomy has begun to be accepted by the dependent child, a new form of emotional connection becomes possible—"identification"—making reciprocal recognition possible in theory, even if it is not necessarily and always accomplished in practice. As Sennett suggests,

Your experience becomes like the child touching a mother's skin; gradually I perceive how different the details of your experience are from mine, *but I do not withdraw my mental hand.* . . . Conceived in this way, autonomy is a powerful recipe for equality. Rather than equality of understanding, a transparent equality, *autonomy means accepting in the other what you do not understand*, an opaque equality. In so doing, you are treating the fact of their autonomy as equal to your own. But to avoid the virtuoso's mastery, the grant must be equal. [*ibid.*, 121–122, our emphases]

In marked contrast to Blair, Sennett is ultimately of the view that

Treating people with respect cannot occur simply by commanding it should happen. Mutual recognition has to be negotiated; this negotiation engages the complexities of personal character as much as social structure. [*ibid.*, p. 260]

On the question of what can be done to promote more mutual recognition at the interpersonal level, Sennett is much more circumspect. Fortunately for us, however, Jessica Benjamin's (1998) book, *The Shadow of the Other*, sets out the processes which enable mutual recognition to be achieved in relational psychoanalytic terms.

The Shadow of the Other

Like Sennett, Benjamin is acutely aware of the important role which identification plays in inhibiting the kind of defensive splitting and demeaning projection that expresses itself in racism, violence, and other vengeful attacks on out-groups. She, like Sennett, notes the developmental challenge entailed in being able to contemplate the other's autonomy or "externality". And she, again like Sennett, argues that recognition cannot be experienced as a command to tolerate the other, to become like them, or to make them be known as social types or in terms of stereotypes.

> Identification can serve as a means for bridging difference without denying or abrogating it, but the condition of this form of identification is precisely the other's externality. The other's difference must exist outside; not be felt as a coercive command to "become" the other, and therefore not be defended against by assimilating it to the self. It is here that the notion of recognition as mediated not only through identification, but through direct confrontation with the other's externality, makes a difference. [Benjamin, 1998, pp. 95–96]

But as the quotation indicates, Benjamin's interest is not limited to the way in which denigrated out-groups become the recipients of the in-group's hostile projections. What matters to her is the role which the recipients of hostile projections can play in transforming the in-group—if only they can convince the in-group at a deep psychological level of their autonomous existence.

In what is a critical move beyond Winnicott, Benjamin argues that anti-social, uncaring, and/or hostile tendencies are not the indefinite and inevitable destiny of the child whose experience of parenting was not "good enough". For her, the Winnicottian developmental route of discovering one's mother's independence as a separate being with her own needs is only one of the ways—albeit a very important one—in which the child comes to terms with its own destructive urges. If, for example, other significant adults are able to reassure the child that he or she is also like them, that the child shares their qualities too, the child can develop a capacity to experience, even enjoy, the co-presence of otherness and togetherness across many relationships. It is, therefore, possible, even for those whose childhoods were damaging, deprived, or humiliating, to free themselves from the desire to denigrate others and develop a capacity to recognize their alterity. Critical to such psychic manoeuvring is the question of whether the individual concerned can recapture its ability to identify with multiple others, hostile tendencies often arising—especially in the cases of troublesome boys—out of the child's defensive and overly-exclusive identification with the parent of the same sex.

Benjamin's explanation of how this can happen involves a reappraisal of Freud's (1917e) essay on "Mourning and melancholia". In that essay, Freud reported on how some of his manic–depressive melancholic patients had managed to overcome their grief as the shadow of the object fell upon the ego. What Freud meant by this was that the processes of overcoming depression are akin to what happens when loved ones are lost and successfully mourned. Although they may not be fully conscious of it, the mourners' grief is primarily to do with the psychic loss of the parts of themselves invested in their relationship with the lost person, and not simply about the physical absence of the deceased. Freud hypothesized that, in order to overcome this grief, the mourner had not only to accept the physical loss of the other person as irreversible, but also to realize that this physical loss need not mean the death of those parts of their self psychically projected on to the lost loved one. In the process of mourning, the grief-stricken individual could gradually reclaim these projected parts of the self and reinvest them in new relationships. And this is exactly what had happened in the cases of his recovering manic–depressive patients.

Similar opportunities for psychical transformation, Benjamin argues, arise in our everyday relationships and in political cultures. When our partners survive our angry projections, we can find ourselves confronted by their alterity or externality. As reparation is made for hostile projections, opportunities often arise for regaining contact with "lost love objects" as one partner signifies their acceptance of the other, including both their good (consciously owned) qualities and bad (often unconsciously disowned) qualities. Similarly, when children grow up ("too fast"), parents may be confronted with their own unconscious dependence on the child's recognition, and, hence, the child's alterity. In such circumstances, the contradictions between the parent's idealization of the child as someone like them (whom they may have hoped would accomplish things they never did) and as a precious dependant who looks to them for inspiration are brought into focus alongside a sense of loss that has to be dealt with through mourning if the parent is to "let go" (see also Diamond, 1998). Applied to the political context of South Africa in the early 1990s, Benjamin argues that white South Africans would not have been able to come to terms with the end of apartheid had it not been for the psychic robustness of those othered by racializing discourses:

> The strategy of the African National Congress exemplified the intervention of the Other as subject, achieving through their solidarity and recognition a form of agency despite persecution and denial of recognition by their opponents. The ANC and Mandela assumed an ethical responsibility for the consequences before that responsibility had been honoured by the white government, before symmetrical power had been established. Much of what transpired in the initial transition offered an alternative to the reversal of power relations that silence the silencer. This is the difference the Other can make, precisely because the Other insists on being a subject, not simply attacking the other's subjectivity. [Benjamin, 1998, pp. 98–99]

By way of confirmation of her hypothesis, Benjamin urges us not to forget that it was also the willingness of the country's last white President, F. W. de Klerk, "to envision *surviving* the destruction of the Afrikaner way of life that allowed difference and externality to emerge" (1998, 98–99, original emphasis).

Frank: a case study

In the work of Sennett and Benjamin we have something of a reversal of the assumptions embedded in Tony Blair's "respect agenda". For them, the important task is not how to make anti-social youth, poor problem families, or minority ethnic groups show respect to a majority who already "give respect". It is, rather, to understand how groups which are anxious about their own status, and/or feel humiliated or dishonoured, project their hostilities on to out-groups, frequently using racism as the social vehicle for this projective activity. It is also to appreciate the critical role which denigrated out-groups can play in changing the minds of those caught up in these projective processes; how, in taking an ethical responsibility for the in-group's hostility, the out-group can create unexpected opportunities for mutual recognition to occur. In the case study that follows, we explore how such a process of recognition unfolded in a deprived white working-class neighbourhood from which many of our research participants came, a neighbourhood where racialized intolerance, violence, and anti-social behaviour had become the focus of both local and national political concern.

Discovering Frank

Frank was a forty-four-year-old potteries worker, local odd-job man, and British National Party election candidate who lived in the heart of a former mining community on the outskirts of Stoke-on-Trent. We interviewed Frank three times during the course of our research. The first two biographical interviews took place a week apart in April 2004. Extracts from a brief follow-up interview, conducted six months later, are also presented to demonstrate the subjective change that had occurred in Frank since we first spoke to him. Frank was an eager participant in the research, writing and ringing back on the day he received our letter asking him if was interested in being interviewed. Notwithstanding this enthusiasm, he proved to be a "high maintenance" interviewee, initially responding to questions with short, rather unrevealing answers. When he paused or had finished talking, Frank would lower his head and look down at the floor without making eye contact. Only when prompted by further questioning did he begin to talk in more detail about his memories. Asked to tell the story of his life at the beginning of our first interview with him, Frank sought more guidance almost immediately. (As before, numbers embedded in the text in square brackets indicate a pause timed in seconds.)

> "Well, I was born in [mining neighbourhood], come off a family of seven, five brothers and one sister. [16] Basically I don't really know what you want, like. That's the thing about it. I mean, a lot has gone on in me life, like. What specific points, like?"

Childhood, poverty and domestic abuse

Urged to tell the story of his childhood and adolescence, Frank responded with accounts of a violent upbringing, a criminal youth, imprisonment, and involvement with the far right National Front (NF). He had grown up in a large family that "never had nothing". His father was a "hard man", an ex-prisoner who "wasn't too kind" to his wife and children. While his mother worked in the pottery industry, Frank's father "wouldn't work", preferring to send his children to "pinch" bags of coal from trains rather than to school. When he did go to school, Frank was "always fighting . . . 'Cos me dad said so". While his father beat all the children, Frank felt that he was given special treatment: "He seemed [to] dote on me, like. I mean tried bringing me up the way he was like, you know." Frank's dad "enjoyed fighting" and brought Frank up "to be the same basically", so much so that when he "got in scrapes" at school with children who had seen him "scrounging" coal, his father would "smack" him "around . . . show me how to actually hit someone". On one such occasion, when another boy had split Frank's head open with a car jack, his dad responded by getting Frank in the garden and giving him a "right good hiding . . . I went to the hospital and then I had to go back the following day and beat this lad. And he made sure I did, like." Frank and the other children would be "shoved" outside so they could hear but not see their mother being abused by their father. Frank remembered one time when he came home from school and saw his mother's face "covered in blood . . . he'd obviously hit her, like. We were too young to do anything then so." Yet, when pushed for any other childhood memories of his mother, Frank claimed to have none.

Adolescence, crime, and the National Front

Even though it exposed him to his brother's sadistic pranks, Frank remembered his first labouring job with great fondness—it was "good money and good fun". These pranks included Frank being stripped naked, tied up, and abandoned in one of the towns where he and his brother had been working. Around the same time, Frank had also become involved in stealing cars and thieving from shops, typically in "gangs". At the age of seventeen, Frank was convicted of robbing a local (white) shopkeeper at knifepoint and sent to

Borstal. At the time of the offence, Frank and his friends had run out of money after drinking all day.

"[W]e decided to pull straws . . .who'd go commit, get some money like. Anyway, me and me mate pulled short straws out [laughs] so we had to do it. Well, we didn't have to, but we did like, you know."

Although Frank's mother said nothing to him about the robbery, Frank's father anticipated that his son would serve his time "standing on his head". Frank lived up to his father's expectations and quickly established himself as "one of the top boys" in Borstal, "'cos I like fighting and there were people there waiting to fight me, like". When Frank returned home to his estate, aged nineteen, it was as a skinhead:

"From there it just spiralled . . . In them days you just sort of got out of control. You get into things you didn't really want to get into, [10] like . . . National Front and used to go [to] National Front meetings and all that. [30] . . . So there was a crowd of ten, fifteen of us, but skinheads. I mean they were known to be hard, like, so you sort of got in with them. And you could guarantee, like I say, that you'd be in trouble somewhere or the other. It was shit."

Frank struggled to explain why he considered being an NF skinhead to be "shit". He had enjoyed the adrenaline-pumped fights the skinheads got him into—a stab wound to the stomach further "glorifying" the violence. He found the racism of the NF entirely consistent with having been "brought up racist" by a "dead racist" father who switched television channels whenever he saw "a black in a film". Yet Frank denied that he had done what the National Front wanted him to do. Back then, the NF's philosophy was

". . . anything black you shouldn't have anything to do with. If you can get away with it, you know, give it a good hiding, like. Maybe the British National Party's philosophy is still the same basically . . . There's still people there what actually do that . . . They were saying that the country were going to be over-filled, and all this, over-run with them, and we'd have no jobs and you tend to believe them, like, especially when you're young."

Frank, however, claimed that he did not "pick on people" in this way. As he recalled things, the drunken fights he and the other skinheads got into were always with groups of black and Asian young men who were "up for it" and as keen to fight as they were.

> "I mean, it wasn't a point of picking on somebody. It never got that far. I was never brought up to pick on people . . . It was just like I held me own. I mean, even though me dad really wanted me to pick on people, I never really did. But fighting's different. If they are up for it then we're up for it. That's different, like . . . If they didn't want it, then you never got hit, like. I wouldn't go jump on them just for the sake of it. I never did."

Adult life and keeping out of trouble

By the time Frank was twenty-five, his brothers had grown to "despise" their father, who was confined to a wheelchair after several strokes. Although Frank's brothers had little or nothing to do with their father, Frank, on the other hand, often felt obliged to defend his dad in the pub fights he provoked by running his wheelchair into the legs of other drinkers. None the less, when Frank's father had a final, fatal stroke, the two men were not on speaking terms. After his father had "just got on to" him for coming in late from the pub, Frank had threatened to hit him:

> "So I picked him up out his wheelchair and I was going to hit him, like. And he went in hospital a few weeks after that. Anyway, he died in hospital and I never had the chance to say I was sorry and that, so . . . It hurt me. I still miss him to this day, like."

Married with a newborn daughter, Frank promised his wife that he would "never be in trouble again". He left his friends to keep him informed about the NF's activities but did not get involved himself. Despite maintaining his old NF acquaintances and continuing to live on the same estate where he had grown up, Frank succeeded in settling down. He stayed in the same job for over twenty years and had only ever been unemployed for one day. Five years after the birth of their daughter, Frank and his wife had a second child together, a son, and their marriage remained "happy" and "close".

Joining and leaving the BNP

It was not until Frank had turned forty that he became active in far right politics once more.

> "Well it [4] . . . I can't, like I say, how I got back into it, I don't know . . . Just one day there was a meeting up town and I happened to go, like . . . Me and me wife went, like . . . They [the BNP] was talking, and everything they said seemed to make sense, like. I mean, couldn't fault really anything they said 'cos everything they said is what I believed in . . . They were saying what they get when they come in to the country and you know what our own people were getting . . . It's basically it's going to be over-run, the country is. [DG: You thought the country was going to be over-run?] Yer. Always have done."

Once again things "spiralled" for Frank, and both he and his wife committed themselves to the BNP. Although his interest in the issue owed more to his own preoccupation with the drug-addicted burglars who preyed on his estate (and whose legs he had threatened to break) than to the attractions of the BNP's policies on crime, Frank stood in a local election and got a "big buzz" out of giving speeches about "law and order". However, despite sporting a suit in his new role, Frank felt that some of his audience interpreted his tattoos as "a mark of being a troublemaker". This bothered him so much that he attempted to have the tattoos removed. Worse still, when Frank had tried to talk to some pensioners whose declining living standards were a special concern of his wife's, they had "booed" him off, saying that he and his colleagues "were nothing but racist". His wife's worries about impoverished pensioners may have been related to difficulties in her own family, which Frank had been compelled to resolve by helping both his mother-in-law and his own mother settle debts that they could not afford to pay. Unfortunately, this had not brought Frank and his mother any closer: "She'll go out of her way sometimes . . . to try talk to me and [7] . . . but I just can't, like."

As the election campaign got under way, Frank's son had been picked on at school—"'cos, like I say, they got coloureds in their school"—while his daughter was ostracized by some of her work colleagues when her father's political allegiances became more widely known. However, it was only after the elections that Frank began to have doubts about the BNP. His wife resigned from her role as the local party treasurer after the BNP's racism was exposed in the local media. Then Frank himself started to have suspicions about the nature of the racism condoned by the party after he witnessed a senior BNP figure proposing that people with black relatives should be excluded from full membership: "Can't blame the kids . . . To do that is blatantly racist." Frank was "disgusted" with what he had heard and the hatefulness he could see in himself repulsed him so much that he felt obliged to apologize to the eighteen-year-old "half-caste" woman and her mother who worked in his local pub.

> "Them as friends had voted . . . for me, like, even though it's a racist party. That hurt me. It really did, like . . . [4] Felt ashamed, like, 'cos they actually voted for me and I was telling them that it is no longer a racist party . . . 'It isn't National Front' . . . I was telling them lies at the end of the day, because they are."

The "half-caste" woman's mother was so furious with Frank that she was "going to belt" him, but her daughter was willing to accept Frank's apology. "She said she didn't vote for the party, she voted for me anyhow." Since leaving the BNP, things had been looking up for Frank and his family. His employers had enrolled him on an evening course in engineering, which he had enjoyed so much that he was paying to continue his studies. Meanwhile, his daughter had been offered a place at university. As for his son, Frank had provided him with a different kind of upbringing from his own: "I haven't got no problems with him at all. I love him to bits and that's it, you know. Tried give him more than I've ever had, like, you know."

The significance of these closing remarks became more apparent when we spoke to Frank for a third and final time six months after our first pair of interviews took place. Asked what it was that he thought was "shit" about the NF, Frank struggled to explain before ultimately conceding that it was only with the benefit of hindsight, and from the perspective of his children, that he had made this assessment:

> "It was, I mean [4] [sighs] . . . I don't know. I can't really say it. [3] [sighs] You don't . . . you wouldn't want your own kids be brought

up, you know, that way of life like, you know, and do them things
what I used to do, like."

Asked whether he was surprised by recent media coverage
exposing the level of support for racist attacks among members of
Britain's far right parties, Frank responded, "A load of racists, thugs
. . . They will never be any different, as far as I'm concerned. I mean
skinheads aren't they? Exactly what I was them years ago."

Re-reading Frank's life story

The violent child of a violent father brought up in a family afflicted
by domestic abuse, poverty, and the long-term under-employment
of its self-appointed head, the young Frank would have been
exactly the kind of "anti-social" child from a "problem family" the
"respect agenda" was designed to tackle. His criminal career began
during his childhood when his father encouraged him to steal coal,
persisted into his teens when it assumed more intimidating (shop-
lifting in gangs) and violent (fighting in custody) forms, and escalated during his twenties when he joined the NF and participated
in what would now be described as racist attacks. Back then, being
"top boy", having money to spend on beer, and saving his face with
his drinking buddies seemed to matter more to him than the harm
his criminality and violence caused to his victims.

Like many of the white working-class people Richard Sennett
talked to in Boston forty years ago, men such as Frank living in
deindustrialized towns and cities like Stoke-on-Trent tend to equate
respect with honour. They see social honour as something to be
defended (with violence if need be), and as something in short
supply that can only be maintained through the diminution of
others. Beaten by his father if he lost a fight, Frank's introduction to
the zero-sum game of honour preservation was a harsh experience.
Being able to "hold his own" was what mattered, at home, among
his peers, and in Borstal. As it did for many other criminally stigmatized working-class young men, membership of the National
Front provided Frank with a source of excitement and a sense
of belonging, a means of expressing both popular and personal
disquiet about immigration made all the more attractive by the

enjoyment to be had from inflicting violence on others (Billig, 1978; Fielding, 1981).

Like his father, Frank had once believed that anyone or "any-*thing* black you shouldn't have anything to do with. If you can get away with it . . . give it a good hiding". Demanding respect and rediscovering pride among working-class whites was on the agenda of the NF and the other parties of far right long before the advent of the *Respect Action Plan*. Indeed, Frank was one of many criminally stigmatized white working-class men who, come the late 1990s, found an opportunity to disown a shameful past by getting tough on drug addicts, sex offenders, "Asian gangs" and "illegal immigrants" in the political agenda of a resurgent BNP (Copsey, 2004).

Recognition and respect

What Frank's particular story reveals, however, is much more interesting, since it tells us that it is possible for transformative forms of recognition to dislodge the destructive codes of honour on which those whose lives have been blighted by hardship and abuse may come to depend. When he discovered that women like the eighteen-year-old "half-caste" barmaid in his local pub would be excluded even from the "new" BNP, Frank was forced to confront the "blatant" racism in which he and his father had often indulged. Suddenly Frank felt "ashamed", "disgusted", and "hurt" (something he had also confessed to feeling in his melancholic account of his father's untimely death). Although they were his "friends" now, in an earlier era, when Frank, with his father's blessing, had been a "racist thug" and a far right activist, the young woman and her mother might well have been seen as his enemies. It is easy to suppose that, refracted through the prism of racist ideology, the threat of being "over-run", with which Frank had long been preoccupied, could have been linked to fears of miscegenation, fears that the invading foreigners might produce "mixed race" or "half-caste" children, thus compromising the purity of the native white race (Dalal, 2002; Frosh, 1997; Ifekwungiwe,1999; Kovel, 1971). In this context, the "half-caste" barmaid might well have been seen by the younger, violent, NF-supporting Frank as more "other" and more dangerous than her "black" mother.

For the older Frank, however, this othering was inhibited by a remarkable process of mutual recognition. Frank stopped perceiving the barmaid as racially other. She had served him in the pub where he and his father had spent much of their spare time. She was also a teenager, two years younger than Frank's daughter, two years older than his son, and the same age Frank had been when he served time in Borstal. From Frank's perspective, this young woman was still a child. Picking on the children was what made the BNP's racism—like the NF's before them—"blatant" and, thus, unacceptable. Here we should recall that it was Frank's father's unwillingness to let his son be picked on for being a thieving "scrounger" that legitimated his brutal lessons in how to fight. So, Frank apologized to the young woman for persuading her to vote for the BNP. The outcome of this apology was not at all what he expected. The young woman refused to be positioned as a victim, to be assimilated into a universalizing category of minority under threat. Instead, she did what Benjamin advocates in order to make the shadow of the object fall upon the ego. She contained her own outrage, and hence was not as inclined to "belt" Frank as her mother was. The young woman positioned herself, instead, as an autonomous and knowledgeable subject; not a victim or cultural dupe, but someone able and willing to confer recognition on Frank despite his political *naïveté*. She told Frank that she had voted for him because of who he had been and who he was, thus making it possible for him to envisage survival beyond his feelings of shame and disgust. As Benjamin concludes,

> Owning the other within diminishes the threat of the other without so that the stranger outside is no longer identical with the strange within us—not our shadow, not a shadow over us, but a separate other whose own shadow is distinguishable in the light. [Benjamin, 1998, p. 108]

Mourning and loss

Re-reading Frank's story from this starting point, it is possible to deconstruct the pattern of identifications that had to unfold to make this transformative moment of recognition possible. Look again at the contradictions in Frank's early account of his involvement in the NF. Here, Frank made three incompatible claims:

1. That he was never brought up to pick on people;
2. That he was brought up to be "the way" his father was; and
3. That his "dad really wanted" him "to pick on people".

These contradictions were not simply a product of Frank's desire to present himself in a socially acceptable light; rather, they are evidence of the enduring complexity of his love for, and loyalty towards, his father. Frank clearly did not benefit from the kind of "good enough" parenting Winnicottians regard as necessary for the retention of cross-sex, over-inclusive identifications with one's parents. Frank's repeatedly abused mother, probably out working more than most given the family's financial predicament, may well have been too damaged, too depressed, and too terrified to contain the trauma her children suffered at the hands of her husband. Tellingly, Frank had few childhood recollections of her, aside from the fact that he had been powerless to protect her: "We were too young to do anything." Rather than identify with her vulnerability, Frank came to identify with his father to the point of complete idealization: they doted on each other despite the violence. And as Benjamin (1998, p. 56) remarks, the subjective inner world of a boy whose development is marred in this way is liable to feel "too flooded to develop ownership of desire". As a result:

> He must adopt a defensive activity. Unable to be his own container, he must defensively use the activity of discharge into the object who contains. In this sense, the masculine defense entails neither separation nor boundaries but an urgently driven relation to the object. This is activity without authorship or ownership—hence without genuine subjectivity that allows space for another subject. [*ibid.*, p. 56]

Benjamin's notion of an urgently driven relation to the object— "activity without authorship"—resonates with the way in which things repeatedly "spiralled" in Frank's life. Having drawn the short straw, Frank felt he *had to* commit an armed robbery. Then, when he came out of Borstal, "top boy" and a skinhead, things again got "out of control". He started going to NF meetings and hanging around with a crowd of other skinheads. They fought with black and Asian young men who shared their taste for violence, but were also part of the invading army of immigrants which Frank had "always" believed was over-running the country. Frank's ideal-ization of his "dead racist" father and the pervasiveness of his fear of being flooded, swamped, and overwhelmed by immigrants made "race" a seductive container for the feelings and desires he as a teenager was unable to own.

Little by little, this began to change as Frank entered adulthood. Where his father had dominated his mother, Frank and his wife were somehow able to respect each other's difference. She did not try to change Frank when they married. After their first child was born, she only asked him to stay out of "trouble" and to confine his long-standing association with the NF to second-hand accounts of the party's activities gleaned from his friends in the pub. Much later, when Frank was again caught up in a "spiral" of far right political activity, he respected his wife's decision to leave the BNP while he remained active. Similarly, while Frank's own doting father had tried to make Frank a man in his own aggressive, violent, and racist image, Frank loved his son "to bits", but wanted him to have everything he never had. At that point, in his relationship with his son, and in his ability to identify with his daughter's educa-tional aspirations (his decision to enrol in a second course at college coincided with her gaining a place at university), the cycle of vio-lent parental bullying fractured. Gradually, Frank began to engage with those parts of himself that he had previously disowned through projection and to work through the contradictory denials that constituted his position on not "picking on people". But it was not until he was able to confront the "hurt" of his father's death that he was able to fully appreciate the hurt that racism causes. Having pulled him out of his wheelchair and been about to hit his father for criticizing his behaviour, Frank had been left with a painful sense of guilt when his father died before any form of apology could be made. This "hurt" Frank, not only because the offence caused could not be taken back, but also because the guilt it evoked in him derived from "an internal conflict, particularly over the worth of the self" (Hinshelwood, 1991, p. 314). The person who "doted" on him most, and whom he was most like, had died before they could resolve their differences and take back the slights they had both made on each other's (very similar) characters.

Critically, it was these "worth of self" issues which the young barmaid inadvertently stumbled upon when she told Frank that she had voted for him not because of his party affiliation, but because of who he was. This enabled Frank to survive, psychologically, the "disgust" he felt about his identification with both the BNP and the "dead racist" father whose idealization was such a defining part of his sense of self. The success of this young woman in disrupting Frank's psychic defensiveness was ultimately made possible by the successful resolution of a number of intersubjective processes: Frank's identification with her vulnerability; her successful nega-tion of Frank's projection of her as foreign, a victim and a political dupe; and, perhaps most critical of all, her capacity to establish herself as a sovereign other, able to recognize Frank for who he was—a man worth voting for—rather than the foolish trouble-maker uncritically following in the footsteps of his father he knew himself to have been.

Conclusion: towards a new politics of recognition

What are the implications of this analysis for nurturing a culture of respect and promoting greater tolerance? If Richard Sennett's analysis is right and other-denigrating codes of social honour are adopted by those who feel unseen, ignored, and left behind, then a politics of recognition is overdue. In the context of his work on the direction of contemporary welfare reform, Sennett's view is that this could be made more likely "by honoring different practical achievements rather than privileging potential talent; by admitting the just claims of adult dependency"; and "by permitting people to participate more fully in the conditions of their own care" (Sennett, 2003, p. 261). From our reading of the work of Jessica Benjamin and the story told by Frank, our interviewee, we would go further than this and suggest that what needs to be recognized more widely is the extent to which individuals can change over the course of a lifetime. When politicians and other social commenta-tors talk about deprived communities and the problems they face, what tends to get forgotten is that, though their social posi-tion remains unaltered, at least some of the people living in such communities will have travelled a significant psychological dis-tance over the course of their lifetimes, and overcome consider-able adversity in so doing. Although he still lived on the deprived and crime-prone estate on which he had grown up, the Frank we talked to was not the Frank of his youth, still less the man his father had been. Despite his violent upbringing, youthful criminality, fears of being over-run by immigrant foreigners, and (almost) lifelong commitment to the politics of the far right, Frank had held down a job for over twenty years and had never abused, nor sought to dominate, his wife or children. On the contrary, his commitment to his wife and his ability to identify with his children had led him to modify his own behaviour by withdrawing from active involvement in the National Front and going back to study at college at his own expense. Finally, thanks to the intervention of a resilient young woman, he had also managed to confront his own violence and racism and overcome the painful identifications that inspired them. It is these less visible, but still very real, psychological achievements that we believe must be recognized if they are to endure and be matched by others in equally difficult social circumstances.

However, as both Sennett's and Benjamin's analyses make clear, identification is a critical precursor to recognition. The problem with Tony Blair's "respect agenda" was that instead of identifying with the struggles of those in whom they hoped to inculcate a culture of respect, the government sought to deploy a battery of more or less coercive measures against them. Its response to the young person who defined respect as "appreciating someone, even though they're from another country and different" was not to ask why people—particularly those living in "the most disadvantaged communities" at which the *Respect Action Plan* was specifically targeted—might find this hard to do (Respect Task Force, 2006, p. 1). Instead of trying to discover how thwarted ambitions, the shame of dependency, and feelings of neglect, loss, and disappointment might lead many white people in places like Stoke-on-Trent not to respect people perceived to be foreign and different, but to seek social honour in denigrating them, the government resorted to the time-honoured device of directing the hostile feelings of a carefully constructed well-socialized majority towards a disrespectful, anti-social minority. Lost amid the tough political talking about prevention and enforcement was any hope of tackling the roots of violent racism by capitalizing on what Clarke (2003) sees as people's hatred of their hating selves.

Frank's case, like Benjamin's' work, also teaches us that we are dependent on the subjectivity of the denigrated and demonized other to facilitate change—a change which has to be negotiated intersubjectively and cannot simply be dictated top down by the state directing its citizens. The intersubjective negotiation of unconscious meanings and power relationships which recognition entails involve a complex process that is susceptible to defensive resolutions. Nevertheless, we are all exposed to opportunities for recognition, most notably when loved ones are found and lost, when we witness our parents confront their own mortality, and when we identify with the vulnerabilities and strengths of children and young people. In such circumstances, adults are easily confronted by the potency of their own projections, and fantasies, including racist ones, can be exposed for what they are. The more challenging questions, however, are first whether we can expect those on the receiving end of racist projections to help with this work of enabling the perpetrators of racism to survive the unravelling of their psychic defences, and second, whether there is anything which the state—given its tendency to reproduce homogenous constructions of "ethnic minority communities" as victimized, isolationalist, and/or culturally regressive—can contribute to this process. These are questions that we are not fully able to answer here (but see Gobodo-Madikezela (2003) for an indication of what has been possible in post-apartheid South Africa). But perhaps the most positive indication that minority ethnic "victims" can withstand the hostility of their aggressors is the enormous "staying power" shown by those who have migrated to this country (Fryer, 1984). Their desire to live, work, and study in Britain—despite so many attempts to construct them as unworthy, anti-social, and disrespectful—must be part of the recognition process from which all those wedded to racist ideas can benefit when they are forced to confront the psychic defensiveness behind their own prejudices. As for the state, we can only suggest two things. The first of these is that, instead of seeking to construct cohesive communities based on respect for a set of supposedly shared but vaguely defined and inherently controversial rules and values, governments should try to find ways of enabling more people like Frank to come to terms with their past and better equipped to identify with others in spite of (sometimes racialized) social differences. They must also find ways of supporting those, like the young barmaid in Frank's local pub, who, in spite of their exposure to hurtful prejudices and hatred, nevertheless possess the capacity to withstand racialized hostility, contain it, and detoxify it in such a way that it helps transform those most dependent on it.

CHAPTER NINE

Conclusion: losing the race

"Although forgiveness is often regarded as an expression of
weakness, the decision to forgive can paradoxically elevate a
victim to a position of strength as the one who holds the key
to a perpetrator's wish"

(Gobodo-Madikizela, 2003, p. 117)

"To ask for recognition, or to offer it, is precisely not to ask
for recognition of what one already is. It is to solicit a becoming, to instigate a transformation, to petition the future
always in relation to the Other:

(Butler, 2006, p. 44)

The connections between racism and loss have been one of the
main themes of this book. We have argued that getting to
grips with these connections can help us to gain a fuller
understanding of the phenomenon of racially motivated crime, the
contexts in which it occurs, and the circumstances under which the
tangle of psychological and social factors all too commonly but
reductively referred to as "racial motivation" might be unravelled.

In attempting to do this, we started out by drawing on a range of intellectual and empirical resources: the typological, identity, and shame-based approaches to racially motivated offending to be found in the "hate crime" literature; the concept of "institutional racism" adopted by Sir William Macpherson in the Lawrence Inquiry report; the many "why questions" posed by the killing of Stephen Lawrence and other high profile cases; interview-based material derived from research we conducted in and around the city of Stoke-on-Trent; and, finally, our own personal experiences of racism and the difficulties of losing "race" from our everyday thoughts and conversations. We tried to look at racism, loss, and the connections between them in the wider context of white working-class people's perception that they are misunderstood and disrespected, not only by certain minority ethnic groups, but also by their own political leaders. However, we believe that it is important not to limit our search for a clearer understanding of these connections to the conflict between competing interest groups for two reasons: first, because people of similar social backgrounds tend to position themselves rather differently in relation to anti-immigration rhetoric, racism, violence, and feelings of community belonging; second, because we are all inherently conflicted beings, our subjective inner worlds informed by multiple and competing patterns of identification, and by thoughts, fears, and feelings of which we are not always consciously aware.

In Chapter Two, we argued that the critical criminologists of the 1970s were well aware of racism's potential as a source of both unity and division among the white working class. We also saw from the literature reviewed in Chapter One that this insight has been too easily forgotten in the contemporary criminological writing about racially motivated offending. Against this background, it was suggested that the classic studies of prejudice and authoritarianism which had set the parameters for "critical" thinking between the 1940s and 1960s could have shed some intellectual light on this phenomenon had they not been written out of the study of racism by the classed-based sociological analyses that followed in their wake. Drawing on the work of Fromm, Adorno, Frenkel-Brunswik, Levinson, and Sanford, and Allport, we argued that an adequate understanding of racist crime demands a model of the human subject informed by the empirical evidence that demonstrates that racist mindsets are rarely all-encompassing, absolute, and immutable. So, for example, our own research in North Staffordshire, also introduced in Chapter One, yielded many examples of contradictory racist subjects: people who hated "Pakis" but thought that "blacks" and "niggers" were essentially "safe" and "sound"; men with non-white friends, acquaintances, and lovers who claimed that the "only" people they took exception to were "lazy Asians", "asylum seekers", and "Kosovans" (the latter a group of new arrivals neither black, white, nor Asian, who were distinctly difficult to place); offenders from minority ethnic groups who were themselves both victims and perpetrators of racism; white racists capable of expressing the harshest views about asylum seekers and members of settled minority groups generally while feeling grateful to individual Asian doctors and shopkeepers who had been kind to them; BNP activists who condemned acts of racist violence while holding to the belief that "our" culture was in mortal danger; and convicted perpetrators of racially aggravated offences who did not appear to be especially racist. As we explained in Chapter Five, much of the survey and poll evidence concerned with support for the far right points in a similar direction. What is required, then, is a model of the racist subject whose development is much more socially and psychologically contingent than the early studies of prejudice would have us believe, a subject continually working though a shifting catalogue of ethnic referents with meanings rooted in a combination of biographical, vicarious, culturally localized and globally mediated experiences. As we discovered, the role of "race" may be contestable, even in the context of "racially motivated offending" that is intended to be hurtful and is experienced as such by those on its receiving ends.

As we explained in the introduction to this book, this contestability is the source of much of the controversy that arises when it is alleged that an offence is "racially aggravated". One of the reasons why offenders may resign themselves to a conviction for a criminal offence while refusing to accept that their behaviour was racist is that they are often only too aware that the stigmata born by the "racist" are more socially and culturally debilitating than any carried by mere "criminals". At the same time, as our case studies also suggest, many people who say racist things may be oblivious to the offence which their language causes and not consciously aware of the extent of their own psychological dependence on notions of racial difference. Many people cannot stop using ethnic referents because they rely on the symbolism of "race"—the myths of racial difference—to keep at bay a range of psychological injuries from nagging self-doubt to unbearably painful feelings of loss. The apparent capacity of ideas about race to alleviate crises of the self is part of the reason why people's prejudices may seem to come from nowhere, out of the most trivial and fleeting experiences: irritation at an untrustworthy taxi driver; rumours about a sexually aggressive foreign man; the sight of an asylum seeker in a post office queue; or a dark-skinned person wearing an England football shirt; or people speaking quietly in languages other than English. To those most dependent on the symbolism of "race", such trivia may be enough to prompt the wildest generalizations and most fantastical prognoses.

The mutually reinforcing relationship between culturally commonplace expressions of racism and the myriad of meanings—some hostile, some less so—individuals invest in race-thinking are yet another reason why it is almost impossible to distinguish definitively between the perpetrators of hate crime and other, non-criminal members of the communities in which they live. The popular racism in which many people invest as a means of coping with anxiety, loss, and self-doubt relies on a very similar rhetoric to the tropes used by those seeking to justify acts of aggression towards people from ethnic groups other than their own. And these justificatory, neutralizing claims about people who have been abused or attacked may be hard to distinguish from those made by politicians hoping to boost their political standing by "clamping down" on "bogus" asylum seekers, illegal immigration, anti-social behaviour, or "self-segregating" minority ethnic communities. Yet, when we conflate all these behaviours and modes of expression, as the critique of institutional racism has tended to do, we lose sight of the web of subjective meanings which enable the quietly prejudiced patriot to see herself or himself as nothing like the rabble-rousing stump politician (still less the far right extremist), and a world apart from the convicted "hate crime" offender. Ignoring these meanings by focusing on institutional racism as the master narrative of the full range of contemporary prejudices makes it impossible to understand the extremist and the racially aggravated offender in all their psychosocial complexity. What we need to do, rather, is to get behind their words and deeds to what is unsaid, unacknowledged, and unthought and to understand that feelings of hurt and shame may make it impossible for the extremist and the racist offender to reflect on their behaviour, identify and empathize with those affected by it, and respond to them with a greater degree of compassion. As Butler (2009, p. 51) has recently put it, "the critique of violence must begin with the question of the representability of life itself": with "what allows a life to become visible in its precariousness and its need for shelter". This is what we have tried to do in presenting our case study material throughout this book, but most obviously in our lengthy discussion of Nigel's life in Chapter Five.

Summarizing what can be learnt from the mass of case study and focus group material we collated in our own research, we are of the view that the most hostile expressions of racism typically involve the coincidence of multiple failures of containment. There is always the offending individual's failure to keep to themselves— to keep confined within their own mind—feelings of animosity that others would consider too damaging, too unjustified, and too socially unacceptable to articulate. When this animosity is enacted physically, as it is in the case of racist attacks, it is also possible that the feelings involved seemed to the offender as if they could not be contained in language, or in language alone, but instead had to be evacuated immediately from consciousness through violent action. This may be because others involved in the incident, including the victim-to-be, were either unable or unwilling to detoxify the feelings of persecution being experienced by the offender. Sometimes, as our examples from the life story of the man we called Steve (Chapter Three) illustrate, the combined effect of developmental failures of containment across the life course (the failure of the child's carers to instil a capacity to care in her/him, and the inability of friends and lovers to make good that failure) and cultural failures of recognition (such as being the subject of stigmatizing gossip and/or public shaming) are so damaging that those about to be attacked have little or no chance of detoxifying the troubled mindsets of those about to attack them.

While it needs wider empirical validation, our hypothesis is that the lives of many of those who could be considered persistent *hate* crime offenders are distinguished by multiple failures of containment and an acute sense of misrecognition manifested psychologically in acute feelings of persecution and stigmatization, over-riding doubts about self-worth in the face of threats and criticism (many of which have predictably social and economic origins), and an inability to come to terms with such feelings and doubts without resorting to violence. Many of the people who were either referred to us as perpetrators of racially motivated violence or harassment, or revealed themselves to be perpetrators in our focus groups, appeared to fit this pattern, and to be especially susceptible to paranoid–schizoid modes of thinking. They were multiply excluded, frequently destitute or homeless, addicted to drugs and alcohol, mentally ill, children who had grown up suffering abuse which no one had ever really spoken about, young people whose parents had died or left them without explanation, who had themselves been victimized and traumatized only to be perceived as "trouble" by neighbours, teachers, and criminal justice professionals. Almost all of them were people with a reputation for exploding when confronted with (real or imagined) slights, with any sign of misrecognition or disrespect. In so far as they were moved by the experience of us listening to their stories, people who cultivated uncompromisingly harsh (and predominantly, but by no means exclusively, masculine exteriors) often revealed a more vulnerable, desperate, but probably no less dangerous, side to themselves. And herein lies another reason why it is so difficult to distinguish definitively between perpetrators and the communities from which they come: the scars of loss, abuse, humiliation, and estrangement are, in one sense, the inevitable consequences of the hidden injuries of class, race, and gender sustained by many, if not most, of the populations of towns and cities like Stoke-on-Trent, where once thriving industries have closed down, where communities built around the shared experience of industrial production have fractured, and where so little in the way of recognition is offered by local and national political leaders.

As jobs in the pottery, coal, and steel industries disappeared in North Staffordshire, so the stern patriarchal values of industrial working-class life began to lose their grip. Those who found it difficult to cope with this—men like Frank and Nigel, for example, who in their own unique ways were unable to relinquish their identifications with severe and emotionally distant fathers—came to blame the outsiders who were moving in for what was happening to "their" city, rather than appear disloyal to kith and kin. "Class and its hurts" became, in Frost and Hoggett's words (2008, p. 443), "highly fantasized spaces", easily occupied by racism. In time, people like Frank were able to move out of these spaces, at least for some of the time. But others, such as Nigel, were rarely able to escape, because the hurts they had endured were so psychologically crippling. And the longer they stayed, the more afraid they became of what leaving might lead them to discover about themselves.

We believe that our interviewee Steve (Chapter Three) was becoming locked into this way of thinking, resigned as he seemed to be to his reputation as the "bastard of Basford Green". The extreme hostility expressed by some of the participants in our focus groups—Gary and Ben (Chapter Four), Trevor and Helen (Chapter Five), and Rita and Mavis (Chapter Six)—suggested that they, too, were liable to be swept up into the spiralling projection that sustains racist fantasies within social groups. We also suspect that at least some of the men suspected of killing Stephen Lawrence still think in this way, and feel sure that Robert Stewart, the man who murdered Zahid Mubarek, had got to a point where he no longer felt able to escape the convoluted logic of his own racist fantasies. Stewart had become emotionally unreachable by everyone who knew him, and untreatable in the eyes of psychiatric and criminal justice professionals. He was the kind of person clinicians Chris Scanlon and John Adlams (2008) describe as having an "un-housed mind"; someone who felt so stigmatised, debased, violated, and dispossessed that he refused to be touched, however much people tried to reach out to him. Scanlon and Adlams explain how the energies of the un-housed become focused on unsettling all those who try to help them, forcing professionals who could contain and detoxify their feelings to displace their trauma on to other clients and fellow workers. As the Keith Inquiry was to reveal, such psychosocial dynamics were a feature of Feltham Young Offenders Institute at the time of Zahid Mubarek's murder. It was a place where staff at all levels were demoralized, where managers had given up caring about the problems faced by their subordinates, and where some junior staff seemed to have taken pleasure in witnessing the suffering of the young people in their care.

The hatred expressed by Zahid Mubarek's murderer has to be understood in this institutional context, but we must also be careful to remember that Robert Stewart's racism was not the racism of most other "racially motivated offenders". There was much more that was unconscious and sexualized in his thought processes than is the case with the majority of people involved in perpetrating what the police record as "racist incidents". Nevertheless, we believe that there are lessons to be learnt from the case of Robert Stewart; lessons that help to explain why some "hate crime" victims are surprisingly close to those who offend against them. Because of the acutely painful losses of love that characterized his own life, Robert Stewart was more desperate than many men to avoid feelings of emotional dependency. But, as the late Ian Craib (1998) has observed, like most men, the more Stewart repressed his dependency needs the more they made themselves known to him.

> An experience of empathy, of closeness, can reawaken the feelings of . . . threatened dependency. The failure of the other to meet these needs . . . can produce a narcissistic, envious rage . . . Dependency needs and the associated feelings of rage and destructiveness are experienced as existing in, and are perhaps even elicited from, others. [Craib, 1998, p. 95]

Our argument is that Stewart experienced his dependency needs as living in Zahid Mubarek and attempted to kill them off there. Stewart projected his destructiveness into his cellmate, who became the unfortunate target of his narcissistic, envious rage.

Thinking about the aetiology of hate in this way not only helps us to grasp why Robert Stewart killed one of the few people in whom he was still able to confide, but also provides us with the beginnings of an answer to the question posed by the Mubarek family's barrister about why this country keeps producing men like Robert Stewart. Put simply, we suggest that the compounding of hurt, loss, and estrangement with experiences of abuse, neglect, and the sundry failures of institutional care are too much for some young men to bear. The culturally tough, hateful masculine identities in which some young men invest in order to deal with this pain lock them into a spiralling process of projective identification, the force of which is too easily, if inadvertently, unleashed by those seeking to restrain it. When it is released, these hostile projective identifications inflict the torment felt by the perpetrator on to the victim, who then appears to be the source of that torment in an intersubjective process than can leave the offender feeling even more persecuted than before. As Rustin (2000) and Clarke's (2003) adaptations of Klein's work both show, people in paranoid–schizoid frames of mind tend to find it hard to accept that their thoughts, words, and deeds hurt more than other people's. Confronting them with this knowledge only compounds the feelings of persecution that fuels their hatred. This is part of the reason why, even when its deterrent and denunciatory message(s) can be can be heard above the cacophony of other, conflicting communications people receive about minority ethnic groups in Britain, anti-hate crime laws have not succeeded in reducing the incidence of racially motivated crime.

We have also argued, in relation to both the "community cohesion" (Chapter Six) and the "respect" (Chapter Eight) agendas, that successive governments have failed to understand the needs of young people while treating them as either vehicles for, or targets of, doomed policy initiatives. In Chapter Six, we saw how the promise of "social inclusion" made to the young British Pakistani men we interviewed remained unfulfilled, and how they, their families, and other people like them were then blamed for creating "self-segregating" communities. Then, in Chapter Eight, we argued that the government elected in 2005, while demanding that the "anti-social" offspring of "problem families" respect the values of the moral majority, showed little concern for white working-class young people in places like Stoke-on-Trent, who felt unseen, ignored, and left behind. The analyses of focus group discussions we presented in Chapters Four, Five, and Six suggests that there are many people, young and old, from within communities who feel this way who would join with members of professional groups in trying to detoxify some of the hateful feelings felt by their peers, but who struggle to do so in a context in which many have good cause to feel aggrieved, where successive losses of economic standing and cultural history have not been made good, where other-denigrating codes of honour are so readily and widely adopted, and when "uncontrolled" immigration and the threat of the "outsider" are the staples of populist politics. In the halcyon days of Fleet Street, journalists used to say that "If a dog bites a man in Bond Street, that's news: if a man bites a dog in . . . Stoke-on-Trent that is merely to be expected" (Taylor, 2001, p. 127). Too many people living in Stoke-on-Trent, and places like it, suspect that the rest of the world still sees them in this way. It is in this context that those, like the BNP, who are able to position themselves as political outlaws, and to identify with the losses felt by local people, are able to gain widespread support and a degree of respectability, however extreme and illusory some of their proposed solutions to social problems may be.

But what will it take to change the minds of people who have become—as Allport expressed it—"lockstitched" into prejudiced ways of thinking? As Barack Obama's election to the USA's presidency has illustrated, dislodging assumptions about white privilege, unravelling hateful mindsets, and losing race from our language and thought processes are not necessarily the same thing. For some of those who opposed Obama, the (for them) unthinkable prospect of having "a black man in the White House" was their primary reason to campaign against him. That his surname rhymes with Osama (bin Laden) and "Hussein"—his second given name—hints conveniently at a Middle Eastern and Islamic heritage was seized on by opponents who sought to portray him as an alien whose election would compromise national security at the height of America's "war on terror". For some of his supporters, too, and for much of the media, the most important thing was that Obama was black, the first African-American to make a serious (and ultimately successful) run for the highest office. Yet, for others, who did not cleave to the "one drop rule", what mattered was that Obama was both black and white, of mixed ethnic and religious heritage, a living embodiment of America as a functioning, pluralistic, multi-ethnic society. But "race" was by no means the central issue for everyone, and there were those who saw the campaign as an opportunity to come to terms, and to defeat the hateful pseudo-patriotism that had come to define the Bush administration in the aftermath of the terrorist attacks of 11 September 2001, much as the emergence of authoritarian personalities had troubled Adorno, Frenkel-Brunswik, Levinson, and Sanford in 1950s America. Whether he lives up to it or not, Obama's (2009) promise at his inauguration was to re-engage with America's enemies—"we will extend a hand if you are willing to unclench your fist"—in terms which promised to unravel the spiralling hatred that has come to define the war on terror.

It is rare to witness what Clarke (2003) refers to as the "hate for the hating self" working itself through at a societal, perhaps even global, level in this way, hence our reliance in this book on some psychoanalytically informed work on post-apartheid South Africa. At the level of the individual, change can be easier to detect even if it is less dramatic and far-reaching in its consequences. The case study of Frank, the far right activist we discussed in Chapter Eight, illustrates how such a change can happen. A shoplifter and violent racist turned neighbourhood vigilante, the profound but partial transformation we saw in Frank's life story may be as good as it gets for many reforming racially motivated offenders (Gadd, 2006). Frank was probably never going to lose the race from his language, nor was he ever likely to move on from his long-standing investment in meeting violence with violence. But the disgust that he felt when he realized that two minority ethnic women whom he liked and cared about had voted for him as a candidate for a party that would not accept them as members was evidence enough that he had begun to mourn the loss of the "dead racist" father with whom he had identified so closely. Critically, this transformation depended both on Frank's capacity to reidentify with his own childish vulnerability and the remarkable ability of the younger of the two women to survive Frank's othering, to reject the racialized victim status imputed to her, and to see beyond Frank's political affiliation and judge the character of the man for herself. Benjamin (1998, p. 99) would say that this "is the difference the Other can make, precisely because the Other insists on being a subject, not simply attacking the other's subjectivity". It is also a good illustration of why, as Pumla Gobodo-Madikezela (2003, pp. 125–126) insists, one needs to "look the enemy in the eye and allow oneself to read signs of pain and cues to contrition or regret where one might have preferred to continue seeing only hatred". Only if we are prepared to do so, she argues, will we realize possibilities for "steering *individuals* and *societies* towards replacing long standing stalemates out of a nation's past with genuine engagements" (*ibid.*, our emphases).

As we have implied in various parts of this book, the trouble is that popular and political reactions to immigration and diversity in Britain over the past decade have tended to reduce the capacity of victimized groups to establish themselves as sovereign others able to look those who attack them in the eye. How, for example, can we expect British Muslims to recognize the hidden injuries of white working-class racists when they, too, remain one of the most disadvantaged sections of the British population in terms of educational attainment, employment opportunities, and experiences of criminal justice; when they, too, feel themselves to have been unjustly demonized, and when the so-called "war on terror" can seem so hard to distinguish from a "war on Muslims". As Hussain and Bagguley (2006) express it,

> The image of Muslims is that they are irrational fundamentalists, with the book burning of the Rushdie affair being taken as an illustration of this. Now they are also associated with terrorism, and the imprisonment of British Muslims in Guantanamo Bay is seen as proof of this. Increasingly Muslims have found themselves identified in a polarised way, as either terrorists opposed to the West or as apologists for Islam as a peaceful religion. [p. 3]

The excerpts from our discussion with a group of young Asian men we looked at in Chapter Six reveal that this kind of rhetorical polarization may sow the seeds for the splitting and projection on which paranoid–schizoid ways of thinking thrive. The experience of being racially abused and then corralled on a football pitch in Stoke-on-Trent felt like warfare to Tariq, Omar, Ali, Imran, and Mohammed. Indeed, they regarded this abuse, and the way in which they had been treated at an event intended to promote "community cohesion", as evidence that they were already at war with a white population that saw them as "the enemy within".

Necessary though it may be to respond to such incidents by defining them as racist, and dealing with those involved as racially aggravated offenders, defining their behaviour in this way, and punishing it more severely as a result, may do little to alter the racist mindsets of the young white people who abused Tariq and his friends. This was brought home to us when we met a young man—we will call him Wayne—at a youth centre where we held one of our focus groups. Wayne was an angry young man who refused to take part in the discussion. He had recently been involved in an incident outside an Asian family's home during the course of which he had spat at someone or something. Convicted of a racially aggravated offence, he claimed that he had never been a racist before the incident—"only spitting", as he described it—but was proud to be one now, unashamed about hating "Pakis" and "Kosovans" in general, and Asian women—"They're muppets"—in particular. Changing racist mindsets requires a great deal more than the criminal justice process is able to offer. Above all, it requires that we help offenders to find a route out of racism that enables them to come to terms with the hurt they have caused, make amends for it, and relinquish the stigma of being a "racist" as opposed to finding strength in it. In order to tackle the hostility that motivates many racist attacks, we need to find ways of allowing victims and offenders opportunities to re-engage with each other intersubjectively. If we want offenders to lose the race from their thoughts and actions, it may be necessary for victims, or those who can plausibly represent them, to seek out "signs of pain and cues to contrition or regret" among enduring "hatred", and to begin the difficult process of identifying with perpetrators and potential perpetrators in ways that are not mediated by the markers of "race" and the fear of violence (Gobodo-Madikezela, 2003, p. 126). In many ways, this is much more than the perpetrators of hate crimes are entitled to ask, and may well be too much to ask of those who are their victims. As Butler remarks,

> [I]t is most difficult when in a state of pain to stay responsive to the equal claim of the other for shelter, for conditions of livability and grievability. And yet, this vexed domain is the site of a necessary struggle . . . [Butler, 2009, p. 184]

For us, the pain that this working through entails has to be balanced against the consequences of surrendering the problem to the criminal justice system; of persisting with a process which tends to condemn and exclude the small minority of offenders who are successfully prosecuted and punished for racially aggravated offences, in much the same way that generations of immigrants to Britain have been condemned and excluded, leaving them more outraged, more embittered, and no less racist than ever.

What struck us as we came to the end of our research were the similarities between the experiences of many perpetrators and those of the asylum seekers being moved to North Staffordshire as part of the government's dispersal policy: members of both groups had been separated from their families, found themselves unable to

230   LOSING THE RACE

work or support themselves, and had experienced homelessness, criminal victimization, and unwanted attention from the police. We became convinced that with help, and without being made to feel too defensive, many of the white people we had met who had been openly hostile to "Pakis", "Kosovans", and "asylum seekers" might come to realize how much they had in common with those they hated and feared. Indeed, some of the people we spoke to in our focus groups who had experienced warmth, generosity, or affection from those they might otherwise have regarded as outsiders had been so changed by these experiences that they felt uncomfortable about indulging in the wild generalizations of their peers. But, too often, they also lacked the opportunities to make their voices heard and felt reluctant to explain themselves through fear of being shouted down and humiliated by their friends and neighbours.

In all of this we found much evidence to support Gilroy's (2004) hypothesis that British reactions to "race" are profoundly melancholic, that too many of us are so saddled with the legacy of empire that we have become dependent on new forms of xenophobia that do nothing to relieve our feelings of loss and do enormous damage to "others" we fear and despise. Without wishing to downplay the harm caused by racially motivated crime, we want to stress that this chronic melancholia is not the only future on offer. Among those who perpetrate hate crimes, there are a disproportionate number of dangerous but emotionally troubled and socially disadvantaged young people who perceive themselves to have been cast out from communities which are themselves living with an acute sense of loss and where many feel stigmatized as cultural and economic failures. If we are to help people in these positions shake off their dependence on racism, we must find ways of assisting them to mourn the losses that contribute to their hatefulness without feeling destroyed by them. If we are to stand a chance of losing the race from our everyday thoughts, words, and behaviours, a tangled, self-perpetuating web of projective identifications will need to be contained and unpicked knot by knot, generation by generation. It is a formidable task, but not an impossible one. Deeply ingrained prejudices can rarely be undone without a level of emotional engagement, without experiences of shame, guilt, longing, and loss being worked through, and without the psychological investments in race-thinking becoming less valuable than a solidarity born of shared experiences. It is in the nature of prejudice that it does emotional work for those invested in it. Investments in racism cannot be undone without re-engaging the racists with the racialized. That much is clear. But it is in the nature of humanity—including the humanity of even the most committed of violent racists—to want to feel recognized, not only for who one is, but who one might have been under different circumstances, and who one might still become if those capable of surviving the effects of racism are willing and able to identify with a desire to change.

REFERENCES

Adorno, T., Frenkel-Brunswik, E., Levinson, D., & Sanford, R. N. (1950). *The Authoritarian Personality*. New York: Harper & Row.

Alexander, C. (2004). Imagining the Asian gang: ethnicity, masculinity and youth after "the riots". *Critical Social Policy*, 24(4): 526–549.

Allport, G. (1954). *The Nature of Prejudice*. New York: Doubleday Anchor Books.

Altemeyer, B. (1988). *Enemies of Freedom: Understanding Right-Wing Authoritarianism*. San Francisco, CA: Jossey-Bass.

Amin, I. (2006). Words from the Mubarek family. In: M. Gergides, M. Willers, R. Sikand, R. Lachman, & J. Lowe (Eds.), *Zahid Mubarek: A Legacy for Change* (pp. 4–5). London: Garden Court Chambers.

Ashworth, A. (1998). Deterrence. In: A. von Hirsch & A. Ashworth (Eds.), *Principled Sentencing: Readings on Theory & Policy* (pp. 44–52). Oxford: Hart.

August, B. (2007). *Goodbye Bafana*. Film.

Back, L. (2004). Writing in and against time. In: M. Bulmer & J. Solomos (Eds.), *Researching Race and Racism* (pp. 203–213). London: Routledge.

Back, L., & Keith, M. (1999). "Rights and wrongs": youth community and narratives of racial violence. In: P. Cohen (Ed.), *New Ethnicities, Old Racisms* (pp. 131–53). London: Zed Books.

Bagguley, P., & Hussain, Y. (2008). *Riotous Citizens*. Aldershort: Ashgate.

Bamber, D., & Syal, R. (2001). Riot flares in Stoke as BNP stirs hate. *Daily Telegraph*, 15 July.

BBC (2004). *The Secret Agent* [Television broadcast]. First broadcast on *Newsnight*, BBC2, 15 July, 2004.

BBC News Channel (2006). "Victory for freedom" claims BNP, 10 November, http://news.bbc.co.uk/1/hi/england/bradford/6137986.stm (last accessed 5 March 2009).

Benjamin, J. (1998). *Shadow of the Other*. London: Routledge.

Benjamin, J. (2006). Two way streets: recognition of difference and the intersubjective third. *Differences*, 17(1): 116–146.

Berk, R., Boyd, E., & Hamner, K. (2003). Thinking more clearly about hate-motivated crimes. In: B. Perry (Ed.), *Hate and Bias Crime* (pp. 49–60). New York: Routledge.

Bhavnani, R., Mirza, H., & Meetoo, V. (2005). *Tackling the Roots of Racism*. Bristol: Policy Press.

Bhui, H. (2008a). Foreign national prisoners. In: H. Bhui (Ed.), *Race and the Criminal Justice System* (pp. 154–169). London: Sage.

Bhui, H. (2008b). Prisons and race equality. In: H. S. Bhui (Ed.), *Race and the Criminal Justice System* (pp. 83–102). London: Sage.

Billig, M. (1978). *Fascists: A Social Psychological View of the National Front*. London: Academic Press.

Bion, W. (1984). *Second Thoughts*. London: Karnac.

Blair, T. (2006). *Respect Agenda*, news.bbc.co.uk/1/hi/uk_politics/4600156.stm (last accessed 11 March 2009).

Blunkett, D. (2005). A new England: an English identity within Britain (Speech delivered to the Institute for Public Policy Research, 14 March), www.efdss.org/newengland.pdf (last accessed 27 July 2009).

Bosworth, M., & Guild, M. (2008). Governing through migration control. *British Journal of Criminology*, 48(6): 703–719.

Bourne, J. (2002). Commentary: Does legislating against racist violence work? *Race and Class*, 44(2): 81–85.

Bowling, B. (1998). *Violent Racism: Victimization, Policing and Social Context*. Oxford: Oxford University Press.

Bowling, B., & Phillips, C. (2002). *Racism, Crime and Justice*. Harlow: Longman.

Bowling, B., & Phillips, C. (2007). Disproportionate and discriminatory: reviewing the evidence on police stop and search. *Modern Law Review*, 70(6): 936–961.

Brennan, F. (1999). Crime and Disorder Act 1998: racially motivated crime: the response of the criminal justice system. *Criminal Law Review*, January: 17–28.

Bridges, L. (2001). Race, law and state. *Race & Class*, 43(2): 61–76.

Burnett, J. (2004). Community, cohesion and the state. *Race & Class*, 45(3): 1–18.

Burney, E. (2003). Using the law on racially aggravated offences. *Criminal Law Review*, January: 28–36.

Burney, E., & Rose. G. (2002). *Racist Offences—How is the Law Working?* London: Home Office.

Butler, J. (2006). *Precarious Life: The Powers of Mourning and Violence*. London: Verso.

Butler, J. (2009). *Frames of War: When is Live Grievable?* London: Verso.

Cantle, T. (2001). *Community Cohesion: A Report of the Independent Review Team*. London: Home Office.

Casciani, D. (2006a). *The Murder of Zahid Mubarek*, BBC News Channel 29 June, http://news.bbc.co.uk/1/hi/uk/3198264.stm (last accessed 26 July 2010).

Casciani, D. (2006b). *Q&A: Respect Agenda*, BBC News Channel, 11 January, http://news.bbc.co.uk/1/hi/uk/4597378.stm (last accessed 11 March 2009).

Cathcart, B. (1999). *The Case of Stephen Lawrence*. London: Viking.

Cheng, A. (2007). Intimate refusals: a politics of objecthood. In: M. Suchet, A. Harris, & L. Aron (Eds.), *Relational Psychoanalysis Volume 3* (pp. 135–150). London: Analytic Press.

Clarke, S. (2003). *Social Theory, Psychoanalysis and Racism*. Basingstoke: Palgrave Macmillan.

Clarke, T. (2001). *Burnley Speaks, Who Listens?* Burnley: Burnley Task Force.

Coetzee, J. (1999). *Disgrace*. London: Vintage.

Collins, M. (2004). *The Likes of Us*. London: Granta.

Copsey, N. (2004). *Contemporary British Fascism: The British National Party and the Quest for Legitimacy*. Basingstoke: Palgrave Macmillan.

Craib, I. (1998). *Psychoanalysis: A Critical Introduction*. Cambridge: Polity.

Crawford, A., Jones, T., Woodhouse, T., & Young, J. (1989). *The Second Islington Crime Survey*. London: Middlesex Polytechnic Centre for Criminology.

Crisp, R., & Tuner, R. (2007). *Essential Social Psychology*. London: Sage.

Dalal, F. (2002). *Race, Colour and the Process of Racialization*. London: Routledge.

Denham, J. (2002). *Building Cohesive Communities: A Report of the Ministerial Group on Public Order*. London: Home Office.

Denham, J. (2006). Uncomfortable truths. *Guardian Online*, 17 May, www.guardian.co.uk/comment/story/0,,1777023,00.html (last accessed 12 January 2009).

Deo, R. S. (2004). Psychiatric report on Robert Joseph Stewart. Expert testimony presented to the Zahid Mubarek Inquiry, http://a1538.g.akamai.net/7/1538/13355/v001/homeoffice.download.akamai.com/13355/Page/1011/101101426.pdf and http://a1538.g.akamai.net/7/1538/13355/v001/homeoffice.download.akamai.com/13355/Page/1011/101101430.pdf (last accessed 26 July 2010).

Diamond, M. (1998). Fathers with sons: psychoanalytic perspectives on "good enough" fathering throughout the life cycle. *Gender and Psychoanalysis*, 3(3): 248–299.

Dias, D. (2006). Zahid's inquiry. In: M. Gergides, M. Willers, M. Sikand, R. Lachman, & J. Lowe (Eds.), *Zahid Mubarek: A Legacy for Change* (pp. 6–7). London: Garden Court Chambers.

Dixon, B., & Gadd, D. (2006). Getting the message? "New" Labour and the criminalization of "hate". *Criminology and Criminal Justice*, 6(2): 309–328.

Dixon, L. (2002). Tackling racist offending: a generalized or targeted approach. *Probation Journal*, 49(3): 205–216.

Dobbs, J., Green, H., & Zealey, L. (2006). *Focus on Ethnicity and Religion*. Office for National Statistics/Palgrave Macmillan, www.statistics.gov.uk/downloads/theme_compendia/foer2006/FoER_Main.pdf (last accessed 12 January 2009).

Docking, M., & Tuffin, R. (2005). *Racist Incidents: Progress since the Lawrence Inquiry*. Home Office Online Report 42/05. London: Home Office, www.homeoffice.gov.uk/rds/pdfs05/rdsolr4205.pdf (last accessed 27 July 2009).

Dodd, V. (2001). Stoke riot sparked by false rumour. *Guardian*, 16 July, www.guardian.co.uk/uk/2001/jul/16/race.world (last accessed 29 July 2009).

Dodd, V. (2009). Anti-terror code "would alienate most Muslims". *Guardian*, 17 February, www.guardian.co.uk/politics/2009/feb/17/counterterrorism-strategy-muslims (last accessed 29 July 2009).

Edgar, K. (2007). Black and minority ethnic prisoners. In: Y. Jewkes (Ed.), *Handbook on Prisons* (pp. 268–293). Cullompton: Willan.

Ehrlich, H., Larcom, B., & Purvis, R. (2003). The traumatic effects of ethnoviolence. In: B. Perry (Ed.), *Hate and Bias Crime* (pp. 153–170). New York: Routledge.

Engels, F. (1958). *The Condition of the Working Class in England*. Stanford, CA: Stanford University Press.

Ferrell, J., Hayward, K., & Young, J. (2008). *Cultural Criminology*. London: Sage.

Fielding, N. (1981). *The National Front*. London: Routledge & Kegan Paul.

FitzGerald, M. (2001). Ethnic minorities and community safety. In: R. Matthews & J. Pitts (Eds.), *Crime, Disorder and Community Safety* (pp. 145–66). London: Routledge.

Ford, R. (2008). Gordon Brown ditches Respect agenda on youth crime. *The Times*, 11 January, www.timesonline.co.uk/tol/news/politics/article3168611.ece (last accessed 11 March 2009)

Foster, J., Newburn, T., & Souhami, A. (2005). *Assessing the Impact of the Stephen Lawrence Inquiry*. Home Office Research Study 294. London: Home Office.

French, S., & Möhrke, J. (2007). *The Impact of 'New Arrivals' on the North Staffordshire Labour Market*. Report to the Low Pay Commission, www.lowpay.gov.uk/lowpay/research/pdf/t0z96gk3.pdf (last accessed 12 January 2009).

Freud, S. (1917e). Mourning and melancholia. *S.E., 14*; 237–258). London: Hogarth Press.

Fromm, E. (2001)[1942]. *The Fear of Freedom*. London: Routledge & Kegan Paul.

Frosh, S. (1997). *For and Against Psychoanalysis*. London: Routledge.

Frost, L., & Hoggett, P. (2008). Human agency and social suffering. *Critical Social Policy, 28*(4): 438–460.

Fryer, P. (1984). *Staying Power: The History of Black People in Britain*. London: Pluto.

Gadd, D. (2006). The role of recognition in the desistance process: a case study of a far-right activist. *Theoretical Criminology, 10*(2): 179–202.

Gadd, D. (2009). Aggravating racism and elusive motivation *British Journal of Criminology, 49*(6): 755–771, doi:10.1093/bjc/azp046.

Gadd, D. (2010). Racial hatred and unmourned loss. *Sociological Research Online, 15*(3), http://www.socresonline.org.uk/15/3/9.html.

Gadd, D., & Jefferson, T. (2007). *Psychosocial Criminology*. London: Sage.

Gadd, D., Dixon, B., & Jefferson T. (2005). *Why Do They Do It? Racial Harassment in North Staffordshire*. Keele: Centre for Criminological Research, Keele University.

Garland, D. (2002). Of crimes and criminals. In: M. Maguire, R. Morgan, & R. Reiner (Eds.), *The Oxford Handbook of Criminology* (3rd edn) (pp. 7–50). Oxford: Oxford University Press.

Garland, J., & Chakraborti, N. (2004). Introduction: justifying the study of racism in the rural. In: J. Garland & N. Chakraborti (Eds.), *Rural Racism* (pp. 1–14). Cullompton: Willan.

Gau, S.-F., & Soong, W.-T. (1999). Psychiatric co-morbidity of adolescents with sleep terrors or sleepwalking: a case control study. *Australian and New Zealand Journal of Psychiatry, 33*(5): 734–739.

Giddens, A. (1998). *The Third Way: The Renewal of Social Democracy.* Cambridge: Polity.

Gilligan, J. (2000). *Violence: Reflections on Our Deadliest Epidemic.* London: Jessica Kingsley.

Gilroy, P. (1987). The myth of black criminality. In: P. Scraton (Ed.), *Law, Order and the Authoritarian State* (pp. 107–120). Milton Keynes: Open University Press.

Gilroy, P. (2003). *There Ain't No Black in the Union Jack: The Cultural Politics of Race and Nation* (2nd edn). London: Routledge.

Gilroy, P. (2004). *After Empire: Melancholia or Convivial Culture?* London: Routledge.

Gobodo-Madikizela, P. (2003). *A Human Being Died That Night.* Cape Town: David Philip.

Gordon, P. (1983). *White Law: Racism in the Police, Courts and Prisons.* London: Pluto Press.

Grattet, R., & Jenness, V. (2001). The birth and maturation of hate crime policy in the United States. *American Behavioral Scientist, 45*(4): 668–696.

Grover, S. (2006). From Lawrence to Mubarek: lost lives, squandered opportunities? In: M. Gergides, M. Willers, M. Sikand, R. Lachman, & J. Lowe (Eds.), *Zahid Mubarek: A Legacy for Change* (pp. 8–9). London: Garden Court Chambers.

Guardian (1999a). Jamie Acourt's evidence to the Lawrence Inquiry, 30 January, www.guardian.co.uk/uk/1999/jan/30/lawrence.uk crime6 (last accessed 25 February 2008).

Guardian (1999b). The mothers' defence: "Saying silly things, that's all it was", 19 February, www.guardian.co.uk/lawrence/Story/0,, 208288,00.html (last accessed 27 February 2008).

Gunn, J. (2004). Report to the Zahid Mubarek Inquiry. *Expert Opinion Submitted to the Zahid Mubarek Enquiry*, http://a1538.g.akamai.net/ 7/1538/13355/v001/homeoffice.download.akamai.com/13355/ Doc/1013/101301806.pdf (last accessed 26 July 2010).

Gupta, T. (2005). *Gladiator Games*. Sheffield: Oberon Modern Plays.

Haddad, P. M. (1990). Discharge letter to Dr A Frazer, Consultant in Child and Adolescent Psychiatry, *Evidence Presented to the Zahid Mubarek Inquiry*, http://a1538.g.akamai.net/7/1538/13355/v001/homeoffice.download.akamai.com/13355/Doc/1011/101109393.pdf (last accessed 26 July 2010).

Hall, S. (1999). From Scarman to Stephen Lawrence. *History Workshop Journal, 48*: 187–197.

Hall, S. (1980). *Drifting Into a Law and Order Society*. London: Cobden Trust.

Hall, S., Critcher, C., Jefferson, T., Clarke, J., & Roberts, B. (1978). *Policing the Crisis*. Basingstoke: Macmillan.

Hare, I. (1997). Legislating against hate—the legal response to bias crime. *Oxford Journal of Legal Studies, 17*(3): 415–439.

Hendricks, C. (2001). "Ominous" liaisons: tracing the interface between "race" and sex at the Cape. In: Z. Erasmus (Ed.), *Coloured by History, Shaped by Place: New Perspectives on Coloured Identities in Cape Town* (pp. 29–44). Cape Town: Kwela Books.

Hewitt, R. (1996). *Routes of Racism*. Stoke-on-Trent: Trentham Books.

Hinshelwood, R. (1991). *A Dictionary of KleinianThought*. London: Free Association Books.

Holdaway, S., & O'Neil, M. (2004). Institutional racism after Macpherson: an analysis of police views. *Policing & Society, 16*(4): 349–369.

Hollway, W. (2006). *The Capacity to Care*. London: Routledge.

Hollway, W., & Jefferson, T. (2000). *Doing Qualitative Research Differently*. London: Sage.

Home Office (1981). *Racial Attacks*. London: Home Office.

Home Office (2003). *Community Cohesion Pathfinder Dissemination Programme: Finding New Routes Into Local Communities*. Report of the National Conference, 27 November 2003, http://www.homeoffice.gov.uk/documents/findingnewroutes.pdf (last accessed 12 January 2009).

Home Office (2004). *Strength in Diversity: Towards a Community Cohesion and Race Equality Strategy*. London: Home Office, http://www.homeoffice.gov.uk/documents/cons-strength-in-diverse-170904/strength-in-diversity-adults?view=Binary (last accessed 12 January 2009).

Home Office (2005). *Improving Opportunity, Strengthening Society: The Government's Strategy to Increase Race Equality and Community Cohesion*. London: Home Office.

Honneth, A. (2007). *Disrespect*. Cambridge: Polity.

Hudson, B. (2006). Beyond white man's justice: race, gender and justice in late modernity. *Theoretical Criminology*, 10(1): 29–47.

Hussain, Y., & Bagguley, P. (2006). Muslim responses to the 7/7 London bombings, invited presentation to the seminar on *Terrorism and Diaspora*, the RAND Corporation, Washington DC, April 2006.

Hyatt Williams, A. (1998). *Violence, Cruelty and Murder*. London: Karnac.

Ifekwunigwe, J. (1998). *Scattered Belongings: Cultural Paradoxes of "Race", Nation and Gender*. London: Routledge.

Iganski, P. (1999). Why make "hate" a crime? *Critical Social Policy*, 19(3): 386–395.

Iganski, P. (2002). Hate crimes hurt more, but should they be more harshly punished? In: P. Iganski (Ed.), *The Hate Debate* (pp. 132–144). London: Profile Books / Institute for Jewish Policy Research.

Iganski, P. (2003). Hate crimes hurt more. In: B. Perry (Ed.), *Hate and Bias Crime* (pp. 131–138). New York: Routledge.

Iganski, P. (2008). *Hate Crime and the City*. Bristol: Policy Press.

Institute of Race Relations (2008). *Deaths with a (Known or Suspected) Racial Element 2000 Onwards*, www.irr.org.uk/2002/november/ak000008.html (last accessed 28 July 2009).

Jackson, D., & Pratt, S. (2001). The fear of being seen as white losers. *Education and Social Justice*, 3(2): 25–29.

Jacobs, J. (1998). The emergence and implications of American hate crime jurisprudence. In: R. Kelly & J. Maghan (Eds.), *Hate Crime: The Global Politics of Polarization* (pp. 150–176). Carbondale, IL: Southern Illinois University Press.

Jacobs, J. (2002). Hate crime: criminal law and identity politics—author's summary'. *Theoretical Criminology*, 6(4): 481–484.

Jacobs, J., & Potter, K. (1998). *Hate Crime: Criminal Law and Identity Politics*. New York: Oxford University Press.

Jenness, V. (2002). Contours of hate crime law and politics in the United States. In: P. Iganski (Ed.), *The Hate Debate* (pp. 15–35). London: Profile Books / Institute for Jewish Policy Research.

Jenness, V. (2004). The dilemma of difference: gender and hate crime policy. In: A. Ferber (Ed), *Home Grown Hate: Gender and Organized Racism* (pp. 181–204). London: Routledge.

Jenness, V., & Broad, K. (1997). *Hate Crimes: New Social Movements and the Politics of Violence*. New York: De Gruyter.

Jones, T., MacLean, B., & Young, J. (1986). *The Islington Crime Survey*. Aldershot: Gower.

Joseph, P. (2000). Confidential psychiatric report on Robert Stewart, DOB 4/8/80, 17 October 2000. *Evidence Presented to the Zahid Mubarek Inquiry*, http://a1538.g.akamai.net/7/1538/13355/v001/home office.download.akamai.com/13355/Page/1011/101101484. pdf and http://a1538.g.akamai.net/7/1538/13355/v001/home office.download.akamai.com/13355/Page/1011/101101489. pdf (last accessed 29 July 2009).

Joseph Rowntree Charitable Trust (2004). *539 Voters' Views: A Voting Behaviour Study in Three Northern Towns*. York: The Joseph Rowntree Charitable Trust.

Judd, T. (2005). How an angelic-looking child turned into a psychopathic racist who murdered a cell-mate. The *Independent*, 12 March.

Kalra, V., Kaur, R., & Hutnyk, J. (2005). *Diaspora and Hybridity*. London: Sage.

Keith, B. (2006a). *Report of the Zahid Mubarek Inquiry*. London: Her Majesty's Stationery Office.

Keith, B. (2006b). *The Zahid Mubarek Inquiry: Summary and Recommendations*. London: Her Majesty's Stationery Office.

Keith, M. (1993). *Race, Riots and Policing*. London: University College London Press.

Kelso, P. (2000). His crime was theft. He paid with his life, murdered by a rabid racist. *Guardian*, 2 November, www.guardian.co.uk/uk/2000/nov/02/race.world (last accessed 28 July 2009).

Khan, I. (2006). Foreword. In: M. Gergides, M. Willers, M. Sikand, R. Lachman, & J. Lowe (Eds.), *Zahid Mubarek: a Legacy for Change* (p. 3). London: Garden Court Chambers.

Kinsey, R. (1984). *Merseyside Crime Survey*. Edinburgh: Centre for Criminology, University of Edinburgh.

Klein, M. (1935). A contribution to the psychogenesis of manic-depressive states. *International Journal of Psycho-Analysis, 16*: 145–147.

Klein, M. (1940). Mourning and its relationship with manic-depressive states. *International Journal of Psychoanalysis, 12*: 47–82.

Klein, M. (1945). The Oedipus complex in the light of early anxieties. *International Journal of Psychoanalysis, 26*: 11–33.

Klein, M. (1946). Notes on some schizoid mechanisms. In: P. Du Gay, J. Evans, & P. Redman (Eds.), *Identity: A Reader* (pp. 130–143). London: Sage, 2000.

Klein, M. (1955). The psychoanalytic play technique: its history and significance. In: *Envy and Gratitude, and Other Works 1946–1963* (pp. 123–140). London: Vintage, 1997.

Klein, M. (1957). Envy and gratitude. In: *Envy and Gratitude, and Other Works* (pp. 176–235). London: Vintage, 1997.

Kovel, J. (1971). *White Racism: A Psychohistory*. London: Allen Lane.

Kundnani, A. (2001). In a foreign land: the new popular racism, *Race & Class*, 43(2): 41–60.

Lawrence, F. (1999). *Punishing Hate: Bias Crimes Under American Law*. Cambridge, MA: Harvard University Press.

Lawrence, F. (2002). Racial violence on a "small island": bias crime in a multicultural society. In: P. Iganski (Ed.), *The Hate Debate* (pp. 36–53). London: Profile Books/Institute for Jewish Policy Research.

Lea, J., & Young, J. (1984). *What Is To Be Done about Law and Order?* London: Penguin.

Lee, J. (1981). Some structural aspects of police deviance in relations with minority groups. In: C. Shearing (Ed.), *Organizational Police Deviance* (pp. 00–00). Toronto: Butterworth.

Lee-Potter, L. (1999). For Stephen's sake avoid a witch-hunt. *Daily Mail*, 24 February, p. 10.

Lemert, E. (1964). Social structure, social control and deviation. In: M. Clinard (Ed.), *Anomie and Deviant Behaviour* (pp. 57–97). New York: Free Press.

Levitas, R. (2004). Let's hear it for Humpty: social exclusion, the third way and cultural capital. *Cultural Trends*, 13(2): 41–56.

Long, J. (2008). White fears. BBC *Newsnight White Season*, news.bbc.co.uk/1/hi/programmes/newsnight/7281314.stm (last accessed 28 July 2009).

Macpherson, W. (1999). *The Stephen Lawrence Inquiry*, Report of an Inquiry by Sir William Macpherson of Cluny, Cm4262-I. London: The Stationery Office.

Malik, M. (1999). "Racist" crime: racially aggravated offences in the Crime and Disorder Act 1998, Part II. *Modern Law Review*, 62(3): 409–424.

Marks, K. (1999). Lawrence suspects' interview: "I never used knives and I've never used violence", *The Independent*, 9 April, www.independent.co.uk/news/lawrence-suspects-interview-i-never-used-knives-and-ive-never-been-violent-1085987.html (last accessed 28 July 2009).

Maruna, S., & Matravers, A. (2007). The Jack-Roller at 100. *Theoretical Criminology (Special Issue)*, 11(4): 427–542.

McClintock, A. (1995). *Imperial Leather: Race, Gender and Sexuality in the Colonial Contest*. London: Routledge.

McDevitt, J., Levin, J., & Bennett, S. (2003). Hate crime offenders: an expanded typology. In: B. Perry (Ed.), *Hate and Bias Crime* (pp. 109–116). New York: Routledge.

McGhee, D. (2003). Moving to "our" common ground—a critical examination of community cohesion discourse in twenty-first century Britain. *The Sociological Review, 51*(3): 376–404.

McGhee, D. (2005). *Intolerant Britain? Hate, Citizenship and Difference.* Maidenhead: Open University Press.

McGhee, D. (2007). The challenge of working with racially motivated offenders: an exercise in ambivalence? *Probation Journal, 54*(3): 213–226.

McLaughlin, E. (2002). Rocks and hard places: the politics of hate crime. *Theoretical Criminology, 6*(4): 493–498.

McLaughlin, E., & Murji, K. (1999). After the Stephen Lawrence Report. *Critical Social Policy, 19*(3): 371–385.

Messner, D., McHugh, S., & Felson, B. (2004). Distinctive characteristics of assaults motivated by bias. *Criminology, 42*(3): 585–618.

Mills, C. W., & Gerth, H. (1953). *Character and Social Structure.* London: Routledge & Kegan Paul.

Ministry of Justice (2009). *Statistics on Race and the Criminal Justice System 2007/8.* London: Ministry of Justice, www.justice.gov.uk/publications/docs/stats-race-criminal-justice-system-07–08-revised.pdf (last accessed 29 July 2009).

Minsky, R. (1998). *Psychoanalysis and Culture.* Cambridge: Polity.

Morrison, M., Tappin, D., & Staines, H. (2000). "You feel helpless, that's exactly it": parents' and young people's control beliefs about bed-wetting and the implications for practice. *Journal of Advanced Nursing, 31*(5): 1216–1227.

Nayani, T. (2000). Psychiatric report: Robert Joseph Stewart. *Evidence Presented to the Zahid Mubarek Inquiry,* http://a1538.g.akamai.net/7/1538/13355/v001/homeoffice.download.akamai.com/13355/Page/1011/101101437.pdf and http://a1538.g.akamai.net/7/1538/13355/v001/homeoffice.download.akamai.com/13355/Page/1011/101101482.pdf (last accessed 12 January 2009).

Norfolk, A. (2006). BNP leader is acquitted of race hate but faces new trial. *The Times,* 3 February, www.timesonline.co.uk/tol/news/uk/article725723.ece (last accessed 5 March 2009).

Obama, B. (2009). Inaugural address, posted on the *The White House Blog,* 21 January, http://www.whitehouse.gov/blog/inaugural-address/ (last accessed 8 August 2010).

Orr, D. (2000). Stop throwing people to the lions. The *Independent*, 3 November, www.independent.co.uk/opinion/commentators/deborah-orr/stop-throwing-people-to-the-lions-625030.html (last accessed 29 July 2009).

Ouseley, H. (2001). *Community Pride, Not Prejudice*. Bradford: Bradford Race Review Team.

Papastergiadis, N. (1997). Tracing hybridity in theory. In: P. Werbner & T. Modood (Eds.), *Debating Cultural Hybridity: Multi-cultural Identities and the Politics of Anti-racism* (pp. 257–281). London: Zed Books.

Pallister, D. (1999). "All get chivvied up"—street violence that is a way of life. *Guardian*, 25 February, http://www.guardian.co.uk/uk/1999/feb/25/lawrence.ukcrime1 (last accessed 28 February 2008).

Parker, M. (2000). Identifying in Stoke. In: T. Edensor (Ed.), *Reclaiming Stoke-on-Trent* (pp. 255–270). Stoke-on-Trent: Staffordshire University Press.

Parkinson, M., Champion, T., Evans, R., Simmie, J., Turok, I., Crookston, M., Katz, B., Park, A., Berube, A., Coombes, M., Dorling, D., Glass, N., Hutchins, M., Kearns, A., Martin, R., & Wood, P. (2006). *State of the English Cities*. London: Office of the Deputy Prime Minister.

Perry, B. (2001). *In the Name of Hate*. London: Routledge.

Phoenix, A., & Owen, C. (1996). From miscegenation to hybridity: mixed relationships and mixed-parentage in profile. In: B. Bernstein & J. Brannen (Eds.), *Children, Research and Policy* (pp. 111–135). London: Taylor & Francis.

Populus (2008). *Populus—BBC Poll: Executive Summary*, http://news.bbc.co.uk/1/shared/bsp/hi/pdfs/06_03_08_Newsnight_White%20Season_poll.pdf (last accessed 4 March 2009).

Poynting, S., Noble, G., Tabra, P., & Collins, J. (2004). *Bin Laden in the Suburbs*. Sydney: The Sydney Institute of Criminology.

Ratcliffe, P. (2004). *"Race", Ethnicity and Difference: Imagining the Inclusive Society*. Maidenhead: Open University Press.

Ray, L., & Smith, D. (2001). Racist offenders and the politics of hate crime. *Law & Critique, 12*: 203–221.

Ray, L., Smith, D., & Wastell, L. (2003a). Racist violence from a probation service perspective. In: R. Lee & E. Stanko (Eds.), *Researching Violence* (pp. 217–231). London: Routledge.

Ray, L., Smith, D., & Wastell, L. (2003b). Understanding racist violence. In: E. Stanko (Ed.), *The Meanings of Violence* (pp. 112–129). London: Routledge.

Ray, L., Smith, D., & Wastell, L. (2004). Shame, rage and racist violence. *British Journal of Criminology*, 44(3): 350–368.

Reiner, R. (1993). Race, crime and justice: models of interpretation. In: L. Gelsthorpe (Ed.), *Minority Ethnic Groups in the Criminal Justice System* (pp. 1–25), Papers presented to 21st Cropwood Round-Table Conference. Cambridge: Institute of Criminology, University of Cambridge.

Renton, D. (2003). Examining the success of the British National Party, 1999–2003. *Race & Class*, 45(2): 75–85.

Respect Task Force (2006). *Respect Action Plan*. London: Home Office, www.homeoffice.gov.uk/documents/respect-action-plan (last accessed 12 January 2009).

Rich, P. (2005). The "half-caste" pathology. In: J. Ifekwunigwe (Ed.), *Mixed Race Studies* (pp. 73–79). London: Routledge.

Ritchie, D. (2001). *One Oldham, One Future*. Oldham: Oldham Independent Review Team Report.

Rustin, M. (1991). *The Good Society and the Inner World*. London: Verso.

Rustin, M. (2000). Psychoanalysis, racism and anti-racism. In: P. Du Gay, J. Evans, & P. Redman (Eds.), *Identity: A Reader* (pp. 183–201). London: Sage.

Salisbury, H., & Upson, A. (2004). *Ethnicity, Victimisation and Worry about Crime*. London: Home Office.

Sayer, A. (2005). *The Moral Significance of Class*. Cambridge: Cambridge University Press.

Sayers, J. (2000). *Kleinians: Psychoanalysis Inside Out*. Cambridge: Blackwell.

Scanlon, C., & Adlam, J. (2008). Refusal, social exclusion and the cycle of rejection: a cynical analysis? *Critical Social Policy*, 28(4): 529–549.

Scarman, L. (1981). *The Brixton Disorders, 10–12 April, 1981*. London: Her Majesty's Stationery Office.

Scheff, T. (1994). *Bloody Revenge*. Boulder, CO: Westview Press.

Scraton, P. (Ed.) (1987). *Law, Order and the Authoritarian State*. Milton Keynes: Open University Press.

Seabrook, J. (1982). *Working-class Childhood: An Oral History*. London: Gollancz.

Seabrook, J. (2004). Religion as a fig leaf for racism. *Guardian*, 23 July, www.guardian.co.uk/race/story/0,11374,1267567,00.html (last accessed 29 July 2009).

Sennett, R. (2003). *Respect: The Formation of Character in an Age of Inequality*. London: Penguin.

Sennett, R., & Cobb, J. (1993)[1972]. *The Hidden Injuries of Class.* New York: Norton.

Shapiro, J. S. (2004). Psychiatric report on Robert Joseph Stewart, *Expert Opinion presented to the Zahid Mubarek Inquiry,* http://a1538.g.akamai.net/7/1538/13355/v001/homeoffice.download.akamai.com/13355/Page/1011/101101431.pdf and http://a1538.g.akamai.net/7/1538/13355/v001/homeoffice.download.akamai.com/13355/Page/1011/101101436.pdf (last accessed 26 July 2010).

Sherwood, R. (1980). *The Psychodynamics of Race.* Brighton: Harvester Press.

Sibbitt, R. (1997). *The Perpetrators of Racial Harassment and Racial Violence,* Home Office Research Study 176. London: Home Office.

Sim, J., Scraton, P., & Gordon, P. (1987). Introduction: crime, the state and critical analysis. In: P. Scraton (Ed.), *Law, Order and the Authoritarian State* (pp. 1–70). Milton Keynes: Open University Press.

Simpson, L. (2004). Statistics of racial segregation: measures, evidence and policy. *Urban Studies, 41*(3): 661–681.

Singh, R., Jandu, K., & Passley, P. (2003). *The Murder of Zahid Mubarek: A Formal Investigation by the Commission for Racial Equality into HM Prison Service of England Wales.* London: Commission for Racial Equality, http://a1538.g.akamai.net/7/1538/13355/v001/homeoffice.download.akamai.com/13355/Doc/1011/101103404_part1.pdf (last accessed 12 January 2009).

Sivanandan, A. (2001). Poverty is the new black. *Race & Class, 43*(2): 1–5.

Sivanandan, A. (2002). Poverty is the new black. In: P. Scraton (Ed.), *Beyond September 11: An Anthology of Dissent* (pp. 113–117). London: Pluto.

Smart, K., Grimshaw, R., McDowell, C., & Crosland, B. (2007). *Reporting Asylum.* London: City University.

Smith, A. (1993). Screen: A romp in the jungle. *Guardian,* p. 6, 25 February.

Society Guardian (2004). Racist murderer "part of prison gang". *Guardian Online,* Friday 19 November, www.guardian.co.uk/society/2004/nov/19/youthjustice.law.

Stewart, R. (2000). Various personal letters, *Evidence Presented to the Zahid Mubarek Inquiry,* http://a1538.g.akamai.net/7/1538/13355/v001/homeoffice.download.akamai.com/13355/Page/1012/101200320.pdf—http://a1538.g.akamai.net/7/1538/13355/v001/homeoffice.download.akamai.com/13355/Page/1012/101200479.pdf.

Stewart, R. (2004). Statement of Robert Stewart. *Formal response to the Zahid Mubarek Inquiry,* http://a1538.g.akamai.net/7/1538/13355/

v001/homeoffice.download.akamai.com/13355/Doc/1013/101301 649.pdf (last accessed 26 July 2010).

Tajfel, H. (1969). Cognitive aspects of prejudice. *Journal of Social Issues*, *XXV*(4): 79–96.

Taylor, D., & Muir, H. (2005). Protests against decision to deport schoolgirl. *Guardian Online*, 24 January, www.guardian.co.uk/uk/2005/jan/24/immigration.immigrationandpublicservices_(last accessed 1 March 2009).

Taylor, P. (2001). Which Britain? Which England? Which North? In: D. Morley & K. Robins (Eds.), *British Cultural Studies* (pp. 127–144). Oxford: Oxford University Press.

Taylor, R. (2000). Private and Confidential Report on Robert Joseph Stewart, http://a1538.g.akamai.net/7/1538/13355/v001/home office.download.akamai.com/13355/Doc/1011/101109386.pdf (last accessed 26 July 2010).

The Economist (2004). Brutes in suits, 29 April, www.economist.co.uk/world/britain/displaystory.cfm?story_id=2629070 (last accessed 15 October 2008).

The Sun (2004). Bloody Nasty People, 15 July, p. 1.

The Sun (2005). "My heart is broken", 30 November, www.thesun.co.uk/article/0,,2-2005550542,00.html (last accessed 29 October 2007).

Toynbee, P. (2006). The next year is crucial if we are to make poverty history at home. *Guardian*, 31 March, www.guardian.co.uk/print/0,,329447273-103390,00.html (last accessed 12 January 2009).

Various (2004). Robert Stewart's prison and security records, *Evidence Presented to the Zahid Mubarek Inquiry*, http://a1538.g.akamai.net/7/1538/13355/v001/homeoffice.download.akamai.com/13355/Doc/1011/101101296.pdf—http://a1538.g.akamai.net/7/1538/13355/v001/homeoffice.download.akamai.com/13355/Page/1012/101200323.pdf (last accessed 26 July 2010).

Ware, V., & Back, L. (2002). *Out of Whiteness*. London: University of Chicago Press.

Weber, L., & Bowling, B. (2002). The policing of immigration in the new world disorder. In: P. Scraton (Ed.), *Beyond September 11: An Anthology of Dissent* (pp. 123–129). London: Pluto.

Weber, L., & Bowling, B. (2008). Valiant beggars and global vagabonds. *Theoretical Criminology*, *12*(3): 355–375.

Webster, C. (2003). Race, space and fear: imagined geographies of racism, crime, violence and disorder in Northern England. *Capital & Class*, *80*: 95–122.

Webster, C. (2007). *Understanding Race and Crime*. Maidenhead: Open University Press.

Werbner, P. (2005). The translocation of culture: "community cohesion" and the force of multiculturalism in history. *Sociological Review*, 53(4): 745–767.

Whyte, D. (2007). The crimes of neo-liberal rule in occupied Iraq. *British Journal of Criminology*, 47(2): 77–195.

Winnicott, D. (1958). Transitional objects. In: *Collected Papers, Volume 1* (pp. 339–342). London: Tavistock.

Worley, C. (2005). "It's not about race. It's about community": New Labour and "community cohesion". *Critical Social Policy*, 25(4): 483–496.

Young, J. (1994). Incessant chatter: recent paradigms in British criminology. In: M. Maguire, R. Morgan, & R. Reiner (Eds.), *The Oxford Handbook of Criminology* (pp. 69–124). Oxford: Oxford University Press.

Young, J. (1997). Left realist criminology: radical in its analysis, realist in its policy. In: M. Maguire, R. Morgan, & R. Reiner (Eds.), *The Oxford Handbook of Criminology* (2nd edn) (pp. 473–498). Oxford: Oxford University Press.

Young, R. (1995). *Colonial Desire: Hybridity in Theory, Culture and Race*. London: Routledge.

Younge, G. (2002). A land fit for racists. *Guardian*, 4 May, www.guardian.co.uk/Columnists/Column/0,,709887,00.html (last accessed 12 January 2009).

Younge, G. (2006). Let's have an open and honest discussion about white people. *Guardian*, 2 October, www.guardian.co.uk/Columnists/Column/0,,1885282,00.html (last accessed 12 January 2009).

Zahid Mubarek Inquiry (2004). Friday 19th November 2004, www.zahidmubarekinquiry.org.uk/article6064.html?c=387&aid=2928 (last accessed 26 July 2010).

Zahid Mubarek Inquiry (2005). Record of proceedings for Tuesday 1st February 2005, www.zahidmubarekinquiry.org.uk/article9566.html?c=387&aid=3229 (last accessed 26 July 2010).

INDEX